Yes Papa!

To Andy and David

Yes Papa!

Mrs Chapone and the Bluestocking Circle

A biography of Hester Mulso
– Mrs Chapone (1727–1801)
a Bluestocking

with love

Barbara Eaton

Barbara Eaton

Francis Boutle Publishers
272 Alexandra Park Road
London N22 7BG
Tel/Fax: (020) 8889 7744
Email: info@francisboutle.co.uk
www.francisboutle.co.uk

ISBN 978 1 903427 70 5

Printed by Melita Press, Malta

Contents

Acknowledgements

I am indebted to the following:

First and foremost, Melissa Hardie of The Hypatia Trust, the publisher of my first book, *Letters to Lydia: 'beloved Persis'* who lent me a handwritten copy, in nineteenth century copperplate, of *The Anti-Chapone* which aroused my curiosity about Hester Chapone.

Dr Elizabeth Eger of King's College, London, for her kind interest and for writing the preface.

The staff of the following who have been most helpful: The British Library, The British Museum and The National Portrait Gallery, London; The New York Public Library and The Morgan Library & Museum, New York; Cornwall Library Service, The Morrab Library, Penzance, Cornwall Studies Centre, Camborne and The Royal Institution of Cornwall Courtney Library, Truro; Dr Johnson's House, London; The National Trust, Hatchlands Park, Surrey.

Jane Grierson and Tess Barlow for their comments and helpful suggestions on the text. Clive Boutle of Francis Boutle Publishers for his encouragement and faith in the work.

Last but by no means least, my husband, Tim, for his unflagging support.

Illustrations are reproduced by kind permission and courtesy of the following: The National Portrait Gallery (London): Hester Chapone (née Mulso); Samuel Richarsdson reading to his friends; Samuel Richardson, author of *Clarissa*; Dr Samuel Johnson; Benjamin Stillingfleet; Admiral Boscawen; George Lyttelton, 1st Baron Lyttelton; Elizabeth Vesey; David Garrick and Eva Garrick. The Trustees of the British Musem: The Middle Class Companionate Family; Crinum: paper flower by Mrs Delany; Entertainment at Bath. Private Collection: Frances Boscawen. The British Library: The Anti-Chapone. Deal Town Council: Elizabeth Carter. New York Public Library: Breaking up of the Bluestocking Club.

For Charlotte and Ben

Preface

Hester Chapone has long been an elusive, shadowy figure in literary history. Her idiosyncratic character has slipped in and out of view, never completely invisible, never fully illuminated. Barbara Eaton's delightful biography has restored Chapone to her rightful place as a central bluestocking writer while retaining a sense of her awkward individuality. Here we find a vivid portrait of Chapone as both 'spitfire' and dutiful daughter, earnest moralist and irreverent satirist. Eaton draws out the distinctive sense in which Chapone crossed the line between private and public literary spheres with trepidation and uncertainty, only to succeed brilliantly.

Hester Chapone was a profoundly intellectual woman at a time when her sex was not expected to be rational. While her wit and intelligence intimidated many of her peers, she attracted the respect of several writers, including Samuel Richardson, who solicited her opinion of his novel *Clarissa*. Chapone addressed a series of forthright letters to him on the topic of a woman's right to choose a marriage partner. She quoted long passages of Locke in her defence, interjecting occasionally with indignant yet logical asides in order to extend his patriarchal definition of liberty to women as well as men. The reader cannot fail to be impressed by the writer's energy, wit and fierce intelligence, not to mention her withering irony:

> Clarissa says that at *every* age on this side of matrimony, the wings of our parents are our most necessary safeguard, from the vultures, the hawks etc. Suppose a woman lives single till forty, I fancy by that time the HAWKS, *vultures* and *kites* will give her very little trouble; and that she might be pretty secure from the danger of being DEVOURED, though she should have the courage to creep from under the wings of her parents.

As Barbara Eaton's biography explains, Chapone's own family circumstances were difficult. Her father prevented her from marrying the man of her choice for over six years, for financial reasons. She was not able to marry until she was well into her thirties. This startling outburst of angry sarcasm was written before she experienced her own personal frustrations, which makes it all the more poignant.

Chapone found release from the claustrophobia of daily life in her writing, not only as a letter writer and essayist but also a poet. When her friend the scholar Elizabeth Carter published her translation of *Epictetus* in 1758, she included an Ode that Chapone had sent her, with the following explanatory note: 'The translator of Epictetus owes the permission of inserting the following ODE entirely to the Friendship of the Writer of it, who, when she favoured her with it, had no thought of it ever appearing in print.' Chapone's stirring poem explores the relationship between mind and body with painful directness:

> No more repine, my coward soul
> The sorrows of mankind to share,
> Which he who would the world controul
> Did not disdain to bear.

As recent critics have suggested, Chapone's passionate vocabulary can be found echoed in the work of her nineteenth-century successors, Emily Bronte and Emily Dickinson, poets who were similarly preoccupied with tensions between the private and public, passion and reason, and with the search for a space in which women could pursue a life of the mind.[1]

Chapone is perhaps best known for her *Letters on the Improvement of the Mind*, originally written for her fifteen-year-old niece and not published until 1773, on the encouragement of Elizabeth Montagu, 'Queen of the Blues', to whom Chapone dedicated the third edition. Chapone had sold the copyright of the *Letters* for £50 when they were first published in 1773, unfortunately relinquishing a substantial fortune to the bookseller. The success of the volume was immediate and enduring.

One of the most influential and popular educational books for women, Chapone's work was intended to help her niece cultivate rational understanding through her reading of the bible, history and literature. In her otherwise scathing survey of conduct literature and educational writings, Wollstonecraft singled out the work for praise: 'Mrs Chapone's Letters are written with such good sense, and unaffected humility, and contain so many useful observations, that I only mention them to pay the worthy writer this tribute of respect.'

See Michael Moon, 'No coward souls': poetic engagements between Bronte and Dickenson', in *The Traffic in Poems: Nineteenth-Century Poetry and Transatlantic Exchange*, ed. Meredith McGill (New Jersey, 2008), pp.231–250

Barbara Eaton's biography combines historical research with a sympathetic understanding of character. Hester's own story is brought into sharper focus through contrast with others – Beau Nash, Elizabeth Montagu, Samuel Richardson, Elizabeth Carter and Fanny Burney, to name only a few of the individuals who are brought to life in the following pages. Readers will enjoy the fine balance struck between individual and collective identities, entertainment and instruction. Eaton pays elegant tribute to the intellectual and moral aims of Chapone, while allowing readers the distance necessary to reflect upon the differences between the eighteenth and twenty-first centuries.

Elizabeth Eger
King's College London

List of illustrations

'I have an utter aversion to bluestockings. I do not care a fig for any woman that knows even what an author means'.

William Hazlitt (1778-1830)

Part One

Growing Up

Samuel Richardson reading the manuscript of The History of Sir Charles Grandison *at North-End to his friends. 1751, Susanna Highmore. Left to right: Samuel Richardson, T Mulso, E Mulso, Hester Mulso (Mrs Chapone), Miss S Highmore (later Mrs J Duncombe), Miss Prescott (later Mrs T Mulso), J Duncombe.*
Aquatint by Joseph Constantine Sadler after Susanna Highmore.

Chapter 1

'the admirable Mrs Chapone'

In the opening chapter of *Vanity Fair* (1847-8) Thackeray[1] describes the boarding school for young ladies which Amelia Sedley and Becky Sharp are about to leave for the wider world. With all its snobbish and educational pretensions Miss Pinkerton's Academy on Chiswick Mall aims to educate young women to take their place in society and for the marriage market. Miss Pinkerton, 'the friend of Dr Johnson, the correspondent of Mrs. Chapone' presents Amelia with her account for £93-4s-0d[2] and a brief report for her mother in which she lays out the accomplishments which Amelia has achieved:

> 'The Mall, Chiswick, June 15, 18-.'
>
> 'MADAM – After her six years' residence at the Mall, I have the honour and happiness of presenting Miss Amelia Sedley to her parents, as a young lady not unworthy to occupy a fitting position in their polished and refined circle. Those virtues which characterise the young English gentlewoman, those accomplishments which become her birth and station, will not be found wanting in the amiable Miss Sedley, whose *industry* and *obedience* have endeared her to her instructors, and whose delightful sweetness of temper has charmed her *aged* and her *youthful* companions.
>
> 'In music, in dancing, in orthography, in every variety of embroidery and needle-work, she will be found to have realised her friends' *fondest wishes*. In geography there is still much to be desired; and a careful and undeviating use of the backboard, for four hours daily during the next three years, is recommended as necessary to the acquirement of that dignified *deportment and carriage*, so requisite for every young lady of *fashion*.
>
> 'In the principles of religion and morality, Miss Sedley will be found worthy of an establishment which has been honoured by the presence of *The Great Lexicographer*, and the patronage of the admirable Mrs. Chapone. In leaving the Mall, Miss Amelia carries with her the hearts of her companions, and the affectionate regards of her mistress, who has the honour to subscribe herself,
>
> 'Madam, your most obliged humble servant,
>
> 'BARBARA PINKERTON.

'PS. – Miss Sharp accompanies Miss Sedley. It is particularly requested that Miss Sharp's stay in Russell Square may not exceed ten days. The family of distinction with whom she is engaged, desire to avail themselves of her services as soon as possible.'

'This letter completed, Miss Pinkerton proceeded to write her own name, and Miss Sedley's, in the fly-leaf of a Johnson's Dictionary – the interesting work which she invariably presented to her scholars, on their departure from the Mall. On the cover was inserted a copy of 'Lines addressed to a young lady on quitting Miss Pinkerton's school, at the Mall; by the late revered Doctor Samuel Johnson.' In fact, the Lexicographer's name was always on the lips of this majestic woman, and a visit he had paid to her was the cause of her reputation and her fortune.

'Being commanded by her elder sister to get 'the Dictionary' from the cupboard, Miss Jemima had extracted two copies of the book from the receptacle in question. When Miss Pinkerton had finished the inscription in the first, Jemima, with rather a dubious and timid air, handed her the second.

'For whom is this, Miss Jemima?' said Miss Pinkerton, with awful coldness.

'For Becky Sharp,' answered Jemima, trembling very much, and blushing over her withered face and neck, as she turned her back on her sister. 'For Becky Sharp: she's going too.'

'MISS JEMIMA!' exclaimed Miss Pinkerton, in the largest capitals. 'Are you in your senses? Replace the Dixonary in the closet, and never venture to take such a liberty in future.'

'Well, sister, it's only two-and-ninepence, and poor Becky will be miserable if she don't get one.'

'Send Miss Sedley instantly to me,' said Miss Pinkerton. And so, venturing not to say another word, poor Jemima trotted off, exceedingly flurried and nervous.

'Miss Sedley's papa was a merchant in London, and a man of some wealth; whereas Miss Sharp was an articled pupil, for whom Miss Pinkerton had done, as she thought, quite enough, without conferring upon her at parting the high honour of the 'Dixonary.'

Having established the social difference in background of the two girls, and their probable expectations and future roles in society, Thackeray then describes Becky Sharp's ultimate rejection of Miss Pinkerton and her principles of education. As she and Amelia depart Becky hurls the dictionary which Jemima has given her, against her sister's strictures, out of the carriage window. The reference to Johnson and his dictionary is not surprising as school leaving prizes always aim to improve. However, Dr Johnson's dictionary will play no part in Becky Sharp's new life of social climbing and is consigned to the dust.

Who was Mrs Chapone and why is she juxtaposed with Johnson?

The answer is her conduct book, *Letters on the Improvement of the Mind, Addressed to a Young Lady* published in 1773 when Hester Chapone was forty-six years old: it became a best-seller. The list of accomplishments achieved by Amelia at Miss Pinkerton's Academy which Thackeray treats with irony reflect much of Hester Chapone's advice some seventy years earlier to a young woman from the gentry who is about to take her place in an adult society where gentlewomen were not admired for their intellect but rather for their ability to be pleasing in their manners, show obedience to their parents and after their marriage, preferably to a man of means, to their husbands. A successful marriage was of prime importance and this meant marrying well financially so that in transferring her economic dependence from her father to her husband a young woman's future was safely secured.

In the first half of the eighteenth century most young girls from the gentry had a limited education. A few were sent to boarding school but in the main daughters were very largely educated in the home environment by governesses or by their mothers who often neglected their intellectual development in favour of their social development. A fortunate few whose fathers were more enlightened and who very often were members of the clergy were given a better education and encouraged in their intellectual development. One of Mrs Chapone's closest friends, Elizabeth Carter,[3] benefited in this way although later her intellectual powers were regarded with suspicion in some quarters. Elizabeth decided against marriage having realized that her intellectual freedom of thought and expression could be compromised. She felt fortunate to have such a forward thinking father and acknowledged her gratitude to him for respecting her wishes. But for young girls who did not have such fathers it was the highly popular conduct book to which their parents turned for advice on educating their daughters for their future role in society.

These books of prescriptive rules set out a model of education by which to mould young girls from the gentry and emerging middle class into a marriageable commodity and reflected the paternalistic view of women in the eighteenth century. The advice covered every aspect from suitable books to read, behaviour in company, desirable and less desirable personal characteristics, duties as daughter, wife, mother and widow and even, heaven forbid, spinsterhood. The genre of conduct books was not new, indeed in the previous two centuries there were many books on the subject, including Lord Halifax's *The Lady's New-Year's Gift: Or, Advice to a Daughter* (1688) and books on domestic economy that laid down rules for the smooth running of a house. Chapone's model was no different except for the fact that within this straightjacket of prescription she did seek to encourage the development of a more rational outlook on life in which a limited intellectual autonomy was to be encouraged while actively discouraging the over-development of sentiment as portrayed in so many contemporary novels. Hester Chapone's conduct book took the form of a series of letters to her elder niece. This epistolary style was familiar and popular in the eighteenth century when letters were of such social importance. Indeed Samuel Richardson[4] had been working on a handbook on the art of writing letters, *Familiar Letters on Important Occasions*, before he put the project on hold in order to write *Pamela*. The tragic story is narrated through the exchange of letters. The novel was a huge success for Richardson. One of his readers, Hester Mulso, later Hester Chapone, read both *Pamela* and Richardson's later novel *Clarissa* and took issue with Richardson on the key theme of Clarissa's filial duty.

Daughters were not free agents in their choice of a husband. Parental approval had to be sought and often parental choice of husband was enforced on an unhappy young woman in order that her family might benefit from an advantageous marriage settlement. Heaven forbid that one's daughter should run off with some handsome but impecunious young man thus ruining any chance of her and her family's advance in society – the central theme of *Clarissa*. It would be through debate with Richardson that Hester would find her voice and express her deep opposition to the current patriarchal attitudes to women and marriage as portrayed in his two novels. She was encouraged by Richardson to enter into a correspondence over the nature of filial obedience and paternal tyranny. This brought her into the public arena with her controversial views whilst in her early twenties.

Later Hester would be drawn into the Bluestocking movement and become friends with some of its most important and influential women who, like her, shared a passion for intellectual debate and no longer wished to be patronised by men who had relegated them to the role of simpering childlike women incapable of rational thought. Within this polite but paternalistic society intellectual women were viewed with some alarm as an ability to view the world from a rational standpoint was not necessarily seen as a quality to be encouraged in young women in the marriage market.

The England into which Hester was born in 1727 would see major social, economic and political change during her lifetime. Socially there was the growth of the middle class and the emphasis on polite society reflected by the growing provision of commercial entertainment. The fashionable spa towns of Bath and Tunbridge Wells grew in popularity. Both were governed by the strict social code laid down by

Beau Nash.[5] Society in search of health and entertainment flocked there in the season for the assemblies where dancing, cards and gambling were enjoyed. There was very importantly an unprecedented growth in the reading public, especially among women, whose interest and appetite for the printed word was met by the printing industry and the growth in circulating libraries. Periodicals such as *Tatler* (1709) founded by Richard Steele and *The Spectator* (1711), which he and Joseph Addison[6] founded, had fed this appetite and were followed by the hugely popular *The Gentleman's Magazine* (1731)started by Edward Cave, a printer who by 1734 was publishing 9,000 copies a month. Johnson, in *The Rambler* (1750-52), later gave Hester encouragement and provided a platform for some of her earlier work.

With the advent of the Industrial Revolution England would shift from a rural economy to one based on industry with the resulting growth and expansion of towns. By the middle of the eighteenth century the population of London was 600,000 and still growing.[7] The expansion of turnpike trusts led to the improvement in roads, and the introduction of the fast post chaise, drawn by relays of four horses which were changed at regular intervals, made travel time shorter and thus less taxing for the traveller, especially for women. Public coaches, known as fly-machines cut travel times even further after 1750 and by 1770 connected the growing industrial cities with the economic and political centre of London. Hester's brother, John, recounts Hester's using the new service to visit him and his family in Yorkshire. The dangers and problems for women travelling by public coach are well documented by both Hester and her great friend Elizabeth Carter in their correspondence while her very wealthy friend Elizabeth Montagu[8] describes the delights of being driven by her young companion in her 'Whiskey', a light, one horse, two-wheeled carriage.

Politically Hester would witness the military success at Culloden in 1746 which brought to an end the Jacobite Rebellion, the subject she would celebrate in one of her earlier poems. She would also voice her anxiety over the repeated threat of a French invasion but would live to see further great British military and naval successes against the competing European powers of the French, Spanish and Dutch in their quest for colonial expansion in India, America, Canada and the West Indies. This led to a sense of national pride and identity. Victories were celebrated with public fervour and admirals and generals fêted and honoured: the Battle of Plassey in 1757 established the dominance of Britain in Bengal and the expansion of the influence and power of the East India Company; 1758 saw the capture of Louisburg in Canada from the French, followed by Quebec in 1759. Great fame and national adulation attended Robert Clive, General Wolfe and Admiral Boscawen[9] whose wife, Frances, would become a close friend of Hester's.

This sense of national confidence is embodied by exploration. James Cook[10] embarked on the first of his voyages of discovery (1768-71) to the distant southern hemisphere. The great plant collector Joseph Banks[11] who accompanied Cook on the voyage of *Endeavour* brought back exotic non-descript plant species, for study at Kew. At home, the Grand Tour, which young men from the aristocracy and gentry took, was seen as an essential part of their education. The classical influence was reflected in Georgian architecture with its elegance and classical proportions seen in the work of Robert Adam.[12] Fashion in interior decoration is amply illustrated by Elizabeth Montagu whose London homes were on the grandest scale. When Chinese influence came into vogue in the later 1760s she selected none other than Robert Adam to design an exquisite ceiling and carpet in that style. The landscape designer, "Capability" Brown,[13] created an essentially English fashion in great gardens and Elizabeth employed him to redesign the parkland surrounding her Sandford estate in Berkshire.

Hester would embrace the English Enlightenment. She would put behind her the romantic notions of the popular novel and flights of fancy. Reason would inform her self-improvement. She would quote John Locke to underpin her debate with Richardson on the relationship between parents and children, including daughters. Political stability and unprecedented economic growth had flourished after the Treaty of Paris.[14] But Hester would live to see the great political changes which resulted in a shift to a less enlightened atmosphere in the last quarter of the eighteenth century. The American War of Independence (1775-83) culminating in the loss of Britain's American colonies was followed by the French Revolution (1789-99) and its atrocities which sent a shiver down English spines. By then the heyday of the Bluestockings was over.

Chapter 2

'The desire to please polishes the intelligence'

Hester Mulso, the fourth surviving child and only daughter, was born into the landed gentry on October 27, 1727, the year in which George II ascended the throne and over a century before the publication of *Vanity Fair*. The ancient Northamptonshire Mulso or Moulshoe family was established before the reign of Edward I. Owning at one time landed estate in the county and adjacent counties to the value of eight thousand pounds per annum, the family fortune was much reduced by the eighteenth century. Her family lived at Twywell, a small village near Kettering in Northamptonshire, in a large Elizabethan house, on the north side of St Nicholas's church, which was in the diocese of Peterborough.

Twywell was an idyllic setting for Hester's early childhood: the house with its mullioned windows and climbing plants reaching up its walls overlooked a large and well-stocked garden. There was a lake with wild flowers bordering it and large shrubs and trees where small children could explore and play. It was here that Hester's love of the countryside took root. Both she and her elder brother, John, refer to visiting Twywell later in life with their father on one of his visits from King's Square Court, Soho which he had made his chief residence in 1731 when Hester was four years old. The family tie with Northamptonshire remained but by 1749, John reports that the house at Twywell was in ruins. It was demolished in 1832 and a new house built upon the site.

Hester had a confidence in herself and an ability to express her views from an early age for she was by all accounts a precocious child: at the age of nine she wrote *The Loves of Amoret and Melissa*, inspired by the setting at Twywell. Her mother, also a Hester, was a renowned beauty, the posthumous daughter of Colonel Thomas, an officer in the Guards known as 'handsome Thomas'. She was much indulged by her husband, Thomas Mulso, whom she had married in 1719, a country gentleman who held the position of Clerk of Assize. She regarded herself as a wit, shining in company, especially the company of men who pandered to her vanity. She had every opportunity to display her social charms at the long evenings, so popular in the eighteenth century, which revolved around gambling, cards and gossip: pastimes which her daughter would come to despise. The role of the woman, who married in the social circle in which the Mulso family moved, lay primarily within the confines of the domestic scene: wife, mother, hostess and manager of the domestic economy and the servants in the household. The union would hopefully produce a surviving heir and a spare. For the wife the reality she faced was the prospect of spending much of her life bearing further children. Infant mortality was high and she would have to deal with the often devastating consequences. Hester's mother had had numerous children yet only five survived to adulthood. One of Hester's elder brothers, John, writes movingly about the death of one of his infant sons in the same year as a daughter was born. He also describes the difficulties his wife, Jane, had during pregnancy and his fear of losing her in childbirth, a very real risk in those days.

Hester's mother's day was made up of ordering the household and servants, making sure her husband and any guests were comfortable, and participating in their entertainment. She was also responsible for looking after the welfare of her five children. By all accounts she preferred the company of her four sons, the youngest born after Hester, to that of her only daughter who was known by her family under a variety of nicknames – Hecky, Heck or later, 'Yes Papa' and 'The Wanderer'.

Just as mothers were the role model for daughters of the gentry in learning propriety in conducting their lives so they also acted as models in the more private sphere of their households. Hester would have learnt by observation how her mother managed the demands of a busy household: her husband and five children; and her ability to rule over her servants and earn their respect and hopefully their affection while keeping a shrewd eye open for any misdemeanours such as lying, stealing or impertinence. Hester observed how her mother managed the allowance given to her by her husband which covered not only food but also improvements to the house. She saw the skill needed to balance all these factors so that her father was not unduly disturbed and could relax either alone or with visitors. Running repairs to linen and clothes were part of the domestic scene as well as the more decorative needlework done at leisure. Hester herself admitted that she was no needlewoman. There was also the fear of disease in the household – the threat of smallpox, typhoid, measles and dysentery as well as the less serious illnesses which lurked in winter months both for family and servants. Above all Hester would have noted the role of the subservient wife who, although essential to the smooth running of the domestic economy and the happiness of her family, had little independence or voice.

Unfortunately her mother seems to have resented Hester's intelligence, high spirits and strong opinions and little was offered in the way of stretching Hester's active mind by any formal education. Her brothers, who adored Hester but were not governed by the restrictions which would impinge on her education, could engage her in lively argument. Her parents' view of women was typical of the age in which beauty was admired above intelligence and women who were educated often took pains to conceal it in male company. Hester's mother was fortunate in possessing both beauty and intelligence whereas Hester only possessed the latter. By the time she was twenty-seven one of her brothers described her as having become 'a Collar of Brawn' while in later life personal descriptions of her were even crueller: Fanny Burney's sister, Charlotte, writing in 1781 describes her: 'I went one evening last week to the Dean of Winchester's, where we met Mrs Chapone, who looked less forbidding than usual; but she is dead ugly to be sure; such African nose and lips and such a clunch [chunky] figure.'[1]

Hester's mother allegedly was jealous of her daughter's precocious intelligence and her increasing ability to voice strong opinions on most subjects. This coupled with her mother's chronic ill health by the time Hester was in her teens is perhaps why her mother had such a distant relationship with her. Frustratingly for a girl of Hester's intelligence her education was limited and seems to have consisted of little except romantic novels, which were hugely popular at the time although in some quarters they were frowned upon for encouraging and over stimulating the imagination of young women. Most of the books she was encouraged to read up to this time were written by the popular French writer of *romans à clef*, Madeleine de Scudéry,[2] who held that the 'desire to please polishes the intelligence and love inspires more liberality in a quarter of an hour than ten years study of philosophy' which no doubt would have met with the approval of Hester's mother. Scudéry specialised in page after page of long conversations which reflected her love of French salon conversation in the previous century. Hester later castigates romances as being 'the worst of all the species of writing: unnatural representations of the passions, false sentiments, false precepts, false wit, false honour, and false modesty, with a strange heap of improbable, unnatural incidents mixed up with true history.' She recalls having 'drudged through books' which her mother had chosen including: 'Le Grand Cyrus, in twelve huge volumes,[3] Cleopatra, in eight or ten, Polexander, Ibrahim, Clélie, and some others, whose names, I have forgotten; but this was in the days when I did not chuse my own books, for there was no part of my life in which I loved romances' but adds: 'and yet I am still alive.'[4] By the time she was in her teens Hester was developing a love of rational thought and argument. She describes this change:

> I remember that, when I was about fifteen years old, I was charmed by many of the doctrines of the Mystics ... but as my reason gained strength, I discovered, that there was no more reality in these my fancied sentiments than in my dreams; and that the sensations I had produced in my own heart were as entirely the effect of imagination, as the distress I felt in seeing a tragedy.[5]

By the time she is in her early twenties she is able to take on one of the great literary figures in a debate on filial duty. Her correspondent was none other than Samuel Richardson who was at the height of his popularity and fame.

But for Hester growing up in her parents' household there were other important social skills to be learnt, one of which was mastering the epistolary form. The art and social importance of letter writing was central to many women's lives. Letters enjoyed a wide circulation among family members and friends and were often read aloud to the assembled company. The rules of propriety governing letter writing included due deference to the rank of the recipient and would have included enquiries about the health of not only the recipient but also the family and close friends as well as the current state of the writer's health. For married women with small children, like Fanny Boscawen,[6] who became a good friend of Hester's later in life, the state of their health was a major concern as infant mortality was high. Lady Mary Wortley Montagu,[7] who was scarred by smallpox in Turkey in 1715, introduced the Ottoman practice of smallpox inoculation in 1721. Great anxiety is expressed by many correspondents as to the safety and the wisdom of exposing oneself and children to such risk. Fanny describes dosing her beloved son with rhubarb as a purgative which was thought beneficial in preparation for the inoculation. Other topics in letters included the dire state of the roads, footpads, and highwaymen, all of which made travelling dangerous; current political affairs such as the illness of King George III; the threat of a French invasion with the resultant panic it incurred and the fear of mob violence. In lighter vein descriptions of social activities were included. The letters of the young Elizabeth Robinson (later Elizabeth Montagu) to her great friend Lady Margaret Cavendish Holles-Harley,[8] who became the Duchess of Portland in 1734, reveal a witty correspondent. She is well informed of the goings on in the social calendar of assemblies and balls at Bath and Tunbridge Wells. Elizabeth is witheringly critical of the sartorial mistakes of some unfortunate women. For female correspondents comments were eagerly awaited on who has been seen with whom at the theatre and opera and evening visits to the pleasure gardens of Vauxhall, which reopened in 1732 with a *ridotto*[9] *al fresco* which Frederick, Prince of Wales attended. All these public gatherings, some of which were more public than others as many were only open to ticket holders or by subscription, enabled a young woman to see and be seen in the wider social sphere but held dangers for the unwary and foolish young woman whose reputation could either be enhanced or ruined. Propriety in public places was extremely important for unmarried young women. Theatres, assemblies, pleasure gardens, *fêtes champêtres*,[10] opera and masquerades exposed the unwary young woman to possible scandal and set tongues wagging to ruin her reputation. On a more serious note there was much discussion and description, often critical, of what the writer or recipient was currently reading with recommendations for further reading matter and reference to periodicals which found a ready audience in female readers of the period. Writing letters and receiving them was for many intelligent women an opportunity to express and discuss ideas within a close circle of supportive friends and family.

Young women like Hester had to learn social skills among which was the art of polite conversation to ensure that they were agreeable in society. This must have proved difficult for the young Hester as she loved a good argument and did not give way gracefully. Hester also had to learn grace when it came to dancing. Dancing masters were employed to teach both girls and boys to dance and great emphasis was put on correct deportment. Small balls were organised at private houses where the young participants could practise their newly learnt skills without the fear of ridicule or censure in the more public sphere. Mary Delany,[11] with whom Hester would become increasingly friendly in later life, describes organising such an afternoon gathering in 1751 for fourteen young people between the ages of eight and twenty-one. The well-connected Mary no doubt kept an eagle eye on the grace and control with which they danced. One gift Hester did possess was a beautiful natural singing voice which made up for her lack of natural grace in dancing and her limited proficiency in drawing and painting or playing an instrument.

Hester was learning the skills and attributes which would ensure

Vauxhall Gardens

that she made a good marriage. While unmarried, a young woman of the gentry lived at home, guarded her virtue assiduously and obeyed her parents. Filial obedience was accepted by most young women and when it came to selecting a suitable husband she would often have little choice in the matter especially if she was betrothed at a young age to a much older wealthy man, who once married, might well continue to keep a mistress or mistresses to which she would have to turn a blind eye. In most cases she was viewed as an adjunct to her husband. For many women marriage was not based on love but on a beneficial financial arrangement which would enhance the husband's estate and the young woman's standing in society. For women who fell in love, as Hester would do, her independence and freedom of choice were still limited by the necessity of receiving paternal blessing. If a young woman refused to marry the man deemed suitable then paternal censure could be harsh both in real life and in literature. Women who chose independence, like Hester's friend, Elizabeth Carter, were warned by their fathers of the social isolation and possible financial hardship they could face. The woman who failed to marry was pitied and for her there was little chance of autonomy for, as Hester later pointed out, the opportunities for women of the gentry to earn a living were few and far between and those who elected to do so were often treated with suspicion. The spinster would remain dependent on her family, often unhappily so, or inhabit that social no man's land which was so often the fate of the governess. Marriage and its centrality to a young woman's place in society was a highly relevant preoccupation for young women like Hester in the eighteenth century.

However, the view of what a young woman should aspire to be was changing and the over-indulgent aristocratic female model who flaunted her wealth and position in public places was being replaced by the ideal of the married woman who managed her household, social position and husband with discretion within the relatively private sphere of the home. Modesty was to be encouraged whereas pride and vanity were not; frugality was seen as a virtue in household management while the profligate wife was seen as an embarrassment to the husband who had to provide the resources to maintain her, his children and household. At the heart of the role of the wife was the domestic happiness of her family and especially of her husband.

For Hester as she grew into her teens there seems to have been a shortage of happiness in her relationship with her mother within the predominantly male household yet Hester was clearly both very loving and much loved by her four brothers and her doting father. Hester, as an only daughter, played an increasingly important role in the management of the household due to her mother's ill health and after her death would take over the day to day management of her father's home in London. Her day would revolve around the domestic routine with family prayers marking the start of the new day. Meals were family affairs and took place at regular times: breakfast at nine o'clock, followed by a substantial dinner at two in the afternoon, followed by tea and finally supper which was eaten relatively late in the evening. Pastimes included gentle walks, excursions by chair to visit family friends; learning the desirable female accomplishments of playing the spinet, listening to music, painting, dancing, singing, needlework, writing and receiving letters, and reading aloud or privately the popular romantic novels for young women.

But time could hang heavily. Boredom with this vacuous way of life, confined to a regimented daily routine with little to stimulate and interest a lively and enquiring mind, could lead young and intelligent women like Hester to question their role and rebel against it. She would actively seek a wider intellectual education which was denied her because of her background and gender.

Chapter 3

The Gilbert White Connection

Unlike Hester her four brothers did receive a formal education. Thomas,[1] the eldest, after Oxford, became a barrister and worked with his father as Clerk of Arraigns until his patrimony. In 1760 he married, after a long courtship, a Miss Mary Prescott, or 'Pressy' as the family referred to her. They settled in London, living at Rathbone Place, near Soho Square where his father, by then a widower, lived with them until his death. Hester adored her eldest brother and became a close friend of his wife, spending much time at his home once he married. In 1768 Thomas published a somewhat dull romance *Callistus; or the Man of Fashion, and Sophronius; or the Country Gentleman, in three Dialogues* which became highly popular in fashionable Bath. John,[2] the second son, followed his brother to Winchester and then Oxford. He was destined for the church. He was fortunate that his uncle, the Reverend Dr John Thomas,[3] his mother's brother, who was married to Susanna, his father's sister, became Bishop of Peterborough and later of Salisbury and Winchester. Dr Thomas was instrumental in John's appointments of Prebendary of Salisbury and Winchester. Dr Thomas was also the Prince of Wales' (later George III) private tutor and held in great affection by the monarch. John loved company and Hester often stayed with him when he moved to become vicar, first at Sunbury in Berkshire and then in 1760 at Thornhill, near Wakefield in Yorkshire. She became close to his wife, Jane, or 'Missy', and their children to whom Hester grew increasingly attached. At that time it would take Hester four days to cover the journey of 160 miles from London to Thornhill along often very poor roads. Travel in winter was hazardous. Roads became mired and there was the risk of the coach overturning. Travelling in the spring and summer were much safer options and it was usually then that Hester made the journey.

The third brother, Charles, became an officer in the navy. He died at 21 while serving in the Mediterranean. Hester's youngest brother, Edward, or Ned, of whom Hester was fond, went to Cambridge and later became an excise officer. He was a gifted musician and became president of the Anacreontic Society[4] the aim of which was to promote a love of music, wit and to celebrate the god of wine. Ned played both piano and violin. It was he who often accompanied Hester when she sang. Her beautiful contralto singing voice was much admired in social circles, apparently another source for maternal jealousy, and this earned her the soubriquet 'the linnet'. In a letter to Samuel Richardson, from Exeter College, dated June 9, 1754, when Hester was twenty-six, a Dr Kennicott pays her the following compliment when describing a performance at the University Festival at Oxford: 'The first clap of applause was upon Forasi's[5] [sic. Frasi] taking her place in the orchestra; Signora seemed a little too sensible of the honour, &c. But I forgive her; for indeed she sings – I cannot say most delightfully – for, I have not heard Miss Mulso.' Ned remained a bachelor and died suddenly from an apoplectic seizure in 1782 which was a devastating blow to Hester.

Gilbert White,[6] the naturalist, was a close friend of John, Hester's second brother, who had been at Oriel College, Oxford when White was an undergraduate there in 1741. They became life-long friends and correspondents. Gilbert was ordained at Oxford in 1747 and settled in Selborne, where he had been born. He became curate there in 1751 but never became vicar because the living was administered by Magdalene College and he was an Oriel man. He was curate at Farringdon, close to Selborne, from 1761 until 1784 when he once more became curate at Selborne. Gilbert was a diligent curate and took his duties seriously. Although Hester's brother, John, not a country man by heart, was somewhat lazy and admitted to liking 'Company & Gayety' and had an eye for young women, he and Gilbert enjoyed each other's company. John and his family would visit Gilbert at his home, The Wakes, in the village of Selborne, set in a landscape of hills and woods two miles from Farringdon, in Hampshire. John Mulso would always request that he be met at the Southampton or Portsmouth coach road because of his fear of getting lost or stuck in the rough cart lanes which led to Selborne which lies about fifty miles from London. From The Wakes Gilbert could see the Hanger, a hill of 300 feet with beech woods on it while to the south lay a Down with glorious views. Gilbert loved projects and extended his beloved garden, growing fruit, including melons, vegetables and much other produce from his two acre orchard, some of which he sold to boost his funds.

Gilbert, like John, was extremely sociable and enjoyed welcoming friends and family to his home. He would organise melon feasts, tea in the bower, encourage his visitors to climb the steep zigzag path, cut by

Gilbert White's House, Selborne

himself and his brother John, up the Hanger, or take them to the Hermitage he had built where his brother would appear dressed in suitable hermit's garb and surprise Mulso's children. There were outdoor singing parties in the garden. Often as many as twenty guests would attend these tea parties, some dressed as shepherds and shepherdesses. The Mulso family took Gilbert to their heart. John Mulso reports in his letters to Gilbert on July 18, 1744 that their mother is much taken by Gilbert: 'My mother loves you, you have a strong part in a family that you never saw, but I claim your heart' and in the following month: 'My mother loves you so much that I am almost jealous of you. She says you speak her very sentiment in your judgement of the Odyssey.'[7] Gilbert, now a family friend, naturally met John's sister, Hester, not quite eighteen and seven years younger than him, when he stayed with the Mulso family at King's Square Court. John comments in a letter dated September 7, 1745: 'Heck likes your Hair, she confesses so much already. It was a very neat Compliment that You sent her. She can't answer it, so She says nothing.' The shy Gilbert and the opinionated young Hester embarked on a teasing and somewhat flirtatious relationship with Hester referring to him as Busser-White, from *buss*, to kiss, a nickname by which he was known at Oxford. Later she coined the name Whitibus for him much to her brother's amusement. However, Gilbert would remain a bachelor in spite of John's best attempts to tease him into marriage.

Thomas, John, Edward and Hester recount visits to Selborne. Gilbert was popular with John's children and it is another Hester, John's fourth child and youngest daughter who was born in 1764, just after the death of his son George, for whom in 1784 Gilbert wrote *Letter from Timothy the Tortoise to Miss Hecky Mulso* in reply to some verses she had sent him. Gilbert had inherited Timothy from his aunt, Mrs Snooke, after her death in 1780, and transported Timothy from Ringmere, near Lewes, back to Selborne. He writes in April, that year, to Daines Barrington,[8] a friend and fellow naturalist with whom he corresponded for twenty years, with his observations on flora and fauna:

> Pitiable seems the condition of this poor embarrassed reptile; to be cased in a suit of ponderous armour which he cannot lay aside; to be imprisoned as it were, within his own shell, must preclude, we should suppose, all activity and disposition for enterprise. Yet there is a season of the year (usually the beginning of June) when his exertions are remarkable. He then walks on tiptoe, and is stirring by five in the morning; and, traversing the garden, examines every wicket and interstice in the fences, through which he will escape if possible; and often has eluded the care of the gardener, and wandered to some distant field. The motives that impel him to undertake these rambles seem to be of the amorous kind: his fancy then becomes intent on sexual attachments, which transport him beyond his usual gravity, and induce him to forget for a time his ordinary solemn deportment.[9]

His letter to the young Hecky purports to be a tortoise's ground eye view of life at The Wakes, where Gilbert also carried out experiments: shouting loudly at the unfortunate tortoise through a speaking trumpet to test Timothy's hearing and observing his spatial awareness when approaching the top of his ha-ha wall. He reported that Timothy, who in fact was female, showed no reaction to the first experiment but then neither did his bees. Gilbert observed nature with a keen eye recording his observations on the natural habitat of birds and plants in his journals and letters. Mulso was prescient about his friend when he wrote in 1776: 'Your work, upon the whole will immortalise your place of Abode as well as Yourself.' In 1789 *The Natural History of Selborne* was published ensuring Gilbert's place as an eminent natural historian.

Chapter 4

A Wider World

By 1746 Hester's mother is suffering increasingly prolonged bouts of ill health which John reports to Gilbert White. In one letter dated October 27 he explains that Gilbert cannot come to stay because his mother and father are now occupying separate rooms due to her illness. The following year, 1747, Hester's mother died and Hester took over her domestic role at King's Square Court where she continued to live with her father until her marriage.

1747 was a watershed in Hester's life as she was now free from maternal disapproval and restriction. Hester was not only in charge of household management but more importantly was now in charge of her own education which she set about with a determined zeal, encouraged by her brothers. She read widely and selectively. After her mother's death Hester, perhaps as a result of over-exposure to the romantic genre from an early age, had little time for this kind of literature. She loved poetry and tried her hand at writing it although she produced nothing particularly noteworthy during this period apart from *Peace* written when she was eighteen in response to the 1745 Jacobite Rebellion. It is a patriotic call for unity written in 10 four line verses with a simple rhyme scheme. It would remain unpublished until 1775 when it would be included in *Miscellanies, in Prose and Verse* which was published as a result of her literary success in 1773. She taught herself some Latin, French and Italian. As a devout Christian she was very familiar with the Bible but now she began to study theology and to become interested in philosophy. More importantly she met Elizabeth Carter who would have a far greater influence upon her than her mother ever did. Hester's friendship with Elizabeth Carter would last more than fifty years.

Hester and Elizabeth, who would become her mentor, were introduced to each other in 1749 by Mr Duncombe, one of Richardson's circle, and a mutual friend of both women. His son, John Duncombe, would later marry Susanna Highmore, a poet and friend of Hester.

Elizabeth Carter, friend of Hester Chapone

Elizabeth was in Canterbury for the races, staying at the home of the Dean, Dr Lynch. Hester was there on a visit to her Aunt Anne and Uncle, Dr Donne. He was a Prebendary of Canterbury where Elizabeth's father the Reverend Dr Nicholas Carter, Perpetual Curate at Deal church, was one of six Preachers. Elizabeth, who was ten years older than Hester, was the eldest daughter of Carter and his first wife, Margaret, an heiress, whose fortune was lost in The South Sea Bubble.[1] When Elizabeth was ten her mother died. Her father remarried and happily Elizabeth loved her step-mother, Mary, and the children of the marriage. Elizabeth was fortunate in that she received an excellent education from her father. Unusually for the time he believed in educating his sons and daughters equally and took the task on himself. Unlike her younger sister, Margaret, Elizabeth's learning did not come easily as a child. But she was driven by a strong determination and worked tirelessly at her studies: rising before four in the morning having been woken by a bell beside her bed which was attached by a thread operated by the sexton in the garden. To keep herself alert while studying she took to chewing green tea leaves and taking snuff. Her dedication paid off. She became a gifted linguist learning Greek, which she excelled at, as well as Latin and Hebrew from her father. A French Huguenot minister at Canterbury taught her French in which she became fluent; she taught herself German, Spanish, and Italian and, later, a little Portuguese and even some Arabic. She also studied ancient history, geography, astronomy, modern history and science.

Her social skills were not neglected. She was taught dancing, music – she played the spinet – and art, though drawing was not her forte. Elizabeth was highly practical and was an excellent needlewoman, a fact acknowledged by Dr Johnson, who was a friend for more than fifty years and said of her that she 'could make a pudding, as well as translate Epictetus from the Greek, and work a handkerchief as well as compose a poem.' She was also skilled in domestic economy and helped bring up and educate her younger half-siblings, coaching one brother to get into Oxford. However, when it came to the question of matrimony she professed it as 'a very right scheme for everybody but herself.' She had turned down a proposal of marriage in 1738 following her father's veto and rejected two further proposals; the last, in 1749, was favoured by her father as it would have helped the family financially. Her father did his best in trying to persuade her into matrimony by warning her of future economic hardship when he died if she did not marry. But Elizabeth resolutely turned down any suitor in spite of dire paternal warning that unmarried women enjoyed little esteem in eighteenth century society. Not only did she protect her personal independence she also protected her intellectual independence by turning down the possibility of becoming governess in the Princess of Wales's household, recognising wisely that court life would subsume the pursuit of intellectual interests so dear to her heart. Her father's gloomy prophecies failed to materialise and Elizabeth pursued her own course with rationality as her loadstar. As a woman she was held in high esteem, coupled with some male suspicion, for her intellect and scholastic achievement.

Elizabeth became a published poet at the age of seventeen. The poem or riddle – Elizabeth never lost her love of riddles – just signed Eliza, appeared in 1734 in *The Gentleman's Magazine*, published by Edward Cave, a friend of her father, which provided women writers with an opportunity to see their work in print, albeit anonymously. Her anonymity protected her modesty and also helped ensure that any criticism was based on her work rather than her gender. Dr Carter encouraged his daughter in these literary pursuits and in 1735 she left Deal for London to write for Cave's magazine. However, by 1735 her cover was blown and she became a contender for the crown that Alexander Pope[2] had worn for so many years. Throughout her work her classical background and her depth of learning and lively intellect marked her out. 1738 saw not only the publication of *Poems upon Particular Occasions* but also her meeting with Johnson – a name her father did not recognise. He soon would! It was Cave who introduced Elizabeth and Johnson when she came to London. They became friends. Johnson recognised Elizabeth's natural modesty which was partly due to shyness and partly because she did not want to cause offence. Her reputation as a writer and translator continued to grow: she produced poems, riddles and epigrams, essays and translations of works in French and Italian. In 1739 she produced a translation from the French of Jean Pierre de Crousaz's *An Examination of Mr Pope's Essay on Man* and in the same year Cave published her translation from Italian of Francesco Algarotti's *Sir Isaac Newton's Philosophy Explain'd for the Use of Ladies*. Her scholarship was applauded but such public accolades were not deemed fitting for a woman who was unmarried and had apparently no intention of following the accepted norm of young women of her age: she was twenty-two.

She had formed a close friendship with Thomas Birch who was also a journalist on *The Gentleman's Magazine*. In his thirties and a widower, Birch recognised Elizabeth's genius and sought to promote her work. Clearly he was attracted to the younger woman whose learning and independence were unusual and who moreover was establishing a reputation for herself as a writer. Matrimony was far from Elizabeth's mind however and on her father's advice she returned to Deal to live a more retired life signalling that she was not interested in marriage.

Apart from the unauthorised appearance of her *Ode to Wisdom* circulating in manuscript form but reproduced by Samuel Richardson in *Clarissa* she published little for the next few years. She was given a full public apology by Richardson who rectified matters by publishing the authorised version in *The Gentleman's Magazine* 17. Elizabeth was clearly mollified and she and Richardson became friends and corresponded. She later became one of the few outside contributors to Johnson's short-lived periodical *The Rambler* (nos. 44 and 100) in August 1750 and March 1751. The first essay is on religion and the second is an ironic look at life in modish society. It was not until 1758, by which time she and Hester had become friends, that her translation of the Greek Stoic philosopher Epictetus appeared and to which a poem by Hester was prefaced.

The correspondence between Hester and Elizabeth Carter started in 1749 as a result of their meeting each other in Canterbury. Hester's opening letter to Elizabeth reveals some trepidation on her part, combined with flattery:

> I cannot too soon take advantage of the kind permission dear Miss Carter has given me, to begin a correspondence which will afford me so much pleasure; and I will do it without fear, since I have as much reason to confide in her good-nature, as to revere her judgement. I shall still find in her that amiable condescension, and unreserved benevolence, which endears her conversation, and enhances the value of her understanding; which teaches her how to improve her companions without appearing to instruct them, to correct without seeming to reprove, and even to reprove without offending.
>
> I parted from you, dear madam, with more regret than I dared shew; for I could not expect that you should have believed me sincere, had I expressed all the esteem and affection I felt for you, since I could hardly, myself, comprehend how so short an acquaintance should have produced so warm an attachment: but why do I call it a short acquaintance? I have known you long, and long honoured and esteemed you; but it is only since I had the pleasure of conversing with you that I have loved you, because fame could never have conveyed to me any idea of the engagingness of your manner and disposition, though it had raised in me a just opinion of your worth and abilities.[3]

Hester was initially somewhat overawed yet at the same time flattered that someone of Elizabeth Carter's intellectual status should encourage their friendship. The friendship proved invaluable to Hester. It enabled her to discuss and test her opinions with a woman who was highly educated. Furthermore, Hester respected and admired Elizabeth's modesty, independence of mind and outlook on life.

Elizabeth is equally taken by Hester and writes a glowing account to her close friend and intimate, Catherine Talbot.[4] Catherine was born five months after her father died in 1720. He was the second son of the Bishop of Durham and the younger brother of the Lord Chancellor. It was Catherine's father who recommended Dr Secker to his father's patronage. Secker, who later became Archbishop of Canterbury, did not forget this act and when he married in 1725 he invited Talbot's widow and the young Catherine to join his household. Like Elizabeth she was well-educated for a young woman of the time. She had received instruction in religion, astronomy, geography, French (she and Elizabeth often wrote in French to each other and read French authors in the original), Italian, some Latin and later in life taught herself German, but much to her regret could not read Greek. Catherine was regarded as a woman of some intellect having been referred to as 'the celebrated Miss Talbot' in her late teens. It was Elizabeth who asked for an introduction through a mutual friend, Thomas Wright, a well-known astronomer. They were introduced in 1741 at the Honourable Mrs Rooke's home near Canterbury. Elizabeth wrote to Wright:

> I do not know whether you ought to congratulate me upon my good success last Sunday, for what have I gained by it? only a new addition to my impatience, which really was very strong before, but is now out of all bounds of moderation. Miss Talbot is absolutely my passion; I think of her all day, dream of her all night, and one way or other introduce her into every subject I talk of.[5]

Catherine was twenty and Elizabeth twenty-four. Elizabeth set great store on her friendships with other women including Elizabeth Montagu and Hester. Catherine was living in Oxford where Secker had been Bishop since 1737. Secker would become Dean of St Paul's in 1750 and then in 1758 Archbishop of Canterbury.

Catherine, like Elizabeth, was to remain unmarried. Elizabeth's views on marriage did not change:

> To give up one's ease and liberty, and be under perpetual restraint, for the sake of wearing a finer gown, eating a greater variety of dishes, or seeing more company and fewer friends, appears to me a very strange scheme. I have shewed these proposals to my father, and he is so good as to leave me to my own choice, which is the very situation I am in.[6]

Elizabeth Carter's letters to Catherine Talbot reveal a warm and witty, learned woman. Subjects range from books they are reading, often with criticism of plot and characters, recommendations for further reading, the state of their health, family, friends, current affairs, the state of the roads for travel, London, visits to Vauxhall and Ranelagh pleasure gardens, masquerades and life in the spa towns. Elizabeth writes graphic accounts of the threat of a French invasion at Deal; assemblies, where she describes in ironic detail who has partnered her at the balls; the terrible headaches which she suffered throughout her life and often incapacitated her; her insomnia; her trenchant views on marriage; French fashions; the adventures she encounters when travelling by public coach and the discomfort she has to endure when squashed like a sardine by a very fat fellow passenger. On one occasion she bales out of a coach and walks sixteen miles to Deal. She recounts going for long walks along the shore and rambling in the countryside near her home. This love of the countryside was shared by Hester.

Catherine Talbot soon became intrigued by Elizabeth's new correspondent and enquired: 'Who and what is Miss Mulso? She writes very well, and corresponds with you and Mr Richardson. I honour her and want to know more about her.'[7] Elizabeth responds with this description of Hester: 'I found her even more amiable than he had represented; she has an uncommon solidity and exactness of understanding, I was greatly charmed with her, and saw her as often as I could in the short time I was in Canterbury.'[8]

Sadly Catherine suffered from chronic ill health throughout her life and by 1760 when Elizabeth accompanied her to Bristol to take the waters had become an invalid and finally died from cancer in 1770 with Elizabeth at her side. She was forty-nine.

Hester expresses her happiness in the friendship when she writes to Elizabeth on March 25, 1750: 'I believe there are few people who are better pleased and contented with their lot than I; for I am qualified to feel my present happiness; by having early experienced very different sensations.'[9] Sadly none of Elizabeth's letters to Hester appear to have survived but both women held the other in high esteem with the more mature Elizabeth responding warmly to the younger woman. Hester's high opinion of Elizabeth is disclosed in a letter to Samuel Richardson in 1752: 'It is impossible not to be better, as well as happier, for an intimate acquaintance with *Miss Carter*; take her for all in all, I think I may venture to pronounce her *the first of women*.'[10] Clearly she was set on a very high pedestal indeed by Hester. Elizabeth was equally delighted with Hester whom she describes in a letter to Catherine Talbot in 1752 as possessing 'an uncommon acuteness of understanding, and a lively and agreeable turn of conversation, and her conduct seems to be governed by the best and noblest of principles.' Both Hester and Elizabeth found the support of the other through their exchange of letters valuable, although Hester would benefit most from this friendship.

Hester, was actively pursuing her literary interests. In 1749 she produced an Horatian ode entitled *Occasioned by Reading Sonnets Written in the Style and Manner of Spenser, by T. Edwards*, in which she lauds the poet Thomas Edwards, a friend of Samuel Richardson, who had resurrected the Spenserian sonnet form. Edwards is delighted by Hester's sonnet, as he is by a sonnet of her friend Susanna Highmore praising him. Edwards responded with an ode to Hester in 1751, though not a Spenserian one, in which he refers to her as a linnet, applauding her voice.

Sweet Linnet, who from off the laurel spray
That hangs o'er Spenser's ever-sacred tomb,
Pour'st out such notes, as strike the Woodlark dumb,
And vie with Philomel's inchanting lay;
How shall my verse thy melody repay?
If my weak voice could reach the age to come,
Like Colin Clout's, thy name would ever bloom
Through future times; *unconscious* of decay:
But such frail aid thy merits not require;
Thee Polyhymnia, in the roseate bowers
Of high Parnassus, midst the vocal throng,
Shall glad receive, and to her tuneful lire
Present; where, crown'd with amaranthine flow'rs,
The raptured choir shall listen to thy song.[11]

Samuel Richardson in his response to Edwards gave her an even higher accolade in the avian world by describing Hester as a nightingale. In 1752 Edwards writes to Richardson again praising her and requesting him to pass another sonnet he has written to Hester:

> I often entertain myself with reading over those charming Odes of Miss Mulso's and admire them more and more every time I read them, that my gratitude has forced from me another sonnet, (you see how bold I grow upon encouragement,) which I desire you to give to her; and, in hopes of seeing more of her verses, I have presumed to give her a subject. I have sent you a copy; but as there is a name in it which you have scratched out of better verses, I have taken the precaution to seal up that which is for Miss Mulso; and if you either sink it, or alter the name to Robinson, or anything else, I will have the sonnet printed, and hawked under your window "in terrorem."[12]

Both Edwards' and Hester's odes would be published much later in 1775 in Chapone's *Miscellanies*. *The Gentleman's Magazine* gave her poetry a glowing review in February 1775. John Duncombe also paid tribute to Hester in *The Feminiad* (1754) in praise of women poets, on which he was working in 1751. Duncombe refers to the robin, the linnet and the lark who will celebrate her in their song and the poet Spenser smiling on her. He adds: 'Of this lady I shall say little more than that the happiness of her genius is only excell'd by the goodness of her heart. The Muses have attended her in the few poetical excursions she has made, viz. her Odes to Peace, Health, and the Robin Redbreast, which are here alluded to; and she has been celebrated in a sonnet by Mr Edwards, author of the Cannons of Criticism.'

Hester was emerging on the literary scene and making valuable and influential friends, of which Samuel Richardson would be the most important. He would provide the opportunity for her to voice her ideas and engage in rational argument. Here was a highly intelligent young woman who had not enjoyed the benefits of a formal education and was making up for it by improving herself in a university of her own making. There was no question that she would make her mark but in what sphere it was as yet unclear.

Hester had inherited her mother's sociability and as a young woman growing up in London there was plenty of opportunity to enjoy herself within the safe and tight-knit social circle of family and friends. John, her brother, recounts her attending balls where on one occasion he relates her being terrified at the sight of blood when a brawl broke out. She loved travelling around on 'jaunts of pleasure' with her father into Northamptonshire, accompanied sometimes by her brothers, Thomas and John. Her exploits are mentioned regularly by John in his letters to Gilbert at this period and reflect his love and amusement for his young sister: 'that bold Girl Heck ventured into Northamptonshire in the Chair with my Father:' and 'Miss Hecky has been a Rake and deserted us for two whole days, and went to ye Races & Assembly and danced away in Company with Lady Musgrave.' There were jaunts when the roads were less hazardous during the spring and summer to visit friends such as Gilbert White in Oxford or Selborne. There is a planned trip to Oxford in the company of her brother, John, and Jane Young who would become his wife. Mary Prescott, who would become her eldest brother's wife, was also in the party. John jokingly reports that when Gilbert is unable to be in Oxford for their visit 'Heck is in ye greatest alarm, & scream'd out on hearing it "but where's my Busser?" In short she is apprehensive of a Dearth of Civilities, because You are not to be there, and fears she will not get her degree, because she has not her favourite Batchelour to answer under.'

By 1749 Hester is developing a strong critical outlook on literature, openly criticising Gilbert White's translation of verses from Horace in spite of having somewhat shaky Latin herself, much to John's amusement. In a letter dated April 11, 1750 John relates to Gilbert: 'she would not always have you translate & imitate, but give your own invention scope, & I hope you observe what she says!' Hester spent much of that year with her aunt and uncle in Canterbury. She suffers in May from the cool weather and longs for the sun to take away her aches as much as Gilbert longs for the shade to allay his fevers. Hester was clearly fond of Gilbert and enjoyed his company when she refers to 'careering about with Whitibus who heightens and improves all parties.' John comments on Hester's new name for Gilbert: 'whether there is any particular Hint of improvement by ye Termination she is pleased to give to your Name, You best know; as to me, I never see those things, because I do as I would be done by; so You best know ye Meaning of your new Name & whether it is a fond abbreviation of your Oxford Title Busser.' Visits to her relations both in Canterbury, where she enjoyed going to the races, and to Peterborough were a welcome chance to escape from London during the spring and summer. Both of her aunts were particularly fond of her. Winters were spent at home in London, visiting friends and her eldest brother, Thomas and his family.

In October Hester is back in London for the winter and is actively seeking further self-improvement. To her delight she is encouraged by none other than Samuel Richardson. It is now at his invitation that she embarks on a series of critical letters to him on his second novel *Clarissa* which she had been studying for some time and in some depth.

Chapter 5

'Never was woe drest out in gayer colours'[1]

When the first volumes of *Clarissa* were published in 1747 Hester was twenty. Many of the questions she raised with Richardson in her correspondence about the themes in his novel and the treatment of the unfortunate eighteen-year-old heroine, Clarissa Harlowe, were very pertinent to women of that time when it came to marriage and the expectancy of filial obedience. Marriage was for many unfortunate young women a straight commercial transaction in which any romantic longing for a marriage based on love had necessarily to be subsumed. The concept of romantic love which would lead to a marriage based on love and companionship still remained a distant hope for many women. The parental vested interest in their daughters' making a good match in economic terms led young gentlewomen to be viewed as pawns in the marriage market. Some, like Elizabeth Carter, were exceptions in retaining their autonomy by refusing to marry. Elizabeth Montagu,[2] well-educated and beautiful, who loved assemblies and the attendant flirtations from her many male admirers, was married at the age of twenty-four to a man nearly thirty years her senior whose main interest lay in politics, mathematics and coalfields in Yorkshire on which his great wealth was based. It was not a marriage based on love and although her husband, Edward Montagu,[2] was kind to his young wife, their interests were hardly compatible: he preferred to retire to his estate in the country and shut himself away in his library rather than go to Bath or Tunbridge Wells which were so beloved by Elizabeth. Some women such as Mary Granville, born in 1700, were even unluckier when it came to marriage.

The Granville family had close aristocratic and court connections. But with the death of Queen Anne in 1714 the family, who were Tory, had suffered a reversal in fortune as the Whigs came to power. Although by all accounts very attractive Mary was without a fortune. When Mary was fifteen a handsome Jacobite by the name of Mr Twyford fell in love with the now beautiful young woman and proposed. Mary's father had to tell him her circumstances. Twyford's mother refused to consent to a marriage based on love, especially when it brought no financial benefit to the Twyford family. Undeterred, the besotted young man proposed a private marriage in 1716 which Mary refused. This was a wise move on her part as so many such marriages ended in disaster. It was not until Hardwicke's Marriage Act (1753), which proscribed marriage for those under twenty-one unless with parental consent, that the temptation to elope was curtailed unless the couple fled to Scotland.

The unfortunate Mary was forced at seventeen into an arranged marriage with Alexander Pendarves, who was a wealthy Tory landowner of almost sixty and a widower. He was a Tory MP with an estate at Roscrow, near Penryn in Cornwall, and had been Surveyor-General of the Crown and Duchy lands in Cornwall to Queen Anne.[3] He was an old friend of Mary's uncle, Lord Lansdowne of Longleat. Lansdowne saw the opportunity not only to solve the problem of Mary's lack of fortune but also as an opportunity to extend his own political power in Cornwall – he was a Tory – through the alliance.

Mary describes her introduction to Mr Alexander Pendarves at Longleat where she was staying:

> I expected to have seen somebody with the appearance of a gentleman, when the poor old dripping, almost drowned, Pendarves was brought into the room, like Hob out of the well. His wig, his coat, his dirty boots, like his large unwieldy person, and his crimson countenance, were all subjects of great mirth and observation to me ... Pendarves was then nearly sixty, and I seventeen ... He was fat, much afflicted with gout, and often sat in a sullen mood, which I conclude was from the gloominess of his temper.[4]

He was so repulsive to her that she would leave a room if he came into it when she was alone. Mary found the attentions of a younger son of Edward Villiers, Earl of Jersey, who was also staying at Longleat, far more welcome than those of the elderly and physically abhorrent Pendarves who drank heavily. Like Clarissa she is a pawn in the game of marriage with her uncle controlling the moves. Mary obviously realised that she was expected by her uncle to sacrifice any prospect of her own personal happiness. Summoned before him she was more or less forced by him to agree to marry Pendarves so that her father's financial position would benefit: the besotted and jealous Pendarves had resolved to settle his whole estate on her. She fled the interview in tears realising only too bitterly that 'no one considered the sentiments of my heart; to be settled in the world, and ease my friends of expense

Mary, Mrs Pendarves, later Mrs Delany. Her arranged, first marriage was deeply unhappy

and care, they urged it was my duty to submit, and that I ought to sacrifice everything to that one point.' Duty triumphed but at an appallingly high cost to Mary's happiness. She was rewarded with a sumptuous wedding but 'Never was woe drest out in gayer colours, and when I was led to the altar, I wished from my soul I had been led, as Iphegenia was, to be sacrificed. I was sacrificed. I lost, not life indeed, but lost all that makes life desirable – joy and peace of mind.'[5] As might be expected the marriage was not a very happy one with the huge difference in age, his lack of physical attraction and his drinking: there were no children.

Mary was taken down to Cornwall where she found that Roscrow, his estate, had been neglected and was in a dilapidated condition not having been lived in for thirty years. She describes her first impressions to her great friend, the Duchess of Portland in her autobiography which she began in 1740:

> When we arrived at Averno (Roscrow), the name of his seat, I was indeed shocked. The castle is guarded with high walls that entirely hide it from your view. When the gate of the court was opened and we walked in, the front of the castle terrified me. It is built of ugly coarse stone, old and mossy, and propt with two great stone buttresses, and so it had been for threescore years. I was led into an old hall that had scarce any light belonging to it; on the left hand of which was a parlour, the floor of which was rotten in places, and part of the ceiling broken down; and the windows were placed so high that my head did not come near the bottom of them.[6]

In fact Roscrow was not a castle but a barton, a mansion house with huge barns all surrounded by a wall. Much later, in the 1770s Roscrow was used as a prison for over 900 French prisoners of war captured with their ships and brought to Falmouth harbour. The adjoining barn to the mansion was their prison which had an enclosed exercise yard. The unrelieved diet of Cornish pilchards unsurprisingly did not meet with the French prisoners' approval. Many died there.[7]

Mary gave people and places fictitious names in her letters and autobiography, a practice which was highly fashionable at the time. She refers to the Duchess of Portland as Aspasia, her husband as Gromio and her close friend, Sarah Kirkham, who would marry and later become Mrs Chapone's mother-in-law, as Sappho. Poor Mary, it was a gloomy start to her married life. However, she was highly practical and, after her initial despair at her situation, with her husband's permission set about refurbishing the mansion to her liking. Furthermore she loved the beauty of the Cornish landscape which stretched away downhill to the deep harbour of Falmouth. She did her best to humour her elderly husband who continued to be ferociously suspicious and jealous of any attention that his young and beautiful wife enjoyed from the opposite sex. Sadly the unfortunate Mr Twyford never recovered from losing the woman he fell in love with and shortly after her marriage, while she was still at Longleat, he fell ill with palsy and later died. Mary records how after his death 'they found under his pillow a pece [sic] of cut paper, which he had stolen out of my closet.' Richardson could not have improved on this tragic love story which took place in 1717, thirty years before the appearance of *Clarissa*.

By 1724 Mary was a widow and would remain so for nineteen years. As neither of Pendarves' marriages had produced children and he had failed to change his will in Mary's favour, his estate passed to his niece, also a Mary, who paid an annuity of £400 a year to his widow. Mary was young and very attractive. She was pursued by admirers in London where she now lived and mixed in high social circles, attending the coronation of George II in 1727. She received overtures from the Hanoverian ambassador, whom she rejected, and Lord Baltimore who announced that he had been in love with her for five years. He wanted a marriage based on affection which met with Mary's approval. However, he suddenly jilted her and married the wealthy daughter of a merchant. Mary fell ill and at the suggestion of Mrs Donellan, her close friend, with whom she lived in Richmond, went to Dublin for a holiday in 1731. It was then that she met and became friends with Jonathan Swift and with Dr. Patrick Delany, a cleric who would become her second husband after his first wife died in 1740. They married in 1743. The following year Delany became Dean of Down. It was a deeply happy and perhaps surprising union because Mary herself espoused the view that those of high breeding could do more good in the world than those who were not, and among her friends and relations there had been much soul searching because it was felt that she should marry someone with greater social standing and fortune but Mary was determined to marry for love the second time around.

Like many of her circle including both the Duchess of Portland and Elizabeth Montagu she had a strong sense of propriety. Johnson's view of Mary reflects her high position in society: 'I have heard Burke say that Mrs Delany was the highest bred woman in the world, and the woman of fashion of all ages.' Because in her opinion neither Samuel Johnson nor Mrs Thrale, his great friend, belonged to polite society she did not seek their acquaintance. Later she felt fully vindicated in her opinion of Mrs Thrale after the scandal of her liaison and marriage to an Italian music teacher and singer which brought widespread condemnation. However, Hester Chapone fulfilled Mary's criteria as a member of polite society and although Mary was much older they would become friends.

Chapter 6

'I never was a writing lady till you made me one'

In 1750 Hester was introduced into Samuel Richardson's circle. Richardson, at the height of his fame, first writes to her on Mr Duncombe's suggestion on July 13th of that year. This was the start of a correspondence which reveals Hester's growing critical ability. It was through her friendship with Duncombe and the Reverend John Burrows[1] and his family that she met and became a member of Richardson's coterie at North-End,[2] in Hammersmith. It was Richardson's habit to get up early to write in a grotto in his garden. Later his guests would assemble there and he would read from his work in progress. Mrs Barbauld,[3] who edited Richardson's correspondence in1804, describes Richardson as living 'in a kind of flower garden of ladies. They were his inspirers, his critics, his applauders.' She adds that 'Catherine, (Talbot) the Miss Fieldings,[4] and Miss Colliers[5] also flourished in his garden where he encouraged lively debate among his tender female plants.' He encouraged his largely female coterie to engage in lively debate, something which Hester loved. He also offered practical help and advice on their writing. It was Richardson who described her as 'a little spitfire' reflecting Hester's strongly held opinions and her confidence in expressing them: she is twenty-three years old. Hester's brother, John, in a letter to Gilbert in 1750, describes the friendship:

> My sister and ye Family are got into the Acquaintance of Richardson ye Author of Pamela & Clarissa, in which they take great Delight, for the Man is a sort of Original for Goodness & Sensibility … She has likewise ye Acquaintance of Miss Carter of Deal, a suprizing woman, Mistress of most Languages, & of a noble Vein of Poetry, her attempts that way being wonderfully classic, correct, and masculine.

High praise indeed for a woman! On December 13th the same year, after a visit to North-End with Hester and their brother, Thomas, he describes Richardson as:

> ... a short fat man, of an honest Countenance, but he has ill Health & shatter'd nerves. But his gentle Manners, his generous Charitableness, his Studiousness to oblige & improve without ye air of superiority, his extreme Tenderness to every proper Object that comes within his Notice, make him infinitely dear to those who know Him, and studiously sought after by those who do not. Rara Avis in Terris.

Richardson came from a manual working background: his father was a joiner. Like Hester he had received little in the way of a formal education. In 1706 when in his teens he was apprenticed to a London printer for seven years. He was good at his trade and after thirteen years was able to set up on his own. He might well have remained content with his success in printing had it not been for a commission to put together a book of model letters for the unskilled in epistolary matters. His practical guide, *Familiar Letters on Important Occasions*, has a series of letters dealing with the problem faced by a girl in service when her master displays amorous intentions towards her. Her letters are to her father asking for his advice. Richardson became fascinated by the project and the seed of the idea for an epistolary novel was sown. So intrigued did Richardson become with his novel, *Pamela; or Virtue Rewarded*, that its publication in parts took precedence over the guide which was not published until 1741. The story is told through the eponymous heroine's voice in a series of letters. It caused a sensation with its theme of a virtuous and beautiful young servant defying her lascivious master, Mr B., and, by asserting her rights as a woman for respect, becoming his wife. It was highly controversial in a society beset by fixed views on the place of both women and servants. Its huge popularity ensured that when his next novel *Clarissa, or the History of a Young Lady* was published (1747-8) there was an eager audience. One member of this audience was a critical Hester who had studied the novel in some depth.

It was the publication of *Clarissa* which led both Susanna Highmore, and Hester, at Richardson's invitation, to enter into correspondence with him on the subject of filial duty. The fact that Richardson advised Susanna, who was both beautiful and educated, to remain under her father's roof instead of going away on long visits to friends and relations reflects Richardson's view that young women needed the protection of their parents. He argued that she would be safer at home from predatory seducers, such as the fictional and dastardly Lovelace in *Clarissa*. His novel emphasises the dangers faced by impressionable and naïve young women who, in search of romantic love, might well be persuaded to elope with their ardent young suitor and go through a private marriage thus ruining themselves in the eyes of society. The trials of the intelligent and articulate but highly unfortunate Clarissa captured the contemporary female readers' imagination and sympathy as her story unfolded leading Susanna and Hester, both of marriageable age and therefore fully aware of the kind of predicament Clarissa faced, to engage in debate with Richardson at North-End on the subject of unquestioning filial loyalty to tyrannical parents.

Hester set out her arguments in three letters dated October 12 and November 10, 1750 and January 3, 1751. Although Richardson's side of the correspondence does not appear to have survived there are references to it and the progress of the debate is clear: on Richardson's side in correspondence with others in his circle, such as Lady Bradshaigh,[6] a prolific letter writer; and with Sarah Chapone,[7] Hester's future mother-in-law; on Hester's side in her correspondence with Elizabeth Carter, and, most importantly, in the course of Hester's second and third letters to Richardson. What is very clear from Hester's side of the correspondence is her ability to marshal rational argument and underpin it so effectively. Their correspondence would bring Hester a much wider audience. It was privately circulated and much discussed, with Hester receiving censure for her views from some quarters and admiration from others for her ability to argue her corner so cogently and rationally.

Although Richardson was sympathetic and encouraged young women like Hester and Susanna, who sought to widen their intellectual horizons, he espoused the tradition of filial obedience and parental authority based on a sense of duty. The theme is central to *Clarissa* in which the eponymous heroine is viewed as a commodity when it comes to the question of marriage and her compliance with her parents' wishes in the matter is taken for granted. That Clarissa should openly defy her parents by her refusal to marry a man she cannot love leads to the loss of all she holds dear and ends in terrible tragedy. The title page of the first edition continues: *'Comprehending The Most Important Concerns of Private Life And Particularly Showing The Distresses That May Attend The Misconduct Both Of Parents And Children In Relation To Marriage.'*

Clarissa Harlowe is a member of the landed gentry. Familial ties are paramount and the opportunity for aggrandisement of the family through a prudent marriage is expected by her father and elder brother, James, as well as the vindictive Arabella, her older sister. The fact that Clarissa cannot abide the approved suitor, Mr Roger Solmes, matters not a jot to her father who is determined that Clarissa will do her duty and marry this odious man. The family expect the 'obstinate, perverse, undutiful Clarissa Harlowe!' to forego her own personal happiness in order that they may benefit. Clarissa wants to be obedient to her father yet her intelligence will not permit her to sacrifice her independence of mind and spirit and marry a man whom she sees as unacceptable not only in appearance but in his moral outlook on life. However, in a patriarchal society it must necessarily be Clarissa who suffers when her tyrannical father and brother, the scheming and morally hateful James, backed up by her male relations, insist she follows the path of dutiful obedience and marry the man. The unfolding story is narrated through a series of letters and ends in tragedy both for the morally good Clarissa and the dastardly Lovelace who helps her escape from the clutches of her family only to hold her prisoner, isolating her still further while he tries to persuade her to marry him.

Hester's arguments against the conventionally accepted view of parental authority in *Clarissa* brought her into the public arena, a dangerous place for a young woman to be in the eighteenth century when modesty in expressing one's opinions and obedience were qualities expected to be espoused in a young woman: yet here was a young woman displaying shocking temerity in taking on one of the great literary figures of the day. She writes a letter to Elizabeth Carter apologising for not replying to a letter earlier:

> The truth is, then, that I have been engaged in a kind of amicable controversy with my honoured friend Mr. Richardson, which has occasioned letters of so immoderate a length between us, that I have been quite tired of pen and ink, and inexcusably negligent of all my other correspondents. Does it not sound strange, my dear Miss Carter, that a girl like me should have dared to engage in a dispute with such a man? Indeed I have often wondered at my own assurance; but the pleasure and improvement I expected from his letters were motives too strong to be resisted, and the kind encouragement he gave me got the better of my fear of exposing myself.[8]

Richardson writes to Lady Bradshaigh, in 1751: 'I am at present engaged with a most admirable young lady of little more than twenty, Miss Mulso, on the subject of Filial Obedience and Paternal Authority, &c. Miss Mulso is a charming writer, &c. Your ladyship will be charmed with her part of the subject.' He also admits that part of his purpose is to 'but whet, but stimulate ladies, to show what they are able to do and how fit they are to be intellectual, as well as domestic companions to men of the best sense.'[9]

Hester's brother, John, charted the exchange of letters between

Samuel Richardson, author of Clarissa, *correspondent of Hester Mulso*

Richardson and his sister for Gilbert White: 'The first letter was long, Mr Richardson's answer 13 close pages, Heck's reply 17; & Mr R-s 3.' Hester's first letter on the subject is dated Friday, Oct.12, 1750 and is written on her return from a visit to Hampton, Twickenham. She explains her failure to write to Richardson from there as he requested because:

> the business there was to laugh, to sing, and to dance; and I was not allowed to be enough of a rational creature to converse with Mr Richardson. However, don't think me quite lost in dissipation: I am now returned for the winter; and returned with the same taste for reasonable pleasures that I went out with, and shall find the same delight in your conversation, whenever you will favour me with it, as I did when I was so happy at North-End.[10]

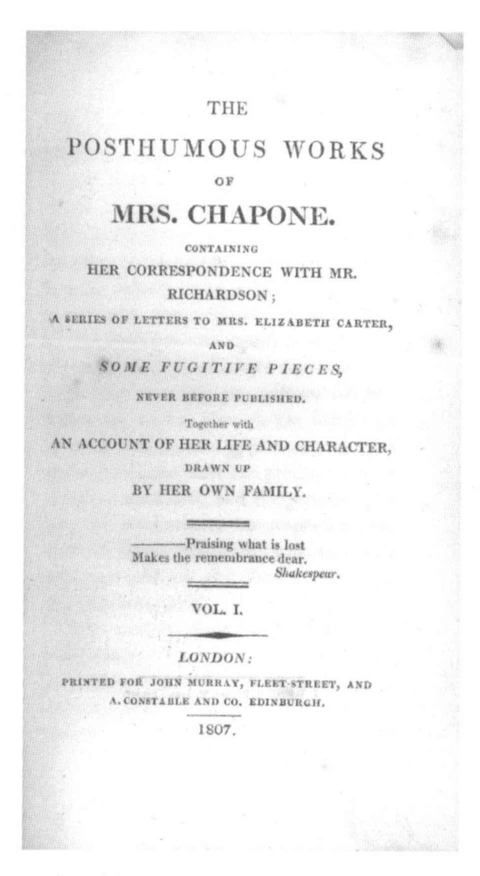
THE
POSTHUMOUS WORKS
OF
MRS. CHAPONE.
CONTAINING
HER CORRESPONDENCE WITH MR.
RICHARDSON;
A SERIES OF LETTERS TO MRS. ELIZABETH CARTER,
AND
SOME FUGITIVE PIECES,
NEVER BEFORE PUBLISHED.
Together with
AN ACCOUNT OF HER LIFE AND CHARACTER,
DRAWN UP
BY HER OWN FAMILY.

———Praising what is lost
Makes the remembrance dear.
Shakespear.

VOL. I.

LONDON:
PRINTED FOR JOHN MURRAY, FLEET-STREET, AND
A. CONSTABLE AND CO. EDINBURGH.
1807.

Title page to Vol 1 of the 1807 edition of The Posthumous Works of Mrs Chapone

She refers to Susanna Highmore as Richardson's 'amiable friend' and looks forward to calling on her and meeting Richardson there.

She then gets down to the reason behind this letter:

> Miss Prescott has desired me not to neglect the proposal you made to me of telling you in writing my sentiments on the subject we touched on at North-End, of filial duty and parental authority. She thinks with me, that to engage you to an explanation of your notions on this, as well as on all other important subjects, cannot but be highly advantageous and improving to her and me; and it is with this in view that I am contented to expose my opinions to you, in order to have them rectified by you.

So it was with the encouragement of her future sister-in-law that Hester sends her first letter. Hester's key objection to the character Clarissa lies in the fact that although Richardson portrays Clarissa as capable of reasoning 'so justly on all other subjects,' she is depicted as 'so superstitious and weak in her apprehension of parental authority' and furthermore 'implicitly joins with her father to condemn herself, when neither reason nor religion condemn her.' Hester has pinpointed the dichotomy in Richardson's view of women: he championed the intellectual development of women yet still viewed them as being sexually vulnerable and in need of parental protection. For any woman the marriage market was a risky business for, denied choice and the power of veto, she could be consigned to an unhappy and loveless marriage. Hester ends this letter by declaring that virtuous characters should not include superstition as a trait but rather religion should be shown as based on precepts which are rational. She expresses her delight on November 10, 1750 at receiving Richardson's response to her arguments:

> How much my heart thanks you for all the trouble you have taken with me, my most kind friend! My excellent instructor! I have no words that can express. I am ashamed to think how much time I have cost you; may but my mind be as much bettered as it has been delighted by your last letter, and then, my dear Mr. Richardson will not think his labour thrown away, even on me.

She continues to adopt the subservient position of a pupil yet recognizes that she is 'so obstinate, so tenacious a girl.' In answer to Richardson's point that she takes the side of the child – hardly surprising as she was still living with her father and had been brought up to accept that obedience, virtue and modesty were key qualities sought in a daughter – she pays a loving tribute to her father who has both her filial obedience and her affection. She has no fear of his displaying any tyrannical power over her and goes on to say:

> I hope my own heart deceives me not, when it assures me that it is ready to sacrifice much of its own happiness to that of my dear papa; and that it will always acknowledge by every act of reverence and submission which may not interfere with its first duties, the great debt of gratitude which it must for ever owe him.

Later, Hester was to prove that when events brought father and daughter into conflict she still upheld these views and acceded to his wishes. She now turns to her defence of her view of parental authority and her argument that a child's obedience can cease. John Locke in Chapter Six of *The Second Treatise of Civil Government* examines parental authority and the bonds which govern the relationship between parents and children:

> Children, I confess, are not born in this full state of equality, though they are born to it. Their parents have a sort of rule and jurisdiction over them, when they come into the world, and for some time after, but it is but a temporary one. The bonds of his subjection are like swaddling clothes they are wrapt up in, and supported by, in the weakness of their infancy: age and reason as they grow up, loosen them, till at length they drop quite off, and leave a man at his own free disposal.[11]

Hester takes up Locke's thesis and poses the question: 'If such a state of reason, such an age of discretion made him free, the same shall make his son free too?' Hester interprets this as to include women:

> ... and if his son, I presume his daughter too; since the duty of a child is equally imposed on both, and since the natural liberty Mr Locke speaks of arising from reason, it can never be proved that women have not a right to it, unless it can be proved that they are not capable of knowing the law they are under.

Hester continues by quoting Locke where he argues that children are bound by gratitude to their parents but this does not entitle:

> ... parents a power of command over their children, or an authority to make laws, and dispose, as they please, of their lives or liberties. 'Tis one thing to owe honour, respect, gratitude, and assistance, another, to require an absolute obedience and submission. The honour due to parents, a monarch in his throne owes his mother, and yet this lessens not his authority, nor subjects him to her government.

Thus Hester argues that Clarissa did not have to obey her parents when they tried to coerce her into marrying the hateful Solmes. Hester rebuts Richardson's argument that a woman can learn to love a husband after marriage in the course of filial duty:

> How little likelihood is there that a man, who, with all the assiduity, all the compliance, all the arts which the desire of pleasing inspires him with, whilst a lover, cannot obtain a favourable thought, should at once become amiable in those very eyes which before regarded him with aversion, and dear to that heart which shrunk at his approach, from the moment he is adorned with the title of *husband*!

Furthermore Hester argues forcefully that had Clarissa married Solmes then she would have committed perjury for clearly she could neither love nor honour him:

> Remember, dear sir, that the minister before he joins the pair, requires

> them, "As they shall answer it at the dreadful day of judgement," to confess if they know any impediment; and bids them be assured that so many as are coupled together otherwise than God's word allow, are not joined together by God, neither is their marriage lawful.
>
> 'Is not hatred on one side an *impediment*?'

Therefore Hester argues that Clarissa is forced to escape although this throws her on the mercy of Lovelace thereby endangering her with fatal consequences. Finally Hester asserts that a father who curses his daughter has 'very little title to be looked upon in this awful light.' Clarissa's concern for her father's welfare in the light of this curse is worthy of a Christian.

This long letter which in printed form is forty-eight pages ends with an apology:

> I am frightened to see what a quantity I have written. You bid me not spare you, and I have not indeed been sparing of your patience, which I fear I have quite exhausted. But forgive me, and as a proof that you do so, let me have the pleasure of seeing you soon; otherwise I shall think I have been too pert, and that my dear Mr. Richardson is angry with his
>
> Ever obliged humble servant,
>
> H. Mulso.

Hester marshals her arguments well and her close study of *Clarissa* is demonstrated by her references to the text. In the final letter of fifty-three printed pages written on January 3, 1751 Hester examines the predicament faced by children whose parents were tyrannical in exacting filial duty. The letter opens with an expression of her gratitude to Richardson and a positioning of herself as open to correction. Her flattery of the much older Richardson reveals she is fully aware of how valuable her relationship with Richardson is and how much she would suffer should he withdraw his friendship and encouragement:

> ... bestowing so much time and pains on one who can so ill repay your goodness; and who for all the pride, the pleasure, and improvement she has received from your friendship and correspondence, has nothing to offer you but her sincere thanks, her best esteem, and an affection and reverence next to filial; nothing to entertain you with but the rude essays of an ignorant girl, the unconnected sallies of a wild imagination, with but little judgement to direct or control it.

By positioning herself as ignorant and lacking in judgment she sets out in the final letter that she is ready to be compliant.

Hester argues that in fact both she and Richardson are on the same side as Locke as their positions are so close. She refers to his letter and seeks to establish how far they agree or differ asking Richardson what children must do when parents treat them with cruel injustice. Must they show the same obedience as to kind and indulgent parents? If this is so then there is no advantage in living in a free country where there is no redress 'against domestic tyrants.' Hester argues her point by quoting from Richardson's previous letters and poses the question 'whether the bare title of father or mother, shall give to such, a right to make their children miserable for life? And if not, what kind or degree of duty is owing to such, and on what grounds?' Hester then examines the case histories of three women who have suffered from parental abuse arguing that when it comes to freedom of choice in marriage parents have no right to force a child to marry and that '… (at any time of the child's life from eighteen to thirty and upwards) the parents shall not, unless they can give superior reasons, refuse their consent to a child who, by her wisdom, prudence, discretion, justifies unexceptionally her passion for a particular object.' John Chapone,[12] to whom Hester had been introduced at North-End, was fast becoming Hester's particular object. Her own filial obedience would be tested.

Hester gives examples of women who have been sorely mistreated by one or both parents even into their thirties if they had not married. These examples are drawn from real life not the fictional world of Samuel Richardson. As a young woman Hester is in the position of being able to empathise more with their predicament than Richardson. She defends herself against Richardson's accusation of being the spearhead and spokeswoman for the 'hastys, the impatients, the impetuous.' Painting a vivid picture of herself leading 'a set of Amazonian soldiers, all dresst in flame-coloured taffety, expert in leaping windows, or scaling walls, but whose conduct is by no means equal to their courage' she rejects his call, suggesting that she is unqualified to lead such an assault. However, she continues to argue for freedom of choice quoting Samuel von Pufendorf,[13] the seventeenth century German political philosopher, whose view on filial duty she concurs with so long as the parental duty has been observed. Richardson had also argued that 'a woman, either as daughter or wife, never can be in a state of independency.' Hester accepts that few women are independent but goes on to state 'whatever differences in particular circumstances, or the customs of the world, may make, these destroy not a general truth, that *women*, as rational and accountable beings, are free agents as well as *men*.' Hester recognises that: 'The rules of the world being made by *men*, are always more severe on *women* than on themselves' but 'though men's ways are unequal, the ways of God are equal, and with him *every woman* shall find justice.'

Although Hester has defended herself from the role Richardson has cast her in as leading assertive females she is asserting the rights of women in the face of Richardson's criticisms. She furthers her argument by stating that a woman's position in society is affected by her class:

> But with regard to parents, I own I do not see that *God* and *nature* have made daughters *more* dependent on them than sons. Custom indeed allows not the daughters of people of fashion to leave their father's family to seek their own subsistence, and there is no way for them to gain a creditable livelihood, as gentlemen may. But amongst the lower ranks of people, daughters are as soon independent as sons. The girls and boys are alike sent out to provide for themselves.

Her scathing view of marriages – 'which are made up by the parents are generally (amongst people of quality or great fortune) mere Smithfield bargains, so much ready money for so much land, and my daughter flung into the bargain!' – reflects her determination to have freedom of choice based on mutual attraction and love when the time came for her to marry. She continues

> I must have been asleep, when I fancied I heard experienced people talk of an honourable engagement with a person of small fortune, however worthy, however suitable by birth, merit and temper, as *madness* and *folly*; and those young women applauded as miracles of discretion and wisdom, who have sacrificed themselves to a fool or knave with a good estate.

Hester questions Richardson's view that the majority of parents seek happiness for their children in marriage rather than securing land and fortune. By espousing such views to Richardson Hester no doubt realised that her chances in the marriage market might be substantially reduced. Her brother, John, records, in a letter to Gilbert White: 'Old *Cibber*[14] *swore* to her Face She would never be married.' Hester was to prove him wrong.

Hester refers to Richardson's reply to her second letter and defends herself against his accusation of depreciating the understanding of parents or casting contempt on them. It was, according to Hester, unintentional but she concedes that if Richardson is right then it was her intent: 'Well then, scratch out of my letter that vile passage, that *seemed* to mean so vile a design.' She however, will preserve and re-read Richardson's admonition to: 'Reign in, on these important subjects, your imagination.' She sees Richardson as discomfited by her assertive arguments. She acknowledges that although she may be lacking in 'the characteristic graces of her sex, in *meekness*, *patience*, *resignation submission*; let not the reading and writing ladies suffer for this; *I* never was a writing lady till you made me one.' She hopes that her arguments will not make him side with the view that it is preferable to offer girls little education, exclaiming:

> Forbid it science! Forbid it Justice! That the sex, and the cause of learning, should suffer for the faults of *one ignorant girl*! For if I have erred, you should impute it rather to my *ignorance* than knowledge. Miss Carter says (and she is herself proof of the truth of her assertion) 'tis certain that every accession of understanding, whether in a man or woman, in its natural tendency, leads to the improvement of the heart. Be not discouraged, good Sir, from your laudable design of "making young ladies better than some of them think they need to be;" and let me obtain mercy, if not for myself, yet for the *reading and writing ladies*.

Hester in her attempts to bring their views closer finally returns to the question of aversion to a forced marriage. She quotes Richardson's response in which he argued that young women must not imagine themselves entitled to non-compliance based on Clarissa's arguments unless they too, like Clarissa, feel absolute aversion. In response Hester argues:

> 'But, dear Sir, will not *less* than an *absolute aversion* be sufficient to give a woman a liberty to refuse an engagement which puts the happiness of her whole life so much in the power of another, that nothing less than a *perfect* esteem should induce her to place so great a trust in his hands? And *whatever* may be the *reason* of a woman's dislike to a man, if she *does* dislike him, has she not a right to refuse to marry him. For my own part, I think, if ever I marry, I ought to give the man I marry a sincere preference to all other men; and I should think myself at liberty to reject any man to whom I could not give such a preference. The marriage vow ought to be perfectly voluntary.'

Hester takes up arms again in defence of Clarissa's position and argues that 'nothing less than perfect esteem should induce her to place so great a trust in his hands.' The risk of committing her future happiness into the hands of a husband who has power over her is too great a gamble if the woman does not love him. She must have the right to refuse and points out that she accepts that good parents have the right of veto but asks Richardson to accept that all children should have the same right. Finally she turns to the Harlowe-curse: she argues that Clarissa with her rational powers would recognise it held no power in the face of God and therefore she would not fear it. She ends her third and final letter on the subject of filial obedience:

> And now may I not flatter myself that we are almost agreed? At least that you begin to think me not *quite so rebellious a spirit* as you did? I will hope so till you tell me otherwise, because I wish to think with you on all subjects; and because I am ambitious enough to wish to emulate the excellence in heart and head of my dear papa Richardson; such is the phaeton-like aspiring of
> His ever obliged
> And affectionate child,
> H. Mulso.

Hester recognises her own tenaciousness. She has argued her points persuasively, cogently and with passion but for many who read the letters at the time her views would have been deemed dangerous by threatening the status quo. However, her brother John is clearly proud of her when he writes to Gilbert White on December 30, 1750: 'Several great men as the Bp of London, the Speaker &c: have seen this Dispute & think Mr R— hard pressed, & Heck has gained great Honour.' He refers to her 'voluminous Dispute with him upon the subject of Parental authority, occasioned by her thinking Clarissa's apprehension of her Father's malediction too strong.' Hester owed much to Richardson's engaging in this correspondence. It gave her the opportunity to mount a spirited and eloquent defence of her arguments. Hester did not disappoint and by producing such a *tour de force* she demonstrated that young women could be rational beings and voice their opinions coherently and cohesively in defence of their rights. Whether or not it impinged on Hester's chances of securing a husband remained to be seen.

Her friend Elizabeth Carter supported Hester's views but then Elizabeth was no meek and mild woman either. She was openly irritated by Richardson's reported prolixity in his side of the correspondence with Hester, although she has not actually seen the letters. Hester refers to this in a letter to Elizabeth when she defends Richardson:

> You say such an unmerciful prolixity upon a plain single subject, where one is not engaged by the interesting events of a narrative, and where there is no room for imagery or beauty of style, is beyond mortal sufferance; but give me leave to assure you that, in my humble opinion, there is great beauty of style in many parts of Mr. R.'s letters, and that he illustrates his arguments by a number of stories, which (though I must own I thought them not much to the purpose) gave me great pleasure, from his agreeable manner of telling them: in short I do not believe that even you would think the time thrown away which would be spent in reading his part of the correspondence; and, if I had you in town, I would punish you for the unjust prepossession you have entertained, by making you read it all through; then indeed I

> would allow you to give your opinion, and I am sure it would be a more favourable one to poor dear Mr Richardson, who never, I believe, wrote any thing that did not shew an excellent heart and a very uncommon understanding.[15]

Elizabeth's reply must have continued her criticism of Richardson for Hester refers to it in her next letter to Elizabeth:

> … and so, madam, you will laugh at me and at my poor dear Mr. R.— why then I do protest I won't bear it! Was there ever so unmerciful, so unjust, so partial a censurer! Nay, don't wonder, for I sat down with a resolution to scold, and I will scold, 'History of Frogs,' 'Conquest of Mexico,' 'Art of flying to the Moon!' 'Thou hast the most unsavoury similies, and art indeed the most comparative rascally, sweet young prince!' but really and truly, dear Miss Carter, I am half angry in earnest at you condemning Mr. R.'s letters in this manner, without even having read them, and a great mind to send them to you in mere spite; for after having set yourself so unreasonably against them, I doubt not but it will be a punishment to you, and yet good breeding will oblige you to read them if I send them. Therefore pray be a little more civil, for you see I have a way to make you repent your unmerciful raillery.

Hester continues by defending Richardson against Elizabeth's accusation of prolixity in *Clarissa* although she does confess:

> As to his letters, I do not allow you to judge them without having read them. – That they are very long I confess, nay I will even grant that the argument would have been clearer had they been much shorter; but there is good sense in every page, wit and humour in some, entertaining narrative in others, which narratives were not concerning the history of frogs, the conquest of Mexico, nor the art of flying to the moon; though I have honestly owned(and thereby given you occasion to laugh, graceless as you are) that I did not think them much to the purpose of the debate between us. They are designed to prove, from the imprudencies of some individuals, how unfit young women in general are to be made independent, and how unhappy those marriages often are which are made without the advice or consent of their natural guardians and protectors. But as I never contended for such undue liberty, as I never disputed the parents' right to a negative in the case of marriage, I do not think that any advantage could be made of these stories against me.[16]

Elizabeth and Richardson did meet at North-End in 1753 when she visited with Catherine Talbot. Richardson was interested in Elizabeth's views and those of Benito Jeronimo Feijóo.[17] In Richardson's last epistolary novel, *Sir Charles Grandison* one of his characters, Mrs Shirley, attacks the male attitude to women and education and the lack of opportunities for women to participate in intelligent conversation which reflects Richardson's knowledge of Feijóo's work. Presumably Elizabeth forgave Richardson his prolixity.

Hester is still in contact with Gilbert White. While she is staying with her brother John in London in June 1751 she borrows a sheet of his writing paper and encloses a letter to Gilbert thanking him for his poem *The Invitation to Selborne*[18] which she and her brother have been reading and offering criticism. John prefaces her comments with: 'I shall leave a page, for Ladies are voluble.' Hester writes:

> I am so much obliged both to the Poet and the Friend in Mr White's gallant and elegant Invitation that I cannot help telling him how much I am mortified that I cannot thank him in Person for his admirable Poem. Your description of Selborne has left nothing to 'the craving imagination of Miss Hecky', and it was very kindly done to send me so lively a Picture, as I fear I am not to see the Original. It is no great compliment to say that I wish to accept your Invitation as I write from this suffocating town, where I am killed with heat, and have no voice or strength. Here, however, I am likely to remain (if I can exist) the greatest part of the summer, with only the refreshing excursion of a day or two now and then to Mr Richardson's at North-End to keep me alive. I shall gratify his Vanity and my own by showing him your verses; and I think yours, if you have any, must taste the praises of Richardson. Pray give my thanks and compliments to your father and sister for their part of the invitation. I hope your father has not seen your more than Poetical Compliments, for if he has, he must not see me unless he has a turn for Poetry, and knows that a Poet must give the Perfection he does not find. When you next drink tea in 'the Pensile nest-like Bower' pity
>
> Your humble servant
> Yes Papa![19]

Chapter 7

'a kind of flower garden of ladies'

Hester's private life at this time was happy. She was living with her father in London, managing the household, enjoying the meetings at North-End, writing and reading with her ever critical eye. Her friendship with Elizabeth Carter was blossoming with a regular exchange of letters. Hester had been delighted when in the summer of 1751 Elizabeth invited her to stay at Deal for three days. She writes:

> 'It might perhaps be more modest in me, dear Miss Carter, to decline your very obliging and most agreeable invitation, but truly I am a very weak creature, and unable to resist so strong a temptation. My aunt has been good natured enough to give me her excuse and permission to leave her for a few days; and next Friday, if convenient to you, I propose stuffing myself into that same lumbering conveyance you speak of, and embracing my dear Miss Carter. How shall I regale upon your *one* dish, with 'The feast of reason and the flow of the soul!' Remember that you have promised me one dish; if I see it even *garnished* I shall take it as a rebuke for my want of modesty in taking you at your first word, and without any ceremony making myself a part of your family.[1]

On returning to Canterbury and her aunt she writes an enthusiastic and amusing letter of thanks:

> A thousand thanks to my dear Miss Carter for the happiness I enjoyed in a visit which will ever give me much pleasure in reflection, though at present the pleasure is mixed with a painful regret … I owe many thanks also to your very agreeable sister, who seems to me to have not only 'refined sense,' but 'all sense,' and an excellent genius for human conveniences. Though she is a wicked wit, and laughs at me, and despises me in her heart, yet I can't for my life be angry with her for it, but patiently consider that 'it might have pleased God to have made me a wit.' I saw her too exult over me in her housewifely capacity; – when I folded up the gingerbread nuts so awkwardly, I saw it was nuts to her; but I forgive her, and hope she will repent before she dies of all her uncharitable insults on a poor gentlewoman, that never was guilty

> of more than four poor odes, and yet is as careless, as awkward, and as untidy as if she had made as many heroic poems as the great and majestic Blackmore!
>
> You were pleased to be anxious about my journey, therefore I must give you some account of it. My company was much better than I hoped, and not a man midwife amongst them. Imprimis, there was Mrs—, sister to Mr—, a very sensible, well-bred old gentlewoman, who knew my aunt, and with whom I scraped acquaintance. Item, a Mrs—, I think was her name, who I fancy was one of your party at commerce, seeing she was fat and vociferous, and looked uncommonly joyous. With her a civil gentlemanlike sort of a sail-maker, (for that he told me was his trade) from Ratcliffe-Cross, very fat and large, with a leg bigger than my waist. Item a maid servant, going to Lady——'s, of a middle size. Item, a very fat gentlewoman, taken up very hot at Sandwich and put down again at Wingham; who in that three miles, with the assistance of the sail-maker, had very nearly finished my journey through this mortal life; but her removal restored me to the faculty of breathing, and I got to Canterbury without any casualty, save breaking my lavender-water bottle in my pocket, and cutting my fingers. I had like to have been overturned upon Sandown, but thought of the stoic philosophy, and did not squeak. At Wingham we refreshed nature, and repaired our clay tenements with some filthy dried tongue, and bread and butter, and some well mixed mountain wine, by which means, as I have told you before, I was brought alive to Canterbury.[2]

Hester's letters reveal an ease of writing and a sharp and amused eye. She also reveals her growing confidence in her own opinions on literature with her critical views on the writer Henry Fielding and his novel *Amelia* (1751) which Elizabeth praises. Hester censures Fielding for his 'low opinion of human nature' especially when it comes to depicting wicked men. Theirs is a lively correspondence ranging from the books they are reading; literary criticism and philosophy; health problems – Elizabeth suffered from terrible debilitating headaches while Hester was prone to fevers, and was seriously ill in 1753; and the practical problems of journeys by stage coach in which the unfortunate female passengers were often jammed closely with their fellow travellers. Hester seems to have viewed these coach journeys with amusement though no doubt she would have preferred the luxury of travelling in her own carriage. Fortunately roads were beginning to improve and journey times would be substantially reduced on major routes by the 1760s.

Hester was also keen to read the Spanish essayist and philosopher, Feijóo, and asks Elizabeth to send her some passages in translation 'in which he speaks so honourably of our sex.' When Elizabeth fails to do so Hester comments: 'I am sorry you could not favour me with a sample of Father Feyjoo's [sic] excellence. I am a little surprised that a Spaniard should think so favourably of women. One would imagine by their manner of treating them, that they had as mean opinion of them as the Turks.'[3] What led Hester to this uncharitable view can only be surmised. Her interest in the author stems from her involvement and enthusiasm for Richardson's last novel, *Sir Charles Grandison*, on which he is working. His creation of the character Sir Charles Grandison is at the behest of many of his female readers and friends, like Mrs Donellan and in response to Henry Fielding's *Tom Jones*. Catherine Talbot is closely involved correcting the manuscript and making suggestions. Also closely involved are Hester and Susanna Highmore. However, Mrs Donellan[4] did not wholly approve of Hester on whom she held Richardson had based his genteel characters deeming Hester to be 'second rate as to politeness of manners' which is why they are 'not so really polished as he thinks them to be.' Was this perhaps jealousy over Hester's close involvement as Richardson's muse? Grandison is a morally good character. He rescues the beleaguered orphan, Harriet Byron, from the clutches of Sir Hargrave Pollexfen who is after her £15,000 inheritance. Hester comments to Elizabeth Carter that the book may induce women to remain single, with the result that the country will be overrun with old maids because no man can live up to Richardson's portrayal of the perfect man. She adds that it will be superior to *Clarissa*.

Susanna and Hester in their correspondence discuss at length the progress of *Sir Charles Grandison* and speculate as to the fate of the heroine, Harriet. Hester writes to Susanna on July 21, 1751, while she is staying at Canterbury with her aunt and uncle, complaining that Pressy has forgotten her while she is in the company of the Duncombes and 'gentlemen that gallant her about so genteelly.' Hester so obviously relishes the meetings with Richardson and his coterie at North-End and continues that she longs 'to know the progress of the story, but must wait for that pleasure till I return to be one of our dear papa's happy auditors.' For Hester the chance to discuss and analyse Richardson's novels with the great man himself provided her with the intellectual stimulation and excitement she craved. She confides in Susanna: 'yet is my fancy never so well pleased as when it places me amongst the dear circle at North-End, which your pencil so prettily described. You do not know how much pleasure I take in surveying that sketch, nor how often I contemplate every figure in it, and recal the delights of that day.' The sketch[5] she refers to shows Richardson, reading from the manuscript of *Sir Charles Grandison* to a circle of friends which includes: Hester's two brothers, Thomas and Edward, Hester, Miss Mary Prescott, whom Thomas would marry; the Reverend John Duncombe,[6] who praises both Richardson and Hester in *The Feminiad* and Susanna Highmore,[7] who would marry Duncombe in 1761 and live in Canterbury. The sketch was drawn by Susanna, who was the daughter of the celebrated painter, Joseph Highmore. He was a friend of Richardson's and painted a series of pictures based on *Pamela*. Susanna, who was both a poet and artist, was on intimate terms with Hester and a favourite at Richardson's gatherings. It was her future father-in-law, William Duncombe, who had effected Hester's introduction to Richardson. Richardson had written to Susanna in July 1750: 'Mr Duncombe, sen. brought me an admirable letter from Miss Mulso, from Canterbury; a letter that has made me in love with her.'

Susanna responds to Hester's letter: 'Your charming epistle, your tender and affectionate expressions of friendship, gave my heart more delight than it has felt of a long time. Oh my dear Hecky, could I say with truth, that our souls are sister souls, how pleased I should be with myself! – how sweet the idea of an irresistible sympathy between us!' She then turns to the subject of key interest to both young women the fate of 'our lovely favourite … and our beloved Sir Charles.' She suspects that Richardson has included Harriet's 'foreboding dream …

> … to revenge himself on you and I, two saucy girls that pretend to be so sure that happiness must reward virtue and heroic sufferings of the exalted lovers, for whom we interest ourselves so strenuously; let us remember he can cut the thread of life at pleasure; their destiny is in his hands, and I am not certain that our security may not provoke him to destroy them, for that has set his imagination on the glow; and he can draw instructions equally from every catastrophe, and can wind nature as he pleases; she presents him with events for every purpose, so probable, that we shall think no other than the chosen fortune could have attended them with propriety. … Every paragraph of your letter gives me very great satisfaction, save only one, and for that one, I could almost, nay I can quite, chide my dear Miss Mulso, who makes me repent of the frankness of my heart, which told her of the preface I had written – a silly girl was I to do so, and too severely punished for my folly, if she persists in a refusal of that gratification, to her papa Richardson.
>
> By the time this reaches you, the happy visit to Deal will be over, and the sweet recollections and reflections concerning improving conversations, agreeable walks, and every pleasing employment, when there will dwell upon your mind. While I am writing this, methinks I see the two women most formed to give each other the highest satisfaction, enjoying, in each other's company, the inexpressible delight of friendly communications, equally sensible, benevolent, and affectionate.[8]

Susanna is of course referring to Hester's visit to Elizabeth Carter. For the two young women, both in their early twenties and both in the marriage market but both determined to marry a man they had fallen in love with, the plot line of the novel was heady stuff and Richardson's readings avidly awaited. Both Hester and Susanna refer to Richardson as 'papa Richardson' and being 'saucy girls' revealing a flirtatious yet seemingly respectful and subservient relationship with the much older author at the height of his fame.

Richardson is interested in Hester and Susanna's reactions to his new novel. He is well aware that as an elderly man he cannot share the emotions of young women so asks Hester to write some scenes for him. At the end of July while on a visit to Peterborough she had received a letter from Richardson with the following request: 'I only want a description of the room you all generally sit in; then shall I have in view the benign countenance of my good Lord of Peterborough'. He continues with a compliment to Hester describing her 'intelligent sweetness shining out.' In a second letter to her the same month he chides her:

> London, July 27, 1751.
>
> CROSS THING!
>
> You cannot, you will not, give me a description of the rooms, in which you and your truly worthy friends mostly sit and converse, which I desired you to do, that I might imagine myself now and then among you! – "Come, and see them." Churl! – Yet, in another letter, tell me, that you are so happy, that you dread the coming in of visitors. Very well, Miss Mulso. But you might have gratified me in the requested description; because you could hardly expect that either my disorders or business would permit me to take such a journey.
>
> Could it be done, however, it would be inexpressibly delightful to me to honour myself with the cognition, shall I call it? of my two new nieces. God bless them all three!
>
> You do Clarissa great honour. But I hope you'll get through the last volumes without hartshorn; yet you'll hardly have been able to find an hour to read them in, in which I have not a bottle of it in my hand.
>
> "How could I be so wicked, as to mean to provoke you, and make you saucy?" – Must one be the consequence of the other? Remember, child, where you are.
>
> "You would not give a fig for a man who at twenty-six is too wise to be in love." How unfair is your inference, that the people who boast of philosophy must be those who are born without hearts!
>
> A fine task have I set myself! To draw a man that is above the common foibles of life; and yet to make a lover of him! to write, in short, to the taste of girls from fourteen to twenty-four years of age. Let me ask, Did you ever know a girl who in that ten years was not in love

either secretly or avowedly? No, say. Well, then, is it not a common failing? It is. And shall a wise man at twenty-six not be able to get above it? Let me tell you, Madam, as the world goes, I think I do a marvellous thing to make a young woman in love with a man of exalted merit. Think you that I don't? And is she to have him with a wet finger, as the saying is? But will you have the story end with a fiddle and a dance: that is to say with matrimony; or will you not? If you will, Harriet must have her difficulties. If not, the dance may be the sooner over, in order to make the happy pair shine in the matrimonial life. And yet you girls generally care not a farthing for the honesty of the honest couple after the knot is tied.

But set your charming imagination at work, and give me a few scenes, as you would have them, that I may try and work them into the story. You will be in time: for I am not likely to proceed with the girl. Only tell me what you will undertake. I expect that you will.

But difficulties must be thrown in. Give me half a score of them, Miss Mulso: look but among your female acquaintance, and you will be able to oblige me. Nay, if you yourself are a philosopher, and have always been so, I shall judge that you were born without a heart.

"Your pride feels for Harriet." Prettily said! But your pride, my dear, must feel, I doubt, a little more than it has felt. A serene man has great advantages over a girl who finds herself, after roving about in the field of liberty and defying twenty fowlers, just caught. She must part with a few feathers, I doubt. For she will not perch in quiet in her golden-wired cage. But the man shall be rather unhappy, I think, than in fault. How, Mr. R.? But hush. I don't know how I shall order it as yet. Once more; do set your charming imagination at work, and do it for me.

And here let me own, that you have a manifest advantage over me, in your inference drawn from what I say of Platonic love, and in relation to person; when I cried out, with an unjustifiable archness, Ah, my Miss Mulso! – This was also said to provoke you. And I submit to your really deserved censure.

"You believe you have been saucy!" You have not, you cannot be saucy. We are not upon the argument of filial duty, are we? – Though never father could be more affectionate to daughter than I profess myself to be to Miss Mulso. Witness her

S. RICHARDSON.[9]

Richardson writes to Hester later that year, on September 3, seeking her definition of love. He quotes her as saying: 'that you have known few girls, and still fewer men, whom you have thought capable of being in love.' He continues that he wishes to make the character of Sir Charles 'to your liking, than to the liking of three parts out of four of the persons I am acquainted with.' He flatters Hester: 'You are one of my best girls, and best judges.' Richardson is asking Hester to help him make Sir Charles more appealing to his female readers by creating a character 'capable of being terribly in love' rather than them thinking him 'too wise.' As a young woman Hester's view of men and romantic love is proving invaluable to Richardson as he develops the morally good hero and he requests: 'Dear, dear girls, help me with a few monkey-tricks to throw into his character, in order to shield him from the contempt for his wisdom.'[10]

The following year on June 20 Richardson asks her to write a short preface:

> But pray, my dear, before I go any further, remember, I expect from you a short preface for my piece. I am greatly in earnest in my request. I hope to get Miss— to give me one. And I will take liberties with both. You must not praise much, promise much. – But as it will be said "preface by a friend," you may say more than it will become the writer of the piece to say.[11]

Their correspondence on characters and the themes of love and marriage continues as well as his requests for Hester to contribute:

> "What a proposal!" say you. Why, what a proposal, my dear? Miss C. has refused, you have refused, and been the cause of a more obliging lady's refusal. Well, I can't help it. I was very much in earnest in my request to you all three. Another trial – I will see, thought I, if they value the poor story so much, as to wish it to be continued for one volume more? If they do, surely they will contribute each one letter. "You cannot write like Clementina." Have you try'd? You would on either the occasions I hinted to you, write better than she.[12]

Chapter 8

A Matrimonial Creed

Hester recognised the problem facing women who wanted or needed to lead independent lives and support themselves like Elizabeth Carter. Elizabeth would not achieve financial independence until 1758 with the publication by subscription of *All the Works of Epictetus Which are Now Extant* when she was forty-one. For Hester, who was still living at home with her father, it was encouragement that she sought at this stage rather than independence and it was through her contact with Richardson at North-End that she began to develop her writing. Hester acknowledges Richardson's role in her literary development in their debate on filial obedience: '*I* never was a writing lady until you made me one.' This had brought Hester to the attention of a much wider audience which for Hester was valuable as a young aspiring writer. However, the criticism engendered by her views on filial obedience raised questions as to whether she had damaged her own position when it came to marriage. She had stressed her willingness to be compliant to Richardson's arguments and had stressed her gratitude to him in helping her on her journey of self-improvement through this correspondence. She had cast herself in the role of an obedient daughter to the much older father figure of Richardson and castigated herself for appearing undisciplined, flattered his greater knowledge before adding: 'Forgive me, dear sir, if I have expressed myself too peremptorily on this subject, and spare not to *take me down*, whenever I forget myself so far as to argue with you with unbecoming tenaciousness or decisiveness.'

Hester would have been only too well aware that by taking on the great Richardson and expounding her arguments with such passion she might well be regarded as a threat to the status quo with her views on female equality and rights which could affect her status as a young woman in the marriage market. It was after her correspondence with Richardson on filial obedience that Hester wrote *A Matrimonial Creed addressed by Miss Mulso to Mr Richardson in consequence of his questioning her*

The Middle Class Companionate Family

strictly on what she believed to be the duties of the married state. Written probably in 1751 when she was twenty-four its tone reflects a softening in her approach to the subject of marriage along more traditional and accepted lines. In the introduction she writes:

> Being told one evening that I could not be quite a good girl, whilst I retained some particular notions concerning the behaviour of husbands and wives; – being told that I was intoxicated with false sentiments of dignity; that I was proud, rebellious, a little spit-fire,&. I thought it behoved me to examine my own mind on these particulars, to distrust its rectitude, and endeavour to detect those erroneous principles and faulty passions, which could draw on me censures so severe from some of my best friends ... if the opinions here set down shall be found to vary from those I set out with, be it imputed, not to designed evasion, but to the gradual effects which the arguments I have since heard, and the reflections I have made, may have imperceptibly produced in a mind, which, however tenacious, is not disingenuous, and would have acknowledged those effects at the time, had it, at the time, been sensible of them.[1]

Hester is carefully setting out to soften her approach to the whole vexed question surrounding filial duty and obedience. Hester needs to salvage her public reputation and establish herself as espousing the propriety expected of a young woman of the time. With this in mind she carefully avoids entering into the same subject of filial obedience which she had already examined so rigorously and rationally, but so tenaciously, in her three letters on the subject to Richardson earlier. Instead she examines the marital relationship. In prime position she places a husband as having 'a divine right to the absolute obedience of his wife, in all cases where the first duties do not interfere … he is undoubtedly her superior.' Therefore, Hester agrees, it follows that a woman should choose a husband whom she freely considers her superior. Next she holds a wife should be her husband's first and dearest friend '… with all the privileges, rights and freedoms of the most perfect friendship' but that friendship can be cancelled by the husband 'if the wife does not deserve it.' She recognises that in order for a marriage based on friendship to flourish:

> … inequality and subjection as must check and restrain that unbounded confidence and frankness which are the essence of friendship be laid aside or suffered to sleep, till such time as the woman shall shew herself unworthy of the high title of friend, with which her husband had honoured her, and shall return to the common state of wives; for though she has, by his marriage vow, a right to his love and kindness, it is not so with respect to his friendship, which is a free and voluntary gift, or conditional loan, and may be withdrawn without breach of vows, according to his discretion and her merits.

She continues by pointing out that many women are capable of filling the role of the traditional obedient and faithful wife but are not able to fulfil the companionacy that she is seeking to promote in order that mutual marital happiness may be attained. She is treading a very careful line here: apparently espousing equality in this friendship while at the same time adding that a husband has the right to bestow or remove it. The wife is key to either winning his friendship or losing it. Companionacy is therefore a privilege not a right. She continues by laying down advice on how to promote companionate marriage: each must respect the other and be solicitous for their spouse's happiness rather than seeking purely their own happiness.

Hester seeks to represent herself in a more acceptable light to Richardson and critics of her views as expressed in *Letters on Filial Obedience* by stating at the end of *A Matrimonial Creed* that after self-examination she is fully convinced that her thoughts on matrimony are not:

> … founded in pride, or in aversion to being governed, or in jealousy of power. … I have never yet been the mistress of myself, nor ever wished to be so; for I am convinced that it is generally a happiness, and often a relief to have some person to determine for us, either to point

> our duty, or direct our choice. If I know myself in this respect, I should be a loyal subject, but a rebellious slave.

In her final paragraph she refers to Richardson:

> I have also examined myself on the article of tenaciousness, imputed to me so often by Mr Richardson, and some other of my good friends, who probably know me better than I do myself. I am very far from denying the charge, which I think is very likely to be true, but what I wish is, to find the cause of this defect, and the remedy. That I am not insincere and disingenuous, I can boldly and safely determine; and if I felt myself convinced, I am certain I could own it freely. Whether my understanding or temper be in fault, I cannot tell. – Perhaps I am still tenaciously persisting in the wrong, but I do not find I *can* from any argument I have yet heard, retract from, or concede any of the opinions contained in it.

Hester is not about to change her opinion completely and has the courage to say so. In *A Matrimonial Creed* Hester defends herself against criticism levelled at her as being over tenacious, improper and ungovernable and at the same time argues that friendship within marriage is the key to lasting happiness. She would take up this theme again and expand on it later. Hester knew that *A Matrimonial Creed* would be circulated by Richardson and her views would be discussed and debated for the subject of marital choice was a topical one. In 1753 the Hardwicke Marriage Act would be passed. No longer was a purely oral contract sufficient; the Act required public marriage ceremonies, preceded by banns. Furthermore the marriage had to be registered with the couple's signatures and those of the minister performing the ceremony and two witnesses. For those under twenty-one freedom to choose one's marriage partner was dependent on parental consent. In a letter to Elizabeth Carter, in August 1753, Richardson suggests that his debate with Hester has had some influence on the Act:

> Miss Mulso, whom you know, has great reasoning powers, some time ago set up for such an advocate for children, and argued so strenuously against the parental authority, (herself one of the most dutiful of children, her father one of the most indulgent of parents,) that I the less wonder that (ingenious and excellent as she is) if the debate got wind, that it obtained the notice of those who brought in and carried through a bill, which should, by a national law, establish the parental authority, so violently attacked by a young lady, who is admired by all that know her.[2]

Delighted as she was to have debated with Richardson on filial duty, she was even more delighted to meet with a Mr John Chapone, an attorney who was part of Richardson's circle. He was the son of Mary Delany's childhood friend, Sarah Kirkham who had married the Reverend John Chapone in 1725. Sarah, the daughter of a clergyman in Gloucestershire, was the same age as Mary, her neighbour at Buckland near Campden in Gloucestershire where Mary's father, Bernard Granville, a Tory, took refuge after he was released from the Tower. He had been imprisoned in 1715, with his brother Lord Lansdowne after the death of Queen Anne and change of government, for supposed complicity with Lord Oxford[3] to exclude the Hanoverian monarch from the English throne. The two girls became friends and they played together in the garden overlooking the Vale of Evesham. Sarah [also known as Sally] was, by Mary's account, somewhat suspect to her father who thought she lacked 'gentleness ... and could not bear anything that had the appearance of being too free and masculine.' She went on to run a boarding school for girls in Gloucestershire in the 1730s and championed education for women. She was the author of *The Hardships of the English Laws in Relation to Wives, with an Explanation of the Original Curse of Subjection Passed Upon the Woman, in an Humble Address to the Legislature* (1735) in which she examined married women's inequality before the law and cited lack of education for their ignorance. Unlike Hester's mother she saw education as a means of empowerment for women.

It was Mrs Dewes, Mary Delany's sister, who introduced John Chapone into Richardson's circle. Like her sister, Anne Dewes was a friend of Sarah and both women championed Richardson's novels. To a letter to Richardson Anne adds:

> P.S. I end where I should have begun, which is, to beg the favour of you to oblige with your countenance and conversation the young gentleman who brings you this; his name is Chapone; a remarkably sober, good young man; his father is a very worthy clergyman; his mother who has been a particular friend to me and my sisters from their childhood, and has most uncommon sense and improved understanding, thinks, with great justice, that your good judgement and friendly advice(which I am sure you will not refuse) must be of great advantage to her son, now he is just advancing upon the most dangerous stage of life.[4]

When Hester met John he was practising law in the Temple and at first the attraction seems to have been one-sided. For Hester it was love at first sight. John obviously made a good impression on Richardson who writes on August 20 1750:

> Most heartily do I thank good Mrs Dewes for her recommendation of Mr Chapone to my acquaintance and friendship. I am greatly taken with him. A sensible, an ingenious, a modest young man. Methinks I am sorry that this kingdom is likely soon to lose him. (A reference to John's moving abroad. In fact he remained in London.)[5]

Before long John had fallen in love with this somewhat argumentative young woman who was critical and confident enough to take on Richardson. However, parents could still exercise their power of veto, especially over the financial position of a daughter's suitor: Hester's father, Thomas, did not approve of his daughter's choice, because of John's poor financial standing, and made her promise that she would not enter into an engagement with John without his permission. Hester agreed and was willing to wait, presumably relieved that her father did not forbid an engagement completely. Hester was able to see John at the family home and finally in 1754 with her father's permission they became engaged. Hester was twenty-seven years old. However, it would be a further six years before her father would give his blessing to their marriage.

Like so many others John's mother, Sarah Chapone, had followed the debate between Richardson and Hester and was impressed by 'the Strength and Penetration of Miss Mulso's Genius.' In her correspondence with Richardson she even went so far as to add that she would welcome a daughter-in-law of such understanding.[4] Mary Delany, also a member of Richardson's circle, comments to her sister, Anne Dewes, that Sarah is 'charmed with Sally the younger.'[6] Sarah Chapone and Richardson entered into further debate by letter. She supports Hester's view that Clarissa would have been committing perjury in the sight of God had she married Solmes and argues with the same passion as Hester on the subject of female dependence. However, when Richardson chides her for some of her views Sarah, as a mature and educated woman, does not take refuge behind the child/parent relationship and flattery of Richardson which Hester felt obliged to do.

Among the leading literary figures of the day who were part of Richardson's circle was Samuel Johnson whose great work *A Dictionary of the English Language* would be published in 1755. Hester recounts meeting the great man at Richardson's in 1753:

> Mr Johnson was very communicative and entertaining, and did me the honour to address most of his discourse to me. I had the assurance to dispute with him on the subject of human malignity; and wondered to hear a man who by his actions shows so much benevolence, maintain that the human heart is naturally malevolent, and that all the benevolence we see, in the few who are good, is acquired by reason

> and religion. You may believe I entirely disagreed with him, being as you know, fully persuaded that benevolence, or the love of our fellow-creatures, is as much a part of our nature as self-love; and that it cannot be suppressed, or extinguished, without great violence from the force of other passions. I told him I suspected him of these bad notions from some of his Ramblers, and had accused him to you; but that you had persuaded me I had mistaken his sense. To which he answered, that if he had betrayed such sentiments in his Ramblers, it was not with design; for that he believed the doctrine of human malevolence, though a true one, is not a useful one and ought not to be published to the world.[7]

Hester is clearly not overawed by a man of strong opinion and vast intelligence but rather welcomes the opportunity to engage in argument. Johnson was open-minded, liked the company of young people and encouraged women writers. However, Johnson was not short on wounding criticism. When Elizabeth Montagu published *Essays on the Writings and Genius of Shakespeare* in 1769 he made the following comment to Joshua Reynolds:

> Yes, Sir; it does her honour, but it would do nobody else honour. I have indeed not read it all. But when I take up the end of a web, and find it packthread, I do not expect by looking further to find embroidery, Sir. I will venture to say there is not one sentence of true criticism in her book.[8]

Relations somewhat cooled between Johnson and Montagu as a result. Hester did not limit her critical views on current opinion to marriage alone: she had also contributed two essays to Samuel Johnson's periodical *The Rambler* (1750-52) in which essays, largely written by Johnson, appeared on a wide range of subjects including social issues. The periodical appeared twice weekly on Tuesdays and Saturdays. In issue No.10. Saturday April 21, 1750 Hester attacks card playing on Sundays, a pastime which was fashionable at the time. Hester describes these card playing assemblies as too trifling when she was grave, and too dull when she was cheerful and warns against the dangers and miseries of gambling. Conversation was limited at these gatherings and to many women they were wearisome occasions for drinking, gossip, gambling and displaying the latest fashion. Hester views that world as a sham: a view that many other intelligent women shared.

In 1753 Hester began working on a much longer piece for Johnson's periodical *The Adventurer* (November 1752-March 1754). Founded by Johnson and John Hawkesworth it was also published twice a week and proved to be more popular than *The Rambler*. Hester's contribution was a highly moralistic tale in prose entitled *The Story of Fidelia*. It

Dr Samuel Johnson

owes much to both *Pamela* and *Clarissa* with its central theme of mercenary marriage, the perils facing a young woman who refused to bow to the demands to make such a match and the centrality of Christianity in the eponymous heroine's salvation. Hester agonised over whether it should be published. It was Elizabeth Carter – both she and Catherine Talbot were involved in the periodical – who persuaded her that she should go ahead.

Published in three instalments in 1753, it is the story of a well-born girl, Fidelia, whose mother dies when she is twelve. She is educated by her loving and free-thinking father. However when he dies she is thrown on the mercy of her uncle who takes her into his own home. At the age of twenty she is told that she will marry a man whom she feels she must love and respect. She refuses this mercenary match. Her uncle throws her out of his house and she is forced to take refuge with one of her much loved father's servants. Some days later she is summoned to a male cousin who rebukes her for turning down the offer of marriage, implying that even had she not loved her husband, once married she could have a host of male admirers. The second instalment opens with Fidelia seeking out a female friend, Amanda, who is about to marry. Instead of being sympathetic to Fidelia's plight she lectures her on accepting a mercenary marriage as being preferable to remaining a spinster. Their conversation is interrupted by the arrival of Amanda's suitor who is accompanied by a dashingly handsome young man by the name of Sir George Freelove. The wicked Freelove finally manages to seduce Fidelia. In the third and final instalment Fidelia moves into Sir George's home and for eight months he heaps his attention on her. But then she discovers he is about to marry and flees his house. She is saved from throwing herself into a river by a passing clergyman who takes her back to his home. Here she meets his wife who, although her eighth child has just died, does not waiver in her Christian faith. Fidelia remains with the saintly couple until the wife dies then leaves to go into service having found her salvation in religion. This early attempt at writing fiction is not particularly memorable. Rather it acts as a framework for Hester to put forward her arguments against the subjugation of women at the hands of unscrupulous men.

Part Two

The Bluestocking Connection

Benjamin Stillingfleet, "blew stockings"

Chapter 9

'Come in your blew stockings'

At the same time as Hester became part of Richardson's circle, a group of women who had grown disenchanted with their lack of opportunity for intellectual stimulation began to set up social gatherings where conversation was celebrated. This movement which encouraged women to engage in openly displaying their intelligence and love of learning, became known as the Bluestockings. The founder members were Elizabeth Montagu and Elizabeth Vesey.[1] Influenced by the seventeenth century French salons in Paris of Madame de Rambouillet and Madeleine de Scudéry they established a network of like-minded men and women who celebrated the art of polite conversation in the privacy of their homes. Here was a more public opportunity for the dissemination of ideas and opinions where women could have a more equal voice. Importantly they would also find support and encouragement in expressing their ideas in the published form.

The term Bluestocking was first used in the mid 1750s to describe not women but a man by the name of Benjamin Stillingfleet.[2] He came from an academic background and was a man with a wide range of interests: a botanist, publisher – he published the first English edition of the Swedish botanist Linnaeus – translator, poet, philosopher, and mountaineer – he had climbed Mont Blanc. Stillingfleet, who had a reputation for stimulating intellectual discussion was also a very popular and sought after member of the early circle of women who started throwing conversation parties. It seems that it was Elizabeth Vesey who originally coined the term when she met him in Bath and invited him to one of her gatherings. When he protested that he could not afford the customary formal silk stockings worn by men at evening functions she dismissed this sartorial worry with: 'Don't mind dress. Come in your blew stockings,'[3] a reference to the blue worsted stockings he wore ordinarily. As the majority of the other guests would be dressed in brocades and satins and the men would wear silk stockings he would have stood out. He soon became a much sought after member of the

Admiral Edward Boscawen

parties. As a botanist, a subject in which Elizabeth Montagu was interested, he was invited to stay at her country estate, Sandleford, in Berkshire. In 1756 Samuel Torriano, a friend of hers from early Tunbridge days, writes: 'You shall not keep Blew stockings at Sandleford for nothing.' But by the following year Elizabeth was bewailing the absence of Stillingfleet to her friend and physician, Dr Monsey:

> 'I do not believe our friend Mr Stillingfleet is more attached to the lilies of the field than to the lilies of the town, who toil and spin as little as the others, and like the former are better arrayed than Solomon in all his glory. I assure you our philosopher is so much a man of pleasure, he has left off his old friends, and his blue stockings, and is at operas and gay assemblies every night so imagine whether a sage doc-

> tor, a dropsical patient, and a bleak mountain are likely to attract him who has deserted the gatherings for the opera and assemblies.'[4]

Although the term Bluestocking initially was applied to Stillingfleet it became adopted to describe both male and female members of the enlightened intellectual movement. Women predominated as the hostesses: some from very wealthy and privileged backgrounds while others entertained on a less sumptuous scale. Literary and contemporary ideas were discussed in an enlightened atmosphere: women were not seen as being intellectually inferior and were encouraged to enter into rational debate. Such male luminaries as Samuel Johnson, Horace Walpole, Edmund Burke, George Lyttelton, William Pepys, Joshua Reynolds and David Garrick[5] were members. By the 1770s the term Bluestocking came to be exclusively applied to women indicating that they were women who were no strangers to intellectual ideas. Furthermore, some Bluestockings were appearing in the public sphere through publication of their works, often anonymously initially. The early Bluestockings who played such an influential role in Hester Chapone's life and became her friends included among others Mary Delany, Elizabeth Vesey, Elizabeth Carter, Elizabeth Montagu, and Frances Boscawen. Both Elizabeth Carter and Elizabeth Montagu, like Hester, saw their work published: the former to great praise while some critics such as Johnson were less than kind about Montagu's foray into literary criticism. They were followed by the younger group of whom Hester Thrale,[6] Laetitia Barbauld, Hannah More[7] and Frances Burney,[8] all played a role in Hester's later life, and all became published authors. Through their writing they established themselves as female writers of note. Hester describes herself of being fond of Fanny Burney as a person and championed her novels *Evelina* (1778) and *Cecilia* (1782). However, her opinion of Mrs Barbauld was less favourable although she admired her intellect. The term Bluestocking would later become a disparaging reference to a woman who dedicated her life to intellectual study at the expense of any social life and would remain unmarried.

Admiral Edward Boscawen, a Cornishman, is also credited as the alternative inventor of the term, referring to the gatherings as the Blue Stocking Society: a somewhat derisive reference to the fact that the men were not formally dressed. As a man of courage and action he was reputedly somewhat impatient about these literary meetings which his wife, Frances, hosted. Edward, born at Tregothnan, near Falmouth, was the second son of the first Viscount Falmouth. Boscawen had started his naval career, which was a distinguished one, at the age of twelve which was not uncommon in the eighteenth century. Boscawen was involved in the war with Spain which the Prime Minister Sir Robert Walpole had finally declared in 1739. He had already distinguished himself at Cartegena leading a landing force of 500 men against the Spanish and destroying two forts in 1741. After his marriage he had entered Parliament in 1742 as member for Truro in his native county. Two years later he was back at sea and his reputation as a courageous leader in naval warfare grew. His naval career was one of glory: he was promoted to Rear-Admiral of the Blue in 1747 following his role in the great victory over the French off Finisterre; his expedition to India and the recapture of Madras in September 1749 further enhanced his naval career. Aged forty-six he was made Admiral of the Blue prior to his part in the great victory in capturing Louisburg from the French in 1758 which made him deservedly a national hero and a favourite of William Pitt.[9] In 1750 he returned to England from the East Indies and the following year was made one of the Lords of Admiralty. He stayed in England until 1755 before returning to action against his old enemy, the French, in America. This was followed almost immediately by command of the fleet blockading the French at Brest and the start of the Seven Years' War.

Boscawen, who was also known as 'Old Dreadnaught' or 'Wry-necked Dick', married Frances Glanville in 1742. Fanny and Edward's marriage was a very happy one although shortly afterwards Fanny's new husband was back at sea on his ship *Dreadnaught*,[10] patrolling the Channel. For Fanny it necessarily meant long separations from her husband whom she loved so dearly, most notably from October 1747 until April 1750 when Boscawen finally returned from India. In his absence she had to cope with all the day to day problems of bringing up a growing family and dealing with the practicalities of finding suitable lodgings until 1751 when they would move to their Surrey estate, Hatchlands Park. Fanny wrote long and loving letters to Edward describing her domestic life and always her concern and love for him. A letter written to him on October 14, 1748 illustrates Fanny's feelings about the long separations she endured:

> This day twelve month we parted. I can shudder at the thought of it but am thankful that my mind is now at ease and not as it was then when I did not say much, nor desire everybody I met to pity me. But when I returned to town every creature said to me, "How you are fallen-away" and I believed them. But I am since arrived at great composure of mind – always think the best and never look on the dark side of the pillar, or raise devils. No, I always suppose my husband suc-

> cessful, triumphant, returning home with health, riches and honour. I suppose him vastly well pleased when he is come home: thinking of his wife the best of all wives and his children the loveliest of all children. Thus my dearest I paint the scene and fixing my eyes on so pleasing a prospect, I keep them free from tears, unless now and then a tender thought or kind letter steal a few, almost unknown to me.[11]

Unlike Elizabeth Montagu, Fanny much preferred living in the country to being in London recognising that her children's health benefited from country air. She happily and efficiently busied herself supervising the building of their new home on the site of the former house on their estate Hatchlands Park which they bought in 1750. This building project was financed from Admiral Boscawen's prize money[12] based on the value of captured enemy ships. With her husband at sea it was Fanny who oversaw much of the work according to his wishes and instructions. In a letter from his ship *Invincible* he writes in 1756:

> I have a plan of the building every day in my head and shall be glad to hear you have seen Leadbetter' [his architect]. 'I forgot to tell him I would not have a parapet wall, they always make the house leak. No care can prevent it, but to have the eaves hang over. I fancy he won't like it, but in this I will be absolute with him.

In a later letter the same year he pays tribute to Fanny:

> I am very sensible of your condescension in letting me have the direction of our buildings, and much more so for you owning you do not understand it. Most wives meddle with all concerns, understanding or not. In return you shall have the principal hand in furnishing, that is in directing all that is to be new...[13]

By autumn the following year the outside shell of the house was almost complete. It was to the young Robert Adam, freshly returned after three years in Italy, that the Boscawens turned to for much of the fine interior. It was one of Adam's first commissions. The exquisite and sumptuous interiors reflected the Italianate influence in the beautiful plaster work on ceilings. Taking Boscawen's maritime connection as a theme, there are cannon, anchors and dolphins incorporated in the designs. A very personal touch included Edward's favourite dog, Becca, carved in marble on a chimneypiece.

Sadly Boscawen did not live to see Britain's victory over the French and her mastery of the seas which led to peace in 1763 with the Treaty of Paris and the end of the Seven Years' War. After nine months at sea in command of England's battle fleet Fanny's beloved husband returned. Exhausted, he fell ill with a fever and died in January 1761, cutting short an illustrious naval career and a happy marriage. When he died he was a member of the Privy Council and General of Marines with a salary of £3,000. His heartbroken wife composed a fitting epitaph on the tomb designed by Robert Adam at St Michael Penkivel church in Cornwall. Included in the inscription is a reference to the home they built together which Fanny loved so much. It states that it was built 'at the expense of the enemies of his country', a reference to his prize money. Fanny never remarried. It would be her youngest son, George, who would inherit Tregothnan in Cornwall in 1782 when he became 3rd Viscount Falmouth on the death of Edward's elder brother whose marriage had produced no children. Fanny's two older sons had both died: William, her second son, had followed his father into the navy. He drowned in 1769 while swimming in Jamaica at the age of seventeen. Edward Hugh, the eldest, who suffered from ill health and was described by Mary Delany as a 'coxcomb' and a 'fop' was a disappointment to Fanny. He died in 1774 in France where he had gone to seek a cure at Spa on the advice of Elizabeth Montagu.

Perhaps it is Fanny Boscawen, of all Hester Chapone's Bluestocking friends, who encapsulates most nearly the values which Hester would espouse for her niece in 1773. Renowned for her kindness and fine conversation Fanny became an important hostess of literary gatherings especially after her husband's death. She was a close friend of both Elizabeth Montagu and Elizabeth Vesey. Elizabeth Montagu in a letter to her sister, Sarah Scott, wrote this paean of praise to Fanny in 1757 after Fanny had been staying at Sandleford:

> I was very happy in her company, and we really looked very foolish at parting. She is in very good spirits, and sensible of her many felicities, which I pray God to preserve to her. But her cup is so full of good, I am always afraid it should spill. She is one of the few whom an unbounded prosperity could not spoil. I think there is not a grain of evil in her composition. She is humble, charitable, pious, of gentle temper, with the very finest principles, with a great deal of discretion, void of any degree of art, warm and constant in her affections, mild towards offenders, but rigorous towards offence, and speaks her mind very freely to young people in regard to the fashionable levities.[14]

Chapter 10

'the little fidget'

Elizabeth Montagu was born Elizabeth Robinson in 1718, the fourth child and eldest daughter. The family was wealthy and well connected. The Robinson family was blessed with intellect and beauty both of which Elizabeth inherited. Her mother had received her education at a school where its owner, a Mrs Makin, had the avowed intent of educating young girls to develop a rational mode of thought and outlook. It is not surprising that Elizabeth's mother set about inculcating these into her own large family; she had twelve children of whom nine survived into adulthood. She would preside at the dinner table directing and controlling discussions thereby encouraging the participation of all her children irrespective of their gender.

Elizabeth and Hester both had enquiring minds when young but unlike Hester Elizabeth had the benefit of an early education. As a child she stayed with her grandmother and her second husband Dr Conyers Middleton, a classical specialist at Cambridge. Middleton trained Elizabeth to listen to intellectual discussions and then repeat what had been discussed later to him. It was in Cambridge when she was twelve that she met and became a close friend of Lady Margaret Cavendish Holles-Harley who was seventeen. Lady Margaret was the daughter and only surviving child of the second Earl of Oxford and his wife, Lady Henrietta Holles, who was extremely wealthy in her own right. Wimpole Hall, a few miles from Cambridge, was one of her estates and it was here that Lady Margaret spent part of her year. She had the good fortune as a child to be surrounded not only by books but also such great literary figures as Alexander Pope, Jonathan Swift and Matthew Prior, who wrote this charming poem to her:

A Letter to Lady Margaret Cavendish Holles Harley, when a Child

MY noble, lovely, little Peggy,
Let this my First Epistle beg ye,
At dawn of morn, and close of even,
To lift your heart and hands to Heaven.
In double duty say your prayer:
Our Father first, then Notre Père.
And, dearest child, along the day,
In every thing you do and say,
Obey and please my lord and lady,
So God shall love and angels aid ye.

If to these precepts you attend,
No second letter need I send,
And so I rest your constant friend.

The young Elizabeth was intelligent and always eager to be doing something: so much so that she was known affectionately as 'the little fidget' by Margaret, who became Duchess of Portland in 1734 when she married William Bentinck, second Duke of Portland. Margaret was now an extremely rich woman who could afford to indulge her interest in botany. She was extremely knowledgeable herself and knew leading botanists and plant collectors of the time. On their estate at Bulstrode near Gerrard's Cross, in Buckinghamshire, she developed a large botanic garden and an aviary as well as a large library and collection on Natural History. Bulstrode was under four hours from London and during the spring and summer months of the year the young Duchess surrounded herself with a wide circle of interesting and stimulating visitors, among whom was her old friend, Elizabeth Robinson, later Elizabeth Montagu. The way of life at Bulstrode was congenial with learning and leisure combined in a rural setting. Part of the delight lay in reading aloud to the assembled company and in the subsequent discussion and conversation which followed among the group of guests. This intellectual activity was nicely balanced with gentle walks and picnics on the beautiful estate which could be combined with some form of nature study or handiwork. Mary Delany, who would become one of the most loved members of the Bluestockings and a friend of Hester, wrote of Bulstrode where she was a welcome and regular guest: 'Surely an application to natural beauties must enlarge the mind? This house with all belonging to it is a noble school for contemplations.'

The Duchess of Portland, friend of Elizabeth Montagu and Mrs Delany

Mary was a fine needlewoman: her embroidery was exquisite. After Dr Delany's death in 1768, Mary spent summers at Bulstrode with the Duchess of Portland, and the remainder of the year in London, first at Thatched House Court then at St James's Place. Through the encouragement of the Duchess Mary began to create collages in the form of flowers made from cut paper shapes at Bulstrode. She records how 'The paper mosaic work was begun in the 74th year of my age' to give her employment and amusement while staying at Bulstrode:

> Having a piece of Chinese paper on the table of bright scarlet, a geranium caught her eye of similar colour, and taking her scissors she amused herself with cutting out each flower, by her eye, in the paper which resembled its hue; she laid the paper petals on a black ground, and was so pleased with the effect that she proceeded to cut out the calyx, stalks and leaves in shades of green, and pasted them down; and after she had completed a sprig of geranium in this way, the Duchess of Portland came in and exclaimed 'What are you doing with that geranium?' having taken the paper imitation for the real flower.[1]

Crinum: Paper Flower by Mrs Delany

So skilled did she become that Joseph Banks, the great eighteenth century plant collector and the unofficial director of Kew, where he and George III would meet to discuss their mutual interest in agriculture, sent specimens for her to copy. There are now almost 1,000 of these exquisite plant collages in The British Museum. Through this new and exquisite art form that she created she became famous and was introduced to King George III and Queen Charlotte. A lasting friendship was born and it was they who provided a small annuity after the Duchess of Portland died in 1785 and omitted to make any financial provision for her great friend. Such was the affection the royal couple held her in that she was also given a small house at Windsor.

Before she married, Elizabeth Robinson kept up a spirited and amusing correspondence with the Duchess describing a fun-loving social life attending the races, parties, balls and evening visits to Vauxhall. She wrote about Bath and Tunbridge Wells, both fashionable at the time. Here there was the opportunity for flirting and gallantry amid the heady atmosphere of the social scene and Elizabeth was never short of suitors. She wrote witheringly caustic comments about the lack of sartorial judgment in other women.

Mrs Montagu's House, Portman Square. Her May Day Chimney Sweeps' Feast

At the age of twenty-four Elizabeth Robinson married Edward Montagu, the nephew of Lady Mary Wortley Montagu, the poet. As was still the custom she was accompanied on her honeymoon by her sister Sarah, as chaperone.[2] Edward was perhaps a surprising choice for such a beautiful and vivacious young woman. He was by 1742 in his fifties and was MP for Huntingdon. Although it was not a marriage based on romantic love it was one in which both parties respected each other. She took a highly practical interest in his business. Edward had made his money from collieries and farms on his estate at Denton Hall in Northumberland and in Yorkshire When he began to ail towards the end of his life Elizabeth would prove herself to be an extremely capable business woman. She also had a strong philanthropic streak. She set up schools and held annual feasts for the colliery and farm workers and May day feasts for boy chimney sweeps on her lawn at Montagu House in Portman Square in London. Elizabeth led an enviable life of privilege and comfort. Edward owned country estates at Allenthorpe in Yorkshire, Denton in Northumberland, and at Sandleford in Berkshire which she loved especially. Elizabeth became a gifted hostess in London, first at Hill Street, Berkeley Square and then at Montagu House, where she entertained on a lavish scale. Her wealth also enabled her to become a patron of the arts. She continued to attract male admirers such as Lord Lyttelton,[3] the Earl of Bath and Samuel Johnson: later there would be a rift when Johnson wrote withering comments about Elizabeth's literary output and published critical remarks on Lyttelton. Like many women of her time she was an avid letter writer. Her large circle of friends with whom she kept up a prolific and entertaining and socially insightful correspondence included, among many others: Elizabeth Vesey, Lord Bath, Lord Lyttelton, Lord Chesterfield, Lord Hardwicke, Sir Joshua Reynolds, David Garrick and his wife, Eva, Laurence Sterne, Edmund Burke, the Duchess of Portland, Benjamin Stillingfleet, Mary Delany, Fanny Boscawen and somewhat surprisingly the modest Elizabeth Carter whom she met in 1758 and recognised as being her intellectual superior although she herself was extremely well read.

Chapter 11

Beau Nash

Elizabeth Montagu had been hit by a series of family tragedies in the 1740s: in August 1743 the death of her only son, John, nicknamed Punch, from convulsions while teething; followed by the death of her mother in 1746 from cancer and the death of her favourite brother, Thomas Robinson, a brilliant young lawyer, in 1747. Elizabeth sought solace at the spa towns of Bath and Tunbridge Wells, both of which she knew well, and set about recovering both mental and physical equilibrium. The marriage of her sister, Sarah Scott, the novelist, to whom she was very close, had also collapsed and Elizabeth herself was coming to terms with the realisation that essentially she and her husband were becoming increasingly incompatible. She enjoyed an ostentatious display of wealth and appearing in society whereas her husband was happiest in his library

It was Richard Nash, or Beau Nash, who made Bath the most fashionable spa in England in the early eighteenth century. Nash was born in 1674 in Swansea and came from a relatively modest background: his father was partner in a glassworks which produced quart bottles on a small scale. The hopes of his father lay in his only son who matriculated at Jesus College, Oxford, in 1692, where he had spent a year allegedly doing little in the form of academic study, and was briefly in the army, before he became a student of the Inner Temple in London. Richard had the talent for reinventing himself and his next role was as a gamester. This led him to Bath which, with the visit of Queen Anne in 1702, was enjoying even greater popularity among those seeking alleviation or cures for their physical ailments by imbibing the mineral water and immersing themselves in the baths to which they were transported, cocooned in towels and already dressed for immersion, in half-tub chairs. It was also attracting those seeking their fortune at the gaming tables. It was this latter fraternity of which Richard was a member when he arrived in Bath in or around 1705. By 1716 Nash had established himself as a regular visitor to Bath and had become friendly

Entertainment at Bath

with Captain Webster who was responsible for the running of the amenities in Bath. Soon Nash became assistant to Webster and when in 1723 the latter was killed in a duel he became Master of Ceremonies of Bath. There was much to manage. The King's Bath was mixed: it boasted the highest water temperature and was for the physically ill. The Queen's Bath was cooler. The fashionable Cross Bath had a gallery from which the male gentry could espy young women in a state of undress, their heads and shoulders bobbing above the water while they or their aquatic male admirers kept a watchful eye on little floating bowls in front of them which held nosegays, a handkerchief and sweet smelling unguents. Elizabeth Robinson describes attendant dangers: 'The dowager Dutchess [sic] of— bathes, and being very tall, had nearly drowned a few women in the Cross Bath, for she ordered it to be filled till it reached her chin, and so all those who were below her stature, as well as her rank, were forced to come out or drown.'[1] There were balls to attend, which were paid for by subscription. These were held at Harrison's where in 1720 a new ballroom was added onto the assembly rooms. It already catered for the card players with tables for the various games such as faro which was played for high stakes, ombre with its extremely intricate rules and the more innocent pastime of whist. In 1730 second assembly rooms were opened with the entertainment alternating between the two. There was plenty to entertain the visitors: breakfast concerts were popular and musicians were brought down from London to entertain the clientele. There were coffee houses like Morgan's and The Ladies' Coffee House where gossip was exchanged and papers read; gentle walks could be enjoyed in the Grove. Attendance was *de rigeur* at the Pump Room to drink the waters. Here Nash would appear in his black wig and cream *tricorne* to imbibe the health-giving waters and view his court.

Nash started to mould Bath into a spa governed by a code of conduct to promote a more polite society. He laid down a series of rules to safeguard the smooth running of the Bath season, which became extended and divided into spring and autumn. The rules, posted up in the Pump room for all to see and observe, ranged from the highly practical:

> 2 That Ladies coming to the Ball, appoint a time for their Footmens coming to wait on them Home; to prevent Disturbances and Inconveniences to Themselves and Others;

to sartorial matters:

> 3 That Gentlemen of Fashion never appearing in a Morning before the Ladies in Gowns and Caps, shew Breeding and Respect;

to an attempt to limit the gossip which played such a part in life at Bath:

> 10 That all Whisperers of Lies and Scandal be taken for their Authors;
>
> 11 That all Repeaters of such Lies and Scandal be shun'd by all Company:– except such as have been guilty of the same Crime.[2]

The Company referred to was the system by which subscriptions were levied for the right to attend the twice weekly balls on Tuesdays and Fridays, music at the Pump Rooms and other amenities. Names were entered into the subscription book, run by the notoriously efficient Sarah Porter at the Pump Room. This enabled visitors to check out the guest list at forthcoming events where members of the landowning gentry and those from the growing middle class of merchants would mix with members of the landed aristocracy. From the point of view of seeing and being seen the season at Bath became increasingly important especially for marriageable young women. Nash, known as the King of Bath, observed social precedence with a keen eye, himself leading out the most important lady at a ball for the opening minuet. Nash's rules extended to governing behaviour at the balls: a gentlemen was only to give tickets to gentlewomen if he was not acquainted with any; it was bad manners for men to crowd in front of the ladies; children and older women were to occupy the second row of seats because he stated they were 'past or not come to perfection.' Nash did not exclude the fairer sex from gambling, taking the view that it displayed 'such boldness as raises them near that lordly creature man.'

The streets of Bath were not only relatively clean but also relatively safe as Nash prohibited gentlemen from wearing swords. Nash loved ceremony and the great and good were greeted on their arrival by the peal of the Abbey bells. This was followed by musicians playing outside their lodging the following day, often at an early hour, for which privilege and recognition of social status payment was exacted from the bleary-eyed visitors. Social life at Bath was marked by certain activities at fixed times. Elizabeth Robinson's view of Bath, which she describes to the Duchess of Portland, charts her typical day. She comments on The Ladies' Coffee House and grumbles about having to listen to people describing their ailments which for the beautiful nineteen year old Elizabeth, who was in the best of health and loved gaiety, must have been both depressing and boring. She continues: 'The waters employ the morning, visits the afternoon, and we saunter away the evening in great stupidity. I think no place can be less agreeable; how d'ye do, is all one hears in the morning, and what is trumps in the afternoon.'[3]

Having established his authority in Bath Nash turned his eyes to Tunbridge Wells in Sussex, and by 1735 had established himself as Master of Ceremonies there and set about making it more fashionable. Tunbridge Wells had first become fashionable in the seventeenth century when Queen Henrietta Maria took the waters there after the birth of Prince Charles. Unlike Bath there were no hot baths to assuage aches and pains. Instead there was the Chalybeate Spring which had a high iron content. Drinking the water was beneficial to invalids. Tunbridge also attracted those who wished to escape from the dust and heat of London in the summer months, among whom were politicians and foreign diplomats.

Like Bath, life centred around taking the waters, visiting the coffee houses to indulge in gossip and promenading along the Pantiles, a colonnaded walkway, while musicians played and a restorative dish of tea could be enjoyed. Groups of friends who rented houses for the season also enjoyed reading aloud, gentle walks, jaunts by carriage to the surrounding countryside, riding, enjoying a picnic, meeting new people and making new friends. Like Bath, balls were held twice weekly on Tuesdays and Fridays, card parties and assemblies took place on other evenings. When it came to young women of marriageable age, being seen and admired by society at Tunbridge was a key social aim. This led to a bookseller on the Pantiles establishing a large book in which a public airing could be given to comments and poetry on the fairer sex in general or more particularly in praise or censure of one particular individual. The texts would be commented on by the promenaders which in turn led to gossip and speculation. Sometimes the comments could be cruel. Elizabeth Montagu with her observant eye and sharp wit could also be scathing about her fellow visitors at Tunbridge: 'I think the Miss Allens sensible, and I believe them good; but I do not think the graces assisted Lucina at their birth.' She goes on to attack Lady Parker and her two daughters' lack of sartorial taste: 'Such hats, capuchins, and short sacks as were ever seen! One of the ladies looks like a state-bed running upon castors. She has robbed the valance and tester of a bed for a trimming. They have each of them a lover.'[4]

The season at Tunbridge Wells lasted from the end of May till the end of September. Elizabeth would go with a group of friends and spend about six weeks drinking the waters or, if the weather was good, would spend longer there. She obviously loved the company as much as the cure which she describes so entertainingly:

> Indeed this is a strange place, for one has neither business nor leisure here, so many glasses of water are to be drank, so many buttered rolls to be eaten, so many turns on the walk to be taken, so many miles to be gone in a post-chaise, or on horseback, so much pains to be well, so much attention to be civil, that breakfasting, visiting, &c. &c. leave one no time even to write the important transactions of the day ... In the beginning of the season there are many people of quality whose behaviour is extremely bourgeoise; at the end of it, citizens who by their pride and impertinence think they are behaving like persons of quality and each by happily deviating from the manners and conduct their condition of life seems to prescribe, meet in the same point of behaviour, and are equally agreeable and well bred. Tunbridge seems the parliament of the world, where every country and every rank has its representative; we have Jews of every tribe, and Christian people of all nations and conditions. Next to some German, whose noble blood might entitle him to be Grand Master of Malta, sits a pin-maker's wife from smock-alley; pickpockets, who are come to the top of their profession, play with noble dukes at brag. For my part I am diverted with the medley; the different characters and figures are amusing, especially at the balls, where persons of every age, size and shape, step forth to dance; some who have just quitted their leading-strings, others whom it would become to shift into the lame and slippered pantaloon; but who will believe it is too soon to attempt, or too late to endeavour, to charm![5]

Elizabeth, in spite of all the distractions while at Tunbridge, found time to write such vivid and entertaining letters to her friends and her husband. One great advantage of a visit to Tunbridge was its relative acces-

George Lyttelton, 1st Baron Lyttelton

sibility from London: it was only a journey of thirty-six miles and this could be undertaken in a day whereas the longer journey from London to Bath necessitated overnight accommodation: Elizabeth reports it taking her four days on very bad roads in 1740. Added to this was the discomfort of the long journey, the added expense and the risk of highwaymen who frequented the route. In 1750 the stage coach from London to Bath would take three days but by 1776 the journey was cut to only twenty hours. With the introduction of the post-chaise, a means of transport much loved by Elizabeth, the travelling time to Tunbridge Wells was cut to just four hours.

Elizabeth's husband, was happy to let her visit Tunbridge without him. Although it was less hectic than Bath he was still far happier ensconced in his library with his books on mathematics. By 1745 Tunbridge was less fashionable than Bath although it still attracted visitors such as Richardson, Garrick, Colley Cibber and William Pitt, and his sister who later so admired Admiral Boscawen's heroic exploits.

Visiting spa towns was popular not only for the beneficial effects of the waters but it also provided the gentry with an opportunity to meet new people and make new friends. It was at Tunbridge that Elizabeth made lasting friendships based on shared intellectual interests. She met Frances Boscawen in 1749 and Sir George Lyttelton, who became Lord Lyttelton in 1756. He referred to Elizabeth as Madonna in his letters to her. Elizabeth took an immediate liking to Fanny. She reports: 'about twenty yards from our house lodges the wife of Admiral Boscawen, a very sensible, lively, ingenious woman, and who seems to have good moral qualities.'[6] Elizabeth describes how their evenings often centred around conversation and reading aloud to each other. Almost immediately on her return to her home in Hill Street in London Elizabeth starts a correspondence with Fanny which includes their views on *Clarissa*. The next year, 1750, Fanny Boscawen rented a house at Tunbridge Wells for the summer and it was then that their close and enduring friendship was cemented. Fanny's new home, Hatchlands, near Guildford, was only thirty miles from Sandleford, Elizabeth's much grander estate, making it relatively easy for the two friends to visit each other.

Chapter 12

'the Sylph'

Elizabeth Montagu began giving large breakfast parties in London in 1750. She was a hostess who entertained in some style and relished her role. Hannah More describes her: 'She is made for the grand world, and is an ornament to it. It is an element she was born to breathe in.' Madame du Boccage, a French visitor, reports on one such gathering in 1750:

> In the morning, breakfasts, which enchant as much by the exquisite viands as by the richness of the plate on which they are served up, agreeably bring together the people of the country and strangers. We breakfasted in this manner today, April 8, 1750, at Lady Montagu's in a closet lined with painted paper of Pekin, and furnished with the choicest moveables of China. A long table, covered with the finest linen, presented to the view a thousand glittering cups, which contained coffee, chocolate, biscuits, cream, butter toasts, and exquisite tea. You must understand that there is no good tea to be had anywhere, but in London. The mistress of the house, who deserves to be served at the table of the gods, poured it out herself. This is the custom, and, in order to conform to it, the dress of the English ladies, which suits exactly to their stature; the white apron and the pretty straw-hat become them with the greatest propriety, not only in their own apartments, but at noon, in St James's Park, where they walk with the stately and majestic gait of nymphs.[1]

Soon these literary breakfasts were to be replaced by evening gatherings at which orgeat – a cooling syrup originally made from barley and later from almonds and orange flower water – lemonade, tea and biscuits would be served.

Elizabeth Vesey and Elizabeth Montagu first met in July 1755 at Tunbridge Wells. Never inhibited about giving her views on new acquaintances Elizabeth Montagu writes to Gilbert West, a cousin and close friend of hers who knew Elizabeth Vesey, hence the introduction:

> ... make my bows to half a dozen ladies, and say half a dozen words to

> each of them and if I can, select some to converse with; among these I find none so agreeable as your friend Mrs Vesey, who arrived at Tunbridge the day we came; and took occasion soon after to begin a conversation with me, by inquiring after you since that time we are become acquainted, and seem to like one another very well.[2]

Four days later she writes:

> I am glad you are acquainted with Mrs Vesey, she is a very amiable, agreeable woman, and has an easy politeness that gains one in a moment, and in reserve she has good sense and an improved mind, to keep the approbation she acquired by her manners. She is so entirely polite, that it is a wonder if one ever reflects, that she is polite at all, her behaviour "shews no part of study but the grace."[3]

It was at Tunbridge that the two women who enjoyed the polite art of conversation discussed the idea of setting up gatherings in their own homes at which conversation on literary subjects was to be encouraged and celebrated. Politics and cards were to be banned. In order to lead the discussion eminent men of letters were to be invited but women would be encouraged to regard themselves as intellectually capable of contributing and supporting other women by their friendship. Women like Elizabeth Carter were only too well aware that most men did not view women as being capable of offering intellectual companionship which forced many to conceal their learning in company. She gives a jaundiced view when she writes some twenty years later:

> As if the two sexes had been in a state of war, the gentlemen ranged themselves on one side of the room where they talked their own talk and left us poor ladies to twirl our shuttles and amuse each other by conversing as we could. By what little I could overhear our opposites were discoursing on the old English Poets, and this did not seem so much beyond a female capacity but that we might have been indulged with a share in it.[4]

For someone like Elizabeth Carter with a background in classical languages it was deemed necessary to conceal her learning and at times social life of this kind must have been intensely boring.

Elizabeth Vesey began her conversation parties when she was next in Bath and continued to organise these literary meetings when she returned to London, first in 'the dear blue room' at her house in Bolton Row and then from 1780 in Clarges Street. Elizabeth was Irish by birth, the daughter of Sir Thomas Vesey, Bishop of Ossory. She married twice: first to William Handcock, who was an MP in the Irish Parliament, and then to Agmondesham Vesey.[5] Elizabeth divided her

Elizabeth, Mrs Vesey (the Sylph)

time between her home in Ireland, near Dublin and London. Known as 'the Sylph' she was a few years older than Elizabeth Montagu and very different in temperament. Where Elizabeth Montagu thrived on attention and flattery, Elizabeth Vesey was more retiring and somewhat diffident, preferring to see others enjoying themselves rather than being centre stage. Where Elizabeth Montagu was practical, Elizabeth Vesey was described as somewhat unworldly to the extent that she designed a coffee pot with neither lid nor spout. It is surprising that she was a friend of the moderate and intellectual Elizabeth Carter who describes Elizabeth Vesey's appetite for life: 'she always wants to get every plaything in the whole fair, she would see every place in the world at one time, and all the people at one view.' Elizabeth also wrote: 'though I have always honoured you for having the simplicity of a little child.' It was this quality, her feyness and generosity that made her so much loved by her friends as well as her genuine concern for their well-being and her gentleness of spirit and charm. One story about the Sylph goes that when a friend who was staying with her and was on crutches explained to her solicitous hostess that they were to be used outside on gravel Elizabeth had immediately set into motion plans for the gardener to transport gravel from the garden to put on the floor in the drawing room. Apparently she was dissuaded!

The literary evenings, with their objective of promoting intellectual discussion, in the tradition of French salons, soon became an attractive alternative for intelligent women who had become bored whiling away their time, listening to the often over-extravagant male flattery which Elizabeth Carter complained about, playing cards and gossiping idly. They also acted as a support system which gave women the confidence to express their ideas in a more public setting and lead many of them to publish, often anonymously, reaching out to a much wider audience. Elizabeth Montagu would become known as the Queen of the Bluestockings, or as Samuel Johnson referred to her 'Queen of the Blues', a title she usurped from Elizabeth Vesey, who abdicated gracefully. Hester would be drawn into the Bluestocking circle through her contacts in Richardson and Johnson's circles. She would become friends with not only Elizabeth Vesey and Fanny Boscawen and Mary Delany but more importantly she would become a friend of Elizabeth Montagu: a friendship which would be of great benefit to her later in life.

Part Three

Marriage and Heartbreak

Catherine Talbot, friend of Elizabeth Carter

Chapter 13

'The frivolous bolt of Cupid'

Hester was supportive of Elizabeth Carter's ongoing project of the translation of the works of Epictetus. It was at the request of Elizabeth's great friend Catherine Talbot, who like Elizabeth was a devout Christian, that she began her translation. In 1743 Catherine had referred to Epictetus in a letter to Elizabeth: 'I am infinitely provoked that there is no translation of that part of his precepts which Arrian has preserved, and which I am vastly curious to see.'[1] However, it was not until 1749 that Elizabeth refers to her translation in a letter to Catherine from Deal on June 20: 'Have you concluded, dear Miss Talbot, that I was run away, or that I had determined to translate all Epictetus before I sent you any. Alas! the scraps enclosed will prove how idle I have been; but I have been ill.'[2] She has finally embarked on the translation with the encouragement of Catherine but with no view to its publication. Elizabeth sent parts of the translation up to London as she completed them for Catherine and her mother to read and for Bishop Secker to comment on. Initially Dr Secker offered valuable advice which at times Elizabeth found discouraging. He pointed out that her style had to reflect the plain style of the original so she must avoid being too flowery in her translation. Catherine acknowledges the progress of the translation from the Greek for her benefit in November:

> 'Tis time I should talk to you about the idea and obliging perseverance you exert for my sake. I admire Epictetus more and more every day and the last chapter about the storks nests especially. There is a nobleness in its simplicity very striking. A superiority of thought, and shortness of expression, that makes both my mother and me wish for more. It is fair to tell you that we copy your papers into a little book, so you need not return them. I wish I could deserve half your goodness – But the fig-tree must have time to grow good for any thing. All I entreat is that you will not write and make your head ache for our sakes.[3]

The stoic philosophy of endurance was well known to Elizabeth. Epictetus's view of the equality of man and love of one's fellow human beings would ring true to her and to Catherine with their strong Christian faith. It was a huge undertaking: although it had been translated into Latin and French this was to be the first English translation.

In 1753 Elizabeth went to London from her home in Deal and took lodgings near St Paul's Cathedral where Thomas Secker was now Dean. It was Catherine who encouraged the modest and somewhat diffident Elizabeth to think about publication. Elizabeth had found the demands on her time heavy:

> As soon as I have dispatched Epictetus to St Paul's, Harry to University, and finished my fifteen shirts, I comfort myself with the hopes of being at liberty to grow most delectably idle, to read what books I please, and run wild over hill and dale for the rest of the summer.[4]

In July 1754 Hester was preoccupied with looking after her father who had suffered a stroke. Thomas, her eldest brother, deputised for him on his circuit and John Chapone stood in for Thomas as Clerk of Arraigns. On August 13 she writes to Elizabeth Carter enclosing some verses she has requested including an ode which, she explains, reflects her sober sadness adding:

> I know you will smile at my distress with a kind of pity not much like contempt, but I cannot help it, and comfort myself with thinking that, cased up as you are in philosophy, armour – proof against the 'frivolous bolt of Cupid,' you will at least forgive if not applaud me, if ever you become intimately acquainted with the Caro Ogetto [sic] del mio innocente ardore. Your opinion of the lordly sex I know is not a very high one, but yet I will one day or other make you confess that a man may be capable of all the delicacy, purity, and tenderness which distinguish our sex, joined with all the best qualities that dignify his own.[5]

It is John Chapone, whom she refers to as her *caro ogetto*, she is now engaged to but her father has still not given his blessing to their marriage. For Hester, who is so clearly very much in love with John, the enforced wait of six years would be a trying and testing time and would affect her health. Hester's friendships brought some solace. She and Susanna Highmore were close and exchanged odes in celebration of their friendship: Hester's is addressed *To Stella* and Susanna's response is addressed *To Aspasia*.

Elizabeth finally finished the translation in January 1755. It was decided to publish *Epictetus* by subscription, a popular method by which half the cost could be raised prior to publication with the remainder paid after it appeared. There was no shortage of subscribers: the 1,031 subscriptions of one guinea included those from the Prince of Wales, many bishops (Secker ordered 12 copies), Samuel Johnson, a friend of many years, Elizabeth Montagu, Fanny Boscawen and of course Hester Mulso. It was Samuel Richardson who printed the first edition. Fortunately the contretemps over his unauthorised inclusion of Elizabeth Carter's *Ode to Peace* had been patched up by his public apology. Printing started in July 1757 and was finished by April 1758. Elizabeth earned about £1,000 which enabled her to buy two adjoining properties, one for her father and one for herself, in her beloved Deal, overlooking the sea. Here she could indulge her love of walking on the beach and in the countryside and be close to her father. Elizabeth did not seek public recognition, she was far too modest, but even she could not dispute the status the book had brought her not only in the wider sphere which included Europe but among the Bluestockings. It was after the publication of *Epictetus* that their 'Queen', Elizabeth Montagu, who was impressed by Elizabeth's scholarship, sought her for a friend.

Hester's *Irregular Ode* was prefaced to *Epictetus*. In it she praises Elizabeth's classical knowledge while also stressing that Christ is the true fountain of succour rather than stoicism. Her newly married brother, John, refers to it in a letter to Gilbert White:

> My sister is pretty well & asked after Whitibus very much ... Heck has written a very good Ode to Miss Carter, upon her translation of Epictetus, which is now coming out by subscription. Miss Carter is likely to be much encouraged in this affair, which will be of Use to her Fortune; the Bishop of Oxford is her hearty friend. If You chance to see this Work & think the Language at all stiff by the Translation's being too literal, I give You notice that you should spare the Lady, who was compelled into So narrow a Form: and indeed it is not the Lady's Fault to be oversparing of words.

Elizabeth, on reporting to Hester that she has been suffering from violent headaches, receives a stern reproof from her for being too stoical about them, something Hester feels she has learnt perhaps not always beneficially from Epictetus. The publication of *Epictetus* had brought Elizabeth Carter at the age of forty both fame and financial independence through her writing: a model which other Bluestockings would seek to emulate. However, there was still disbelief in some quarters that Elizabeth had been the author. Hester refers to this:

> I hope your head is in good order; I was told by a gentleman t'other

> day, that if it were not well ballasted, it would be overset by the unreasonable share of honour and praise you have gained by your late work. At the same time I was told that it had thrown the whole learned world into the utmost astonishment, and that they could not otherwise account for the thing, or comfort themselves under it, but by attributing its excellence to the archbishop's assistance. This last part of the story provokes me, but some how or other they would fain strip the honour from our sex, and deck out one of their own with it. I question whether there will not be an act of parliament next session to banish you this realm, as an invader of the privileges and honours of the lords of the creation, and an occasion of stumbling to women, in the article of acknowledging their superiority.[6]

It seems entirely in keeping with Elizabeth's character that she was not interested in capitalising on this success by publishing more. Her next work *Poems on Several Occasions* did not appear until 1762 and consisted of poems that she had written at various times. After this she published no further work. However, her position as the most learned of the Bluestockings was firmly established. She continued to participate in their circles when in London. Her pleasant apartments in Clarges Street, Piccadilly, were convenient for attending Bluestocking gatherings at the homes of various hostesses although she always insisted on being brought home by ten o'clock at night. Her modesty about her intellectual standing brought her both respect and endeared her to the other members.

Chapter 14

'Give me your congratulations'

In 1756 Hester is still waiting with growing impatience for her father to agree to her marriage to John Chapone. A fact her brother John is fully aware of yet he cannot help teasing Gilbert White when he writes to him in April:

> Pray, Gil, let me know a Truth. You stand indicted by the name Gilbert White Clerk, for that you having the whole and sole Property of a thing called a Sermon wrote by Miss M—o, keeping it from the family of the said Miss out of a pretended Pride of having a manuscript value 10,000 etc. etc. etc. etc.: have yet let this manuscript escape out of your Possession … of the said G. White ye delinquent: who is mainly suspected of making undue communications of these Lady-Favours, a thing unpardonable, and till this time unsuspected in the said G. White. Please to clear up these affairs, before condemnation is passed in the King's Square Court.

Hester's health was giving cause for some concern among her family and friends including Richardson. It was not only her physical health – she was prone to catch colds in the winter – but also her mental health. A visit to Canterbury was arranged in August to try to lift her spirits but Richardson was concerned enough to write:

> But with my dear Miss Mulso the case is different. She has youth and genius with her. Yet she must not hurt her health by writing; though she writes with an ease that very few of either sex can equal, as well as with a strength that still fewer can surpass.[1]

The feeling of depression continued into the following year when she writes in August to Elizabeth from Canterbury that:

> Sometimes I seem, like Panthea's lover, to have two souls. The one convinced of the goodness of Providence 'alike in what it gives and what denies,' cheerful and contented, and, considering the whole of its situation, exulting in an uncommon share of earthly happiness. The other lamenting its incapacity to enjoy what it has, or to attain

> what it wishes; endeavouring to account by outward circumstances, for a depression which has its causes in some unknown part of the body or mind, and fancying that a change of circumstance would make it happy; feeling pain and disgust from objects of indifference, and indifference from objects of pleasure.

Richardson was sufficiently concerned to advise her to return to London. But it is not London she pines for. She continues:

> ... my best soul has now the upper hand, by the assistance of medicine and cool weather, much more than of reason; and perhaps by the hope of two or three days of fancied good, in the presence of a fancied essential to my happiness, who has promised to come down and see me some time before the middle of next month.

The fancied essential is of course none other than John Chapone. She ends this letter to Elizabeth:

> 'You see Epictetus has no great chance of getting the better of me, except he can, as the saying is, bring me down in my wedding shoes.'[2]

Hester's clergyman brother, John and his wife, Jane, were living in Sunbury, Surrey, relatively close to Gilbert White at Selborne and to Hester in London. Hester was a regular visitor and when their first child, a daughter named Jane, was born in March 1758 Hester was there. It would be this daughter for whom Hester would embark on writing a conduct book which would be highly influential. John writes to Gilbert about the baby as being 'alive and pretty well, & reckoned a large and well shaped Baby: I think it is like any thing but itself, it is more like me than its Mother.' His optimism was almost proved wrong when not only the baby nearly died but his wife was also seriously ill after childbirth. Happily both recovered and by July John is writing to Gilbert: 'My little Girl thrives & will do very wel, & by a significant leer of her Eye promises to be a Droll.' The proud father continues to report on the baby, Jenny as she is known in the family, and her progress to Gilbert charting her teething at six months and commenting that for a baby she is very quiet which is her only beauty! The risks of pregnancy and childbirth were high in the eighteenth century, many babies did not survive or died in early infancy like Elizabeth Montagu's son. Sadly Jane miscarried twins in the November of the same year when again Hester came to look after her.

In August, 1758, Hester is on one of her regular visits to Canterbury. She writes to Elizabeth that her health is better and her spirits more buoyant than for the past three summers:

> ... and am thereby enabled to keep my very weak and unphilosophical heart in better order than when you so justly reproved its impatience, under circumstances that certainly ought not to be considered as serious evils, yet which have sometimes operated on my mind in such a manner.[3]

The long wait for her father's permission to marry John Chapone is clearly irksome. She reports that she has enjoyed the race week with the Burrows, who came over from Margate for the week, which helped enliven her stay in Canterbury and has drawn her even closer to them.

Meanwhile, John Chapone of Clement's Inn, one of Inns of Chancery, was acting for Admiral Charles Knowles in a high profile case, *Rex versus Smollett*. Tobias Smollett[4] the writer and former ship's surgeon, in the *Critical Review* No. XXVIII, May issue, 1758 had called Admiral Charles Knowles:

> '... an admiral without conduct, an engineer without knowledge, an officer without resolution, and a man without veracity.'

The printer and publisher was Archibald Hamilton of Chancery Lane. Knowles initially set about bringing a libel action against Hamilton. John Chapone despatched his clerk, Samuel Gawler, to buy a copy of the offending periodical from Hamilton. On 2 June, 1759 Hamilton faced trial. The judge was Lord Mansfield. Hamilton pleaded not guilty. Chapone records the dramatic turn of events on June 19 at Lincoln's Inn Fields:

> ... whereupon one Mr Tobias Smollett appeared in open court and did acknowledge himself to be the Author and publisher in London of the whole Article ... In which said Article or paragraphs is contained the scandalous or libellous matter above mentioned. And this Deponent saith that thereupon the said Defendant Archibald Hamilton was accordingly acquitted by the Jury.[5]

Knowles prosecuted Smollett. Chapone in his affidavit cites defamation of Knowles' character and conduct. On June 25 a court order was served on Smollett by John Chapone's clerk. However, it was not until November 24, 1760 that Smollett finally appeared at Westminster Hall before Lord Mansfield and a grand jury of twenty-four. Smollett was fined £100 and imprisoned for three months for libel. John Chapone had won justice for his client and sent a warning shot against the freedom of the press. Winning a case which attracted so much publicity enhanced Chapone's reputation. He had been appointed to the office of a commissioner of bankrupts which was in the gift of the Lord Chancellor in 1758 and with his role in the Smollett case his future seemed promising.

In spite of poor health and her father's reluctance to bless her marriage with Chapone Hester has lost none of her appetite for criticism. In 1759 Johnson published *The History of Rasselas, Prince of Abyssinia* which does not meet with Hester's critical approval. When she writes to Elizabeth Carter in April she reveals that he is not a favourite author of hers. She acknowledges that Elizabeth has always venerated him before going into attack and asking for Elizabeth's view: 'but do for once give your judgement fair play against the man's name, and tell me whether you do not think he ought to be ashamed of publishing such an ill-contrived, unfinished, unnatural, and uninstructive tale?' She continues in her outspoken attack on the moral tale of Prince Rasselas leaving the 'happy valley' in search of earthly happiness before returning home to his former life of luxury. Hester is fully aware of her temerity in pouring such scathing criticism on the great man when she asks:

> By this time I begin to fear you are angry with me, and consider me as a strangely presumptuous animal, thus to lift up my nothingness against the giant Johnson: but I think he has built too much on the blind superstitious reverence he thinks his name exacts from the world, and I will not be one of those whom he will laugh at for being taken in to admire what he must know is unworthy of him. They say he wrote it in three mornings; but as the Spectator says, 'I never do excuse faults through haste.'[6]

In fact it took Johnson a week to write it in order to pay for his mother's funeral. Hester continues her attack in her next letter to Elizabeth in which it appears that Elizabeth has defended Johnson. Hester is scandalized by the 'frightful picture he has drawn of family life' but admits to admiring Johnson's presentation of the pros and cons of each situation. Elizabeth is staying in Bristol with Catherine Talbot and Hester is intrigued to know whether she is finding time to write and philosophise. Hester is reading another stoic philosopher, Antoninus, and asks Elizabeth whether she does not find him 'a better natured stoic than your Epictetus?' She heaps praise on his writings which have caused her to muse on the benefits her friendships have brought her, writing: 'I was not before sensible, my dear Miss Carter, how much I was obliged to you, amongst a few more, whom I count over in my mind with more exultation and delight than a miser does his bags.'[7]

Friendships with influential people were a key essential if Hester was to fulfil her ambition of becoming an established woman writer in a man's world. Influential friends could offer a degree of protection by offering patronage which enabled publication through subscription although some writers did turn on their patrons, as Johnson so famously did with Lord Lyttelton, for not fulfilling his role; or in the bitter financial dispute between Ann Yearsley, 'Lactilla', the 'Poetical Milkwoman of Bristol'[8] and Hannah More.

Hester continues the pattern of deserting London for the more pleasant environment of rural life in the summer and while on a visit to Salisbury in August 1759 she paints an amusing picture of her life for Elizabeth:

> I shall now tell you something of myself, who live here uncorrupted by grandeur; who can see venison pasties without eating them, and great dinners smoke every day without envying those whose noses are always so besmoked. Who come home from an assembly at eleven, without envying those who dance till five, and who could be content to return to my little habitation, and to that poor desart [sic] place you so much despise and hate, without envying those who live in a palace. Who could prefer a *little attorney* even to my Lord Feversham, had he offered to me instead of the fair young lady he has so happily won.[9]

She confesses that she is happier in Salisbury, where her uncle is Bishop, than in Canterbury, describing it as more agreeable a town because she finds its inhabitants polite and sociable. Adding to her pleasure is the presence of her brother, Ned, who accompanied her on piano when she sang at the concerts they held in the palace where they were sometimes joined by the cathedral organist.

In 1760 two key events took place. In March, three months after the birth of their son, Jack, her brother, John, and his family moved up to Yorkshire to live in Thornhill near Wakefield. Here they established a large household which included John's father-in-law, a Miss Chardavoyne, four maid servants, two livery men, stabling for 12 horses and a gardener to tend the sizeable garden with its fruit trees and large kitchen garden. John is now able to share some of Gilbert's enthusiasm for growing his own produce and writes of his gardener's looking forward to availing himself of Gilbert's knowledge and advice on growing melons. Thornhill was a happy move for Hester's brother and by 1766 he had four children: two daughters, Jenny and Hecky; and two sons, Jack and George.

The second event was a momentous one which was to bring Hester both happiness and heartbreak. At last her father put to one side his reservations, arranged his financial affairs and gave his blessing to her marriage to John Chapone and much to Hester's delight agreed to his eldest son, Thomas, also a lawyer, marrying 'Pressy' – Mary Prescott – of whom Hester was so fond. Hester's father was to live with his son and new wife which lessened Hester's responsibility for his welfare. She writes, from London to Elizabeth with the good news, apologising for having neglected her friend:

> I know she will instantly forgive me as soon as she knows in what manner my thoughts and time have been engaged since I left Canterbury. The happiness in my own life, and that of my dearest brother, has been deeply interested in the transactions of these few weeks. Thank God all is settled in the way we wished.
>
> Give me your congratulations, my dear friend; but as much for my dear brother and friend as for myself; for in truth, I could not have enjoyed my own happiness in an union with the man of my choice, had I been forced to leave them in the same uncomfortable state of tedious and almost hopeless expectation in which they have suffered so long.
>
> I shall rejoice to hear that you are coming to town, and shall hope for many a comfortable tête á-tête with you in my lodgings in Carey Street; for there I must reside till Mr Chapone can get a house which suits him, which is no easy matter, as he is so confined in point of situation. In the meantime he will carry on his business at his chambers. I have therefore chosen the spot nearest to them, though farther than I wish from all the rest of my friends.

In spite of this drawback Hester assures Elizabeth:

> … that I flatter my heart may be improved in every virtuous affection by an union with a worthy man, and that my dear Miss Carter, and all my friends, will find it more worthy of their attachment, and better qualified for the best uses of friendship, than it ever was before; at least I think it will not be less kindly disposed towards them, nor less desirous to cherish and cultivate all my valuable connections.[10]

Little did Hester realise how soon those friends would need to play an even greater role in her life.

On December 30 Hester and John Chapone were married at Saint Mary's in Marylebone. Hester began her married life in lodgings in Carey Street, near Lincoln's Inn 'amongst the Lawyers.' When she married in 1760 she no doubt had every expectation of a long and happy marriage to the man she had fallen in love with and whom she admired. Her new found happiness brought her better health; prior to her marriage she had suffered a series of fevers. For Hester it was a wrench leaving her father who doted on her yet she was comforted by seeing his happiness for her. Her own happiness in her new married state is evident:

> I hear with great pleasure, my dear Miss Carter, that you are very soon expected in town. So I snatch up my pen in a hurry to put you in good humour with me before I see you, and to tell you where you may find your old friend, in whom you will find as much affection towards you as ever, and no one alteration, I believe, but that of name, and place of abode. We are at present in lodgings in Carey-street, but have taken a house in Arundel-street, both very wide from Clargis-street,[sic] where I suppose your residence is fixed. Perverse thing! Why are you not now in St Paul's Church-yard? I ought certainly to have thanked you sooner for your kind congratulations and good wishes. I hope, however, you will accept my thanks even now, and consider that new-married people always lead a life of hurry and engagement, which leaves them little leisure or inclination for writing letters. The drudgery of answering all the congratulatory letters, I have put upon poor Mr Chapone, who, poor man, was forced to humour me at first. Those of true friendship, however, must not be esteemed a drudgery. Yet I believe you can conceive it possible to feel very averse to the thoughts of writing, even to a friend one dearly loves.
>
> I dare say you had a real pleasure on reading in the newspapers of the completion of two engagements, the length of which you had so often lamented. And I know you will be really glad to hear, that with every other circumstance of happiness my heart could wish, in the beginning of a union which promises to be the best blessing of my life, I have had the additional comfort of better health since my marriage, than I have known for a long time before it. Certainly, 'a merry heart does good like medicine.' Mine rejoices almost as much for my dear brother as for myself. God be praised we are at present a very happy family, and my dear good father, who has made us so, seems to enjoy a large share of satisfaction and pleasure in what he has done: his cheerfulness enabled me to bear our parting with less pain than I expected.
>
> I have more hours to myself than I wish for, for business usually allows me very little of my husband's company except at meals. This I should be inclined to lament as an evil, if I did not consider that the joy and complacency with which we meet, may probably by this means last longer than if we could always be together. If you *can* love a *man*, I expect you will love him, if ever you know him thoroughly. In the mean time, I will be contented if you love his worse half.
>
> His sister, who I think is a favourite with you, is in town with the Dean of Down. Poor Mrs Delany set out about a fortnight ago, on a very melancholy journey, into Warwickshire, to attend her sister, Mrs Dewes, who is so ill they have but little hope of her.
>
> Miss Chapone always desires to be remembered to you with true esteem and respect. I am happy in having bound her to my heart with the additional tie of sisterly love; for she is a sweet excellent creature, and would be a very great delight and blessing to me, did not Mrs Delany so often run away with her to that ugly Ireland. I have another

> sister, whom you do not know, who is also extremely amiable and good, but she too is kept at a great distance from me by her connexions. I have also a mother too, whom her son is as proud of as she is of him. But, alas, I never saw her, and God knows whether I ever shall, for she grows infirm, and her constitution has been terribly shaken by the death of a son and a husband, both within a few years. Make haste and come to town, and till then adieu, my dear friend. Believe me ever, most affectionately,
>
> Yours,
> Hester Chapone
> Carey-street,
> Feb.4, 1761.[11]

It is a letter full of optimism about her good fortune and present happiness. Yet within the year life would change dramatically.

In July she writes again to Elizabeth from her home in Arundel Street apologising for not writing sooner because she has been busy moving and settling down. Though the house is small she describes their having: 'furnished it neatly, and the cleanliness of a house just fitted up, is not ill recommended to me by the dirt I had lived in before in those *puddling* lodgings.' Her husband, John, was a busy solicitor and Hester at first found it hard adjusting to long hours alone in rented accommodation in spite of having her friends the Burrows relatively close. At the end of this letter Hester refers to her husband:

> Mr Chapone desires his best compliments to you, though you never would let him be acquainted with you. One very pleasing proof of his affection for me, is, the pleasure he takes in my friends, but I have much ado to persuade him that you are of that number, as he hardly ever saw us together. 'Surely, my dear,' says he, 'if she loved you, she would sometimes have spent a day with you; and then I should have known her better. If ever she loved you, I fancy she has left it off on your being married.' This last idea seems to have taken strong possession of him, and I don't know whether I shall not be infected with the same jealousy, unless you convince me to the contrary next winter.[12]

Chapter 15

'her presence was judged injurious to him'

Tragedy struck less than ten months after the marriage. After suffering from a bout of ill health Hester had gone to stay in Islington in the hope that the mineral spring waters and the country air of the spa would be good for her. John joined his wife after a few days but fell dangerously ill with a high fever.

On September 17 Mary, one of the Burrows sisters, who would later marry Culling Smith,[1] is about to set out for London to support Hester. She writes to Elizabeth Carter from Tunbridge Wells where she has been staying with her two sisters:

> Madam,
>
> It is upon a very melancholy occasion I take the liberty of addressing you. Mr Chapone has lain dangerously ill of a fever for these last ten days. The accounts we received this morning put us out of all hope of his recovery. Being well appraised of your affection for dear Mrs Chapone, and the bad state of your spirits, we were fearful, had you first met with the account of this melancholy event in the newspaper, it might have had a bad effect on your health; we thought it most prudent to apprise you of it by this means. Our letters of today informed us they apprehended him dying last night; but that she behaves with most becoming fortitude and Christian patience. I dread the consequences of it upon her health in case the dreadful worst should happen; and there seems to be but little reason to flatter ourselves it will not.
>
> I shall go to London to-morrow, in hopes of being some little comfort to poor Mrs Chapone, who at present I fear is a very miserable being. If you are desirous of further intelligence, you may command me, by directing for me at our lodgings in Southampton-Street. If it shall please God to give us any hopes of Mr Chapone's recovery, you may depend upon hearing from me an account of it; otherwise you may suppose the worst, for the physicians give no hopes at all. You will be comforted, I doubt not, as we are, to hear she bears her present suspense with so much meekness and resolution.
>
> I am, dear Madam,
>
> Your obliged humble servant,
>
> MARY BURROWS.[2]

Ten days later John Chapone was dead. The effect on Hester was devastating. On September 22 Mary writes again having received a letter from Elizabeth the previous night:

> I was very sorry your letter came so late last night that it was impossible to answer it by return of post. I am afraid the suspense has been very painful to you. Mr Chapone died on Saturday night, about ten o'clock. She had not been in his room since Monday last, for as her presence was judged injurious to him she submitted to the advice of her friends not to continue her attendance upon him, she therefore was not made acquainted with his death till Sunday morning. She received the news with her accustomed meekness, and has by the whole of her behaviour during his illness, and since his death, shown an example of patience and resignation that is quite astonishing. You would hardly believe were I to describe to you her calmness and composure, as you are so well acquainted with the strength of her passion for him. Could I tell you half the noble things she says and does, it must convince you of the sincerity of her religion, and infinitely increase your affection for her.
>
> Mr and Mrs Mulso [Thomas and Pressy] are exceedingly friendly to her, and have kindly invited me to their home in Rathbone-Place, together with my dear afflicted friend. I told her I was going to write to you, and she desired me to give her kind love to you. Indeed all her friends, and their kindness to her, are remembered by her, particularly at this time, with so much gratitude and affection, that it quite surprises me, and is a pleasing mark of her gratitude to heaven for those blessings she still possesses.[3]

Her concerned friends rallied round. Elizabeth Carter writes to Elizabeth Montagu on September 25:

> I have lately received a piece of intelligence that gives me very great concern: I know you will be very sorry to hear that Mr Chapone is dead. This was a match of such entire affection, and a plan of happiness which had been concerting for so many years, that one cannot imagine a more melancholy separation. My poor friend is enabled, God be thanked, to behave upon this trying occasion, in a manner conformable to the excellence of her character and principles, and is absolutely calm and resigned. But with so much strength of affection and weakness of constitution, it is much to be dreaded what effect so terrible a shock may have upon her health. I first had this news from Tunbridge from the Miss Burrow's, who came there a few days after we left. I wish they had come sooner, as I should have had a real pleasure in introducing them to you there, as a family distinguished by a most undeviating rectitude of principle, and by an indefatigable activity of virtue. Miss Burrows left Tunbridge as soon as she heard of Mrs Chapone's sad situation, and has been with her ever since, of which I am extremely glad.[4]

Elizabeth Carter wrote several times from Deal but Hester was far too ill to respond. It was Mary Burrows, who kept Elizabeth up to date with the state of Hester's health and spirit, reporting on October 5 that she is drawing great comfort from the support and solicitude of her friends and family. Her fever has abated during the day and she is able to enjoy being read to when she feels better. However, the more positive note in the letter is dashed when she adds a postscript on Friday night, October 9, reporting an alarming deterioration in Hester:

> P.S. The above was written (as you will see by the date)some days since. An accident prevented me sending it in the post immediately, and ever since poor Mrs Chapone has been growing worse. I have been waiting her amendment to give you notice of it, for I was unwilling to let you know how ill she was, fearing the anxiety might be hurtful to you at such a distance. I take the liberty of sending it just as it was written, to convince you, dear Madam, it was not without good reason I detained from you the information you desired in your last letter. She has had a pretty high fever upon her ever since Monday last, has suffered much in her head, stomach, and spirits, but this afternoon finds herself much better, and we all hope will get some rest, as her fever is considerably abated. She has had hardly any sleep for these last four nights and days, which seemed an alarming circumstance. Though the doctor has never pronounced any immediate danger, he and all her friends have been apprehensive for the consequences of the violent restlessness that has attended her. If you desire to hear how she does, I shall with great pleasure comply with your commands, to prevent you indulging any groundless fears. I will promise to take the liberty of writing by the next post if she should be worse; so that if you hear nothing from me you may depend on her being better. I am very sorry to raise these apprehensions in your mind, but thought if I neglected writing any longer, you might justly charge me with carelessness.[5]

Two days later Elizabeth receives a letter from Mary with the news that Hester is much better although she still has a fever at night and is very low and dispirited by day causing Mary to comment: 'I fear it is with some regret she returns again to the world.' Hester has now been confined to bed for twenty-three days and Mary comments:

> She is exceedingly low and faint, and I fear, though she should have no unforeseen drawbacks, it will be a long time before she recovers her strength. The weak state she is at present in, does indeed make her case truly pitiable.[6]

In her next letter to Elizabeth she reports that Hester is much better although once again there has been a crisis:

> We were all exceedingly alarmed about her Sunday and Monday; but as the doctors said it would in all probability be decided in forty-eight or twenty-four hours, I thought it was a pity to send you this melancholy account. On Monday evening she fell into a doze, and continued sleeping in an uneasy way till last night about nine o'clock. She lay quite stupid and almost insensible to everything that passed; when she was awake complained of being like a log; and in short frightened us excessively, as we were anxiously expecting the fatal change that twenty-four hours might make in her. Thank God, this change has been in her favour, for she has had a charming night, is much refreshed by her quiet sleep, and eased of many of her pains. Her pains, indeed, have not appeared so violent for the last two days as before; but till this morning, it seemed uncertain whether this inattention to her sufferings, was not the result of insensibility, rather than any real abatement of them.
>
> When she is well enough to receive it, I shall deliver your kind message, and comfort her by telling her you intend to write to her.[7]

Her brother, John, writes to Gilbert on October 29 voicing his concerns over Hester's health:

> Dear Gil:
>
> If I did not sooner answer your friendly Enquiries about my unfortunate Sister Chapone, … because our Accounts of her have held Us in such suspense about her Life, that I thought it not proper Time to give any Description of her. Her cruel loss She bore with the most patient Resignation, but tho' in her distress She sinned not, nor charged God foolishly, yet it was of that deep kind, that her constitution, before hand weak, and additionally hurt by a close and mournful attendance, was incapable of resisting it. Mr Chapone died at Lodgings in Islington, where my two Sisters were retired for the Benefit of the Waters there & of ye Air. A sharp Feaver carried him off in about ten Days. I may venture to say that He was a very great Loss to his Profession, as he certainly was an irreparable one to my Sister. Upon moving to my Brother's House in Town She caught Cold, which flung her into a Feaver, under which she suffered so much, that Our last Account was that she had just begun to recover her Memory & Understanding, & the Doctors thought it probable that She would recover, but by very slow Degrees. I intend to leave open my Letter, till the Post comes tomorrow that I may, as I hope, insert a more favourable Account.

The following day he adds:

> 'My Sister Mulso's Lr. Of today Oct 30, has these words: "The Doctor finds my Sister Chapone considerably better than before, her Understanding & Memory are recovering & She begins to feel Hunger."'

Hester had been seriously ill, hovering between life and death and her road to recovery was a long one. She had been forced to wait six years before her father finally gave his permission for her to marry the man she had fallen in love with. Yet cruel fate had snatched his life and destroyed her happiness. Weakened physically and coping with her profound grief at her loss she faced an uncertain future. Mary reports to Elizabeth on November 11[8] that Hester is now gaining strength and has recovered her appetite. She is strong enough to sit up all day and is in better spirits. Once Hester is stronger Mary is planning to take her to the Burrows's home in Southampton Street for further convalescence for a month or so. It is from there that Hester writes to Elizabeth on December 6 and she reveals that her financial situation is far from good:

> But my dear Mr Chapone's affairs were left in great confusion and perplexity by his sudden death; which happened just at the time of year in which he should have settled his accounts, and made out his bills. As these are very considerable, his estate must suffer a great loss from this circumstance. At present things are in a very melancholy state, and my own prospects such as would probably have appeared very dreadful to me at any other time. But the deprivation of the sources of all my worldly happiness has, I think, made me less sensible to other calamities.[9]

Hester was now a widow, physically still weak and facing debts which had to be paid. She was forced to move out of the marital home and into lodgings once more. John comments: 'My poor sister Chapone, is, I am afraid, hurt in her fortune by her Match.' Hester was just thirty-four and needed to live on a much reduced income. She did receive a stipend from her uncle, Bishop Thomas, of £20 a year and when her father died in 1763 her financial situation improved: 'He left her an addition to her fortune, but that, in her opinion, was no compensation for the loss of so excellent and kind a parent.'[10] Elizabeth Montagu wrote of her concern to Elizabeth Carter in September 1761:

> I am indeed grieved at the heart for Mrs Chapone; all calamities are light in comparison of the loss of what one loves, uniquement; after that dear object is lost ... the soft and quiet pleasures are over, business may employ and diversions amuse the mind, *but the soul's calm sunshine and the heartfelt joy* can never be regained. Mrs Chapone has great virtues, and if she has the martyr's sufferings, will have the *martyr's reward*.[11]

In July the following year Hester responds to a letter from Elizabeth

Montagu which gives an insight into their relationship and Hester's state of mind:

> If you have not heard from me all this While, my dear Friend, it is not that I have not thought of you, far otherwise. In London where I was confin'd a Week I eat of the Trout of Sandleford, and surely I thought of my Dear Mistress of Sandleford; since I have been here, I talk of you with my Amiable Hostess, but when I shou'd have wrote to you I know not, because I scrupled disturbing the Cheerfulness of your Spirit by the Dejection of Mine; however there is no resisting your kind Letter, which I reced. yesterday & must Thank You for today, concealing if I can every other sensation of my Heart but those of friendship & Gratitude towards Dear Mrs Montagu.

Further on in the same letter she confides:

> Never did my lonely Lodgings appear more uncomfortable than at present, after the delightful Society I have so long enjoy'd. You are very good, my dear Madam to give me the best comfort I can have, that of thinking that my true esteem and Affection for you are not wholly unreturn'd. Nothing but the strong sense of my own defects which a comparison with you naturally produces, could ever give me a doubt on this head, after the innumerable proofs of kindness and friendship I have experienced from you, all which are laid up in my heart, where they produce the most pleasing of all sensations, that of Gratitude accompanied by love.........
>
> Your man will be tired of waiting so I must bid you Adieu! Intreating you to love me as well as ever you can, and to believe me with the highest esteem and gratitude, your most affec, and obliged
>
> H. Chapone.[12]

Hester is invited by Elizabeth Montagu to her home in Hill Street later that month.

Her friends were naturally concerned for her financial well-being and it was mooted later in 1765 that she should become a companion to the Duchess of Beaufort; or a governess in the Bavarian Court: the first, Elizabeth Montagu rejected. She writes:

> Her Graces good nature politeness, etc. would have made a state of dependance as easy as a state of dependance can be, but I imagine Mrs Chapone would not accept of service on any terms whatever. Her brother who is very fond of her is in very good business, her uncle is Bishop of Winchester, and tho she has a very small income of her own yet leisure and liberty are of infinite value to such a person......The Duchess of Beaufort would make any one very happy who was in her service but bad health and a certain turn of mind unfits a person for a

> condition, in which, if they do not converse with Ladies women (the most unlikely in the world to Mrs Chapone and the people she has conversed with) they would be reckoned proud and impertinent. The dapper butler, the spruce groom of the chambers, the house Steward and the friends of all these people must be her future companions, and one had rather live on bread and water than in the tittle tattle and gossipry of that set of people......I must own I should as soon keep a person to blow my nose as to amuse me; connections of friendship are different things.[13]

The second, which Elizabeth strongly backed in 1768, was rejected by Hester herself no doubt for the same reasons and also because she would have been geographically distanced from her family with whom she now spent so much of her time.

Later there was some debate caused by Mrs Barbauld[14] as to how happy Hester's marriage had been. Barbauld at the time of Hester's marriage would have been seventeen and unmarried. When she did meet Hester years later Hester reports herself as being irritated by Barbauld's constant smile which she observed must have made her jaw ache. Her view on Hester's marriage: 'Her married life was short, and not very happy' has been taken up by several biographers yet there does not appear to be any sound evidence to support this. In fact Hester's family wrote a defence of her reputation to disprove any such aspersions. It was published in her *Posthumous Works*.[15] This may of course be an attempt to whitewash any criticism of her. The account of the marriage they present includes a strong attack on Barbauld's version:

> This was a period of her life, on which Mrs Chapone, almost to the last hour of it, reflected as having afforded her complete and uninterrupted happiness. Her tenderness for the lover, never experienced a moment's abatement towards the husband. She loved him with an enthusiasm that admitted not of discerning a fault in him; an affection, which, it is but justice to declare, he returned with every proof of kindness and esteem, and during the short time their union was permitted to last, they lived together on terms of perfect harmony and mutual regard.
>
> Always obliging and accommodating in her disposition, it cannot be questioned that she was peculiarly so to the man of her choice and the object of her fondest partiality; and the absurdity of supposing the contrary, can only be equalled by the shameless effrontery of uttering so unfounded an assertion.
>
> The writers of the spurious production called the Life of Mrs Chapone, in which this unpardonable falsehood is affirmed, have indeed sought to shelter under high and most respectable authority, as will appear from the following sentence. "Her married life," says Mrs Barbauld, speaking from personal observation, "was short and not

> very happy". But in what this infelicity consisted, this lady has no where stated.
>
> The reader will be pleased to take notice that the "personal observation" must have been the invention of the moment. Mrs Barbauld could have been but a child at the time of Mr Chapone's death, and was not acquainted with his widow until many years after the event.
>
> This justly celebrated author of so many invaluable works, will feel herself but little obliged to these writers for being so kind as to supply, from their own imaginations, what they observe she has omitted; and still less so, for their obvious misconstructions of her words. If a rumour had reached her that Mrs Chapone was not happy in her married life, Mrs Barbauld would not be disposed to assign as the cause of it, Mrs Chapone's "want of temper for the cultivation of domestic tranquillity." Her own intimate knowledge of her heart and character must have precluded such a supposition; and indeed Mrs Barbauld has expressed, in conversation, her surprise and concern that so unjust an accusation should have appeared in print, and her decided opinion that it ought to be contradicted.
>
> There yet survive one or two of her most intimate friends, who remember Mrs. Chapone during her married life, and can testify her unceasing fondness for her husband, and her invariable acquiescence in all his wishes. Those of her nearest relations, who only remember her from a later point of time, have been frequent witnesses of the affecting tenderness with which she spake of him, whenever she could assume resolution to do so; and she preserved a miniature picture of him, which she professed that she seldom allowed herself to contemplate, because she thought it improper to indulge the sensations of exquisite grief and regret it always occasioned.[16]

The rebuttal of the rumour of an unhappy marriage is fully understandable. Members of her family wished to protect her name and reputation as the author of the book which had brought her such fame in 1773. Hester was however, known for being both argumentative and very stubborn and had a quick temper. She was also accustomed to living with her doting elderly father as company in more commodious surroundings than the cramped rented accommodation in which she began her married life. Added to which there were still financial worries for the couple, something which Hester would not be familiar with, coming as she did from a background in which the pursuit of pleasure in leisure activities, attending assemblies and balls, visiting the races and staying with her extended family made up so large a part of her life. Once she was married to John, a busy attorney, she complained he spent little time at home. Perhaps the reality of the marriage was a disappointment to her after having been made by her father to wait such a long time to marry the man who she had fallen in love with at first sight at North-End.

Chapter 16

'I begin to love her so much'

Hester's correspondence with Elizabeth Montagu on the subject of her alarming state of health evinces sympathy and concern from Elizabeth who invites Hester, with her friends the Burrows, to dinner. When Hester writes to Elizabeth Carter on July 6, 1762 she reveals that although she is stronger she has lost her pleasure in writing:

> For my own part, writing is become so irksome an employment to me, that were it not the purchase of a comfort I cannot do without, that of hearing of the welfare of my friends, I believe I should never chuse to touch a pen. But this with other ill effects of bad spirits, and a heart ill at ease, will I hope wear off in time. I bless God I am better in all respects than I could hope to be. Indeed I do not think my constitution at all impaired; on the contrary I think it is now able to sustain what in some periods of my life would have sunk me to the greatest weakness and dejection. … … How much am I, and how much the Miss Burrowses are obliged to you, for the very valuable and delightful acquisition you have made for us in Mrs Montagu's acquaintance. We all congratulated each other, as on a piece of high preferment, when she was so kind to invite us to dinner the other day; we looked upon it as a happy token of her inclination to admit us to something like intimacy. I begin to love her so much that I am quite frightened at it, being conscious of my own insignificance will probably always keep me at a distance that is not at all convenient for loving.[1]

This invitation to Mrs Montagu's grand London home in Hill Street brought Hester into contact socially with a wealthy and well-connected circle. Elizabeth Carter, who effected the introduction, had first met Elizabeth Montagu in 1758. In character they were opposites with Elizabeth Montagu describing Elizabeth Carter as 'a most amiable modest gentle creature.' Elizabeth Montagu loved ostentatious display of wealth both in her dress and in her homes; loved to be the centre of society and enjoyed the flattery and adulation which was heaped upon her whereas Elizabeth Carter was content to lead a modest life and dis-

Elizabeth, Mrs Montagu, famed for her opulence

dained any form of flattery. Their friendship is therefore somewhat surprising and it was Elizabeth Montagu who pursued it. For her, Elizabeth Carter represented an intellectual mentor who had proved herself with the publication of *Epictetus*. The friendship bloomed: Elizabeth found lodgings for Elizabeth Carter, during the winter London season, in Clarges Street which was close to her London home in Hill Street on Berkeley Square. Elizabeth Montagu even wanted to offer Elizabeth Carter dinner each day, an offer her friend firmly rejected saying: 'I revel in cake and tea, a kind of independent luxury in which one needs very little apparatus, and no attendants; it is mighty consistent with loitering over a book.' Elizabeth Carter, who loved being in the countryside, was a welcome visitor to Sandleford. With the encouragement of her great friend George Lyttelton, Elizabeth Montagu had written three short dialogues which were published anonymously in 1760, in Lyttelton's *Dialogues of the Dead*. Although she had taken great pains to disguise their authorship rumour began to circulate that they came from her pen. It was Elizabeth Carter who defended Montagu against criticism until public acknowledgement of her work became inevitable.

Elizabeth Carter published *Poems on Several Occasions* in 1762. The volume included the *Ode to Wisdom* which Richardson had published without her permission in *Clarissa*, and a moving poem to her father in which she revealed her deep gratitude to him for his forbearance not only over her rejection of marriage when she decided on a single life, but also her rejection of the possibility to become a governess in the Princess of Wales's household in order to maintain her independence and intellectual development, something which her father had always encouraged.

Through her friendship with Elizabeth Montagu the somewhat diffident Elizabeth Carter was drawn into a wider circle of fashionable people among whom was Lord Bath.[2] Elizabeth Montagu and he carried on a flirtatious correspondence and relationship. They saw each other every day when in London. This very close friendship – he adored Elizabeth – appears to have been possible because he was so much older. In 1763 a party was made up for a visit to Spa in the Ardennes to sample the waters and Elizabeth Carter was included. She met up with the rest of the party at Dover. Unfortunately for the last hour and a half of the five hour crossing she was extremely sea sick whereas the unperturbed Edward Montagu ate cold ham 'all the way,' Elizabeth 'was not in the least sick' and Lord Bath 'was gay in spirits.' The party travelled in a variety of chaises with the two women enjoying the extra comfort of a vis-à-vis. Elizabeth in her letters to her sister, to Elizabeth Vesey and Catherine Talbot describes the terrible road conditions which were exhausting for the two women: it took the party 15 hours to travel the 21 miles from Liège to Spa. Here Edward and the two Elizabeths lodged in a house opposite that of Lord Bath with whom they dined every day. While Elizabeth Montagu enjoyed the European society gathered to take the waters at Spa her friend was less enamoured not only with the company there but also by the weather: it rained seemingly endlessly. There was also the danger posed by robbers who lurked on the mountain walks, which somewhat curtailed Elizabeth Carter's rambles. She had never been interested in sartorial matters and either by design or accident had left behind her hoop so could beg being excused from the more formal gatherings, such as a reception for the Prince and Princess Ferdinand of Prussia at which fashionable ladies appeared in hooped dresses. Nor did the Paris fashion for highly rouged cheeks of the ladies meet with her approval. After their sojourn in Spa the party continued to Aix-la-Chapelle, Cologne, the Hague, Utrecht, Antwerp, Brussels, Lille and Dunkirk before setting sail from Calais for England once more.

Elizabeth maintained that the waters had failed to lessen her headaches and for Lord Bath they failed to bring lasting benefit: he died the following year. Elizabeth Montagu mourned his death deeply. It was Elizabeth Carter who went to Sandleford to help lessen her grief while her husband, Edward, tactfully stayed in London. Elizabeth Carter benefited financially from Lord Bath's death by receiving an annuity of £150 from his heirs, Sir William Pulteney and his wife.

Hester is eagerly awaiting the return of both Elizabeths:

> We stand in great need of you and Mrs Montagu, to produce some pleasing ideas in our minds; for London is now in such a state, that every conversation is tinctured with melancholy and horror. My friends, Miss Burrowses, reproach me often with my insensibility to public affairs, and indeed I generally am guarded, by a sanguine constitution and a most profound ignorance, from those terrors about future evils to the public, which embitter the lives of some of my acquaintance. But even I begin now to be affected with some melancholy apprehensions, and to feel myself shocked at the unbounded torrent of licentiousness which prevails every day more amongst us. Alas, how little able are we, either as a nation or as individuals, to stand the trial of great prosperity! And how constantly are outward blessings counterbalanced by internal evils! How ought this consideration to lessen our dread of calamity, and our impatience under it.[3]

Interestingly this is one of the few occasions that Hester comments on the social or political situation. Hester is delighted to have been introduced into Elizabeth Montagu's circle yet is very conscious of the social distance between her and Elizabeth. Much to her embarrassment she had failed to write offering her congratulations on the publication of Elizabeth's three essays in Lyttelton's *Dialogues of the Dead*. Hester had read them and had been asked by Elizabeth to offer any criticism which again she has failed to do. From her comments in a letter[4] to Elizabeth Carter in 1763 Montagu's cover was blown which for Montagu would make her fears of public recognition a reality. Elizabeth Montagu recognised this danger when she wrote to Lyttelton:

> 'Extraordinary talents may make a Woman admired, but they will never make her happy. Talents put a Man above the World, & in a condition to be feared and worshipped, a woman who possesses them must always be courting the World, and asking pardon, as it were, for uncommon excellence.'[5]

Hester was enthusiastic in her praise of the merit of the three essays but revealed her reasons to Elizabeth Carter for not writing to Elizabeth Montagu as being a lack of confidence in her ability to express herself adequately. A surprising admission given that Hester had established such a reputation for eloquence of style.

Winter always brought a change in Hester's spirits: it meant being confined to London and being deprived of her friends' company:

> I have been rather shabby of late since the wet weather came. My enemy, Winter, begins to lay his fangs upon me. I hate him completely now, as he does not bring my friends about me, the only service the hidden bald-pate ever did me. I now set all my affection on Spring, who comes decked with snow-drops, and Carters, and Burrowses, and such like white and lovely virgins.[6]

Spring and summer meant travelling was easier and Hester seized every opportunity to visit her relatives and friends. Her extended family became even more important than they had been before her marriage. She escaped from London to Hampshire in the spring to visit her uncle, the Bishop of Winchester and his wife. Here she stayed in the grand surroundings of Farnham Castle which at times she found tedious with the long formal meals but delighted in seeing her three cousins: Mrs Ogle, whose husband, Dr Ogle,[7] was the Dean of Winchester; Mrs Buller, whose husband, Dr Buller, later became Bishop of Exeter, and her youngest cousin who married Admiral Sir Chaloner Ogle.

In the spring of 1765 Hester planned a visit to Thornhill where she was always a welcome visitor. Gilbert White whom she regarded as the ideal companion for the long and often hazardous journey from London up to Yorkshire would accompany her. Her brother jokes to Gilbert that at Hester's time of life – she was by now forty-eight – she could embark on such a journey without anyone suspecting that she was eloping. In fact Gilbert did not accompany Hester on this occasion. Hester embarked on her journey alone by the Leeds Machine – also referred to as a flying machine – which was a much faster means of conveyance. This regular coach service had been started in 1760 between London and Leeds and had cut the journey time considerably from four days to two. The coach had steel springs thus making a more comfortable journey for the passengers and, with its increased speed, had the added advantage of cutting down overnight expenses en route at coaching inns. Even so John comments to Gilbert that it was a bold undertaking to set out alone from London 'and be hurried away in chance company.'

Hester helped care for Jane, her sister-in-law, who was still weak from the birth of her fourth child, a son. She had lost a son, George, in infancy, the previous year. It was during this long stay from the beginning of June until August that Hester grew increasingly fond of her eldest niece, Jane, or Jenny, who by then was eight years old and growing up without the benefit of a formal education, which her father did not believe in for his daughters. It was to be this niece for whom Hester started writing a conduct book. The following year in July she went to visit Gilbert at Selborne with her eldest brother, Thomas, and his wife.

In 1767 her brother John left Thornhill and moved to Witney in Oxfordshire which meant that her beloved niece, Jenny, was much closer. When it came to educating daughters her brother, John, reflects the paternalistic outlook on education for women. He writes in 1768: 'We have no thoughts of sending Jenny to a school at present, nor am I very fond of a School for Girls.' Although by then there were more schools for girls available, some were more successful than others. An example of the former was the girls' boarding school started by the three older sisters of Hannah More in Bristol in about 1757, which flourished. Hannah attended the school first as a pupil with her younger sister and then as a teacher. But for the majority of young girls their education still lay in the hands of their parents who, depending on their attitude to educating their daughters, might neglect subjects which they deemed unnecessary thereby denying them whole areas of knowledge systematically taught. Hester knew from her own experience how much she had lacked in the form of guidance when it came to her own education. Through sheer determination she had educated herself. However, she was aware that in comparison with Elizabeth Carter, her friend and mentor, she lacked her intellectual rigour which she so much admired. She felt her youth had been wasted through lack of formal education and determined that her niece should not suffer likewise.

Chapter 17

'I am grown as bold as a lion'

By the summer of 1770 Hester has become one of Elizabeth Montagu's close circle. She has been invited to accompany Elizabeth on a trip north to Scotland. Hester confides to Elizabeth Carter:

> I am grown as bold as a lion with Mrs Montagu and fly in her face whenever I have a mind; in short, I enjoy her society with the most perfect gôut; and find my love for her takes off my fear and awe, though my respect for her character continually increases.[1]

Before continuing north they have been staying at Hagley where Elizabeth's friend from Tunbridge days, Lord Lyttelton, has a palatial estate. Hester finds Lyttelton's company amiable and the grand, Palladian, Hagley Hall, set in beautiful parkland two miles from Stourbridge in Worcestershire, enchanting in spite of the weather being wet in July. Neither Hester nor Elizabeth has been well and they are entertained by George, Lord Lyttelton, reading aloud to them from his work *History of the Life of Henry II* which would be published 1767-71 in three volumes. It had taken thirty years in writing. Whether or not Hester found it dull or not she does not say but certainly when it was published the style was criticised for being so.

Somewhat recovered the party set off for Derbyshire but because of Elizabeth's ill health they are forced to abandon its rural delights. They continue northwards to the Montagu's house, East Denton Hall in Northumberland, close to Newcastle, where they are joined by Elizabeth's husband. The two women set off for Edinburgh in September to visit Dr Gregory, an old friend of Elizabeth's, leaving Edward to manage his business interests. John Gregory[2] knew both Lyttelton and Elizabeth when he and his family had lived in London from 1754 until 1756. A Scotsman, he moved back to Scotland to take up an academic post at Aberdeen and then moved to Edinburgh in 1764.

His wife's death in 1761 left him to bring up his two daughters, one of whom, Dorothea, would later become Elizabeth's companion. Gregory wrote *A Father's Legacy to his Daughters* which he did not intend for publication. However, in 1774 his son, James, also a doctor, published it after his father's death. In the tradition of conduct books it offered parents prescriptive advice on all aspects of their daughters' education and became a best seller.

Gregory puts great emphasis on propriety in public places for his daughters who must conduct themselves with modesty and overcome the female trait of vanity. Vain women will respond to male flattery which could lead them into a relationship which will prove to be unhappy. His advice is genuine he argues because: 'You will have one advantage by attending to what I am going to leave with you; you will hear, at least for once in your lives, the ginuine [sic] sentiments of a man who has no interest in flattering or deceiving you.' When it comes to learning he advises his daughters to 'keep it a profound secret, especially from the men, who generally look with a jealous and malignant eye on a woman of great parts, and a cultivated understanding.' His understanding of the difficulties which intelligent women faced in society would fall on a receptive Bluestocking readership. Elizabeth Montagu was generous in her praise of his virtue after his death in 1773. A view which Mary Wollstonecraft[3] did not share. She attacked the book for its principles in *A Vindication of the Rights of Woman* (1792). She particularly found fault with his views on young women needing to conceal their learning if they were to be successful in the marriage market, scathingly commenting: 'I cannot silently pass over arguments that so speciously support opinions which, I think, have had the most baneful effect on the morals and manners of the female world.'

In Edinburgh Elizabeth Montagu's health is much improved thanks to the ministrations of Dr Gregory. Hester and Elizabeth Montagu are both writing to Elizabeth Carter about their journey. Hester describes the beauty of the landscape once they leave Edinburgh for Taymouth in Perthshire. Although the weather is far from kind Hester is in high spirits maintaining that she has never enjoyed an excursion as much as this. She finds the scenery inspiring with the mountains and lakes around Taymouth adding to her delight. They return to Edinburgh where Elizabeth shines in company, which is drawn together Hester reports 'by the magnetism of Mrs Montagu' although much to Hester's disappointment David Hume[4] is otherwise engaged and unable to attend. Hume had championed the encouragement of women's education arguing that women of sense and education had a civilising role to play in polite society: enlightened views which Hester shared and would later expound in *Letters on the Improvement of the Mind*.

The trip north in the company of Elizabeth Montagu brought Hester great pleasure. More importantly it is probably during this time that Elizabeth encouraged Hester to publish her letters, which she had been writing since 1765, to her niece on education and conduct in order to earn extra income to support herself.

However, she discloses some anxiety to Elizabeth Carter at the end of the letter:

> I am much obliged to you for sending Mrs—'s paper to Lady Dartry, and for your kind intention of bringing me acquainted with her. I can have no doubt of the value of an acquaintance with a person you esteem so much, but have great doubt of answering the expectations your partial friendship may have raised. However that prove, I shall certainly think myself much honoured by her notice. I am a little afraid that the advantage of your's and Mrs Montagu's high opinion of me, will enlarge my acquaintance more than is consistent with my manner of living in town. It will be necessary for me to guard against this, though, in other circumstances, nothing could be more desirable than the acquisition of such acquaintance as your circle affords, and on whose account Mr Burrows rejoices that he never, in any of his sermons, launched out into any common place against the rich and the great.[5]

Mrs Montagu's house at 23 Hill Street, to the west of Berkeley Square, in London had become a main venue for meetings of the Bluestockings. She delighted in lavish decoration and followed fashion in interior decoration somewhat slavishly, writing:

> ... we must all seek the barbarous gaudy goût of the Chinese; and fat-headed Pagods and shaking Mandarins, bear the prize from the finest works of antiquity; and Apollo and Venus must give way to a fat idol with a sconce on his head. You will wonder I should condemn the taste I have complied with, but in trifles I shall always conform to the fashion.[6]

Mary Delany comments:

> If I had paper and time I could entertain you with the acct.[account] of Mrs M's (Hill Street) room of Cupidons; which was open'd with an assembly for all the foreigners, the literati, and the macaronis[7] of the present age. Many and sly are the observations how such a *genius* at her age, and so *circumstanced*, could think of painting the walls of her dressing-room with bowers of roses and jessamins entirely inhabited by little Cupids in all their little wanton ways, is astonishing! Unless she looks on herself as the wife of old Vulcan,[a reference to Edward Montagu's involvement with collieries] and mother to all these little loves![8]

Mrs Montagu's Salon, Portman Square

Clearly some of her interior decoration was not to the taste of her friends. Her husband's death in 1775 did not deter her from embarking on an even grander project, Montagu House in Portman Square. She moved there in 1781. Here her taste in decoration was on an even more sumptuous scale. Ten years later she finally completed a room hung with feather hangings and was rewarded by a visit from the Queen and Princesses at a breakfast gathering.

By the 1770s the Bluestocking gatherings with Elizabeth Montagu, Fanny Boscawen and Elizabeth Vesey as three of the leading hostesses were at their height. Elizabeth Vesey's assemblies had become so large that guests organised themselves into groups beforehand to avoid the crush. Her husband had become a member of Johnson's Literary Club in 1775, which enabled her to attract members including the great man himself to her gatherings. Mrs Vesey was famous for the informality at her parties and the care with which she mixed the guests. The actual management of the parties fell to her more practical sister-in-law, from her first marriage, Mrs Handcock, who was nicknamed 'Body' while Elizabeth went under the nickname of 'Mind'. Hannah More gives a glowing summary of her parties when she writes in 1781: 'I know of no house where there is such good rational society and a conversation so general, so easy, so unpretending.' As the popularity of these private

Hannah More, companion in London of the Garricks

parties spread so did the number of hostesses. Not only did venues vary but also the make up of the group, the grandeur of the occasion, and the time: sometimes gatherings took place in the mornings and sometimes in the evenings. The size and configuration of the meetings also varied depending on the hostess. Hannah More reports offering only cakes and cream to a small gathering which included Johnson and Garrick who reportedly had an uproarious time reminiscing about childhood days in Lichfield. David Garrick had been a pupil at Johnson's school, Edial Hall School, in 1735, before coming to London with Johnson in 1736.

Hannah More was introduced into the Bluestocking circle by the sister of Sir Joshua Reynolds, the artist. Frances Reynolds knew not only Johnson but also the actor David Garrick and his Austrian wife, Eva[9] who became very fond of Hannah. It was Elizabeth Montagu who primarily adopted Hannah as her protégée to rival Mrs Thrale's Fanny Burney. Hannah wrote the poem *Bas Bleu* which was not published until 1786 although it had been in circulation for some three years. It is addressed to Elizabeth Vesey and is a celebration of the Bluestocking circle and the civilising influence of conversation in polite society. The poem describes the social dearth of good intellectual conversation in the eighteenth century, which resulted in dullness in the drawing rooms of the gentry, before describing the brilliance of the Bluestocking assemblies which by the 1770's were firmly established as fashionable meeting places for some of the most important literary figures of the period: Samuel Johnson who was both admired and feared for his intellect; George Lyttelton; Fanny Burney, who was causing a sensation with her novels; the actor, David Garrick, "Capability" Brown and the artist, Joshua Reynolds, were members; politicians, Horace Walpole and Edmund Burke; lawyers such as William Weller Pepys; wealthy society hostesses, with their magnificent country estates and town houses, like Elizabeth Montagu and Hester Thrale who both shone in company; women famed for their good manners and wit such as Elizabeth Vesey, Mary Delany and Fanny Boscawen; scholars like the modest and shy Elizabeth Carter. Hannah More names the female members identifying them by their intellectual achievements or social skills. The male members are graced with Latin names.

THE BAS BLEU, OR CONVERSATION

… …

Long was Society o'er run
By Whist, that desolating Hun!
Long did Quadrille despotic sit,
That Vandal of colloquial wit!
And Conversation's setting light
Lay half obscur'd in Gothic night.
At length the mental shades decline,
Colloquial wits begin to shine,
Genius prevails, and Conversation
Emerges into Reformation.
The vanquish'd triple crown to you,
Boscawen sage, bright Montagu,
Divided fell! – your cares in haste
Rescued the ravag'd realms of Taste;
And Lyttleton's accomplish'd name,
And witty Pulteney shar'd the fame!
The men not bound by pedant rules,
Not Ladies Precieuses ridicules;
For polished Walpole shew'd the way,
How wits may be both learn'd and gay!
And Carter taught the female train,

The deeply wise are never vain;
And she who SHAKESPEARE'S wrongs redrest,
Prov'd that the brightest are the best.
This just deduction still they drew,
And well they practis'd what they knew!
Nor taste, nor wit deserves applause,
Unless still true to Critic laws!
Good sense, of faculties the best,
Inspire and regulate the rest.

See Vesey's plastic genius make
A circle every figure take!

Th' enchantress wav'd her wand, and spoke!
Her potent wand the circle broke;
The social Spirits hover round,
And bless the liberated ground.

Here sober Duchesses are seen,
Chaste Wits, and Critics void of Spleen!
Physicians fraught with real science,
And Whigs and Tories in alliance,
Poets fulfilling Christian duties,
Just Lawyers, reasonable Beauties!
Bishops who preach, and Peers who pay,
And Countesses who seldom play!
Learn'd Antiquaries, who, from college,
Reject the rust and bring the knowledge!
And, hear it, age, believe it, youth,
Polemics, really seeking truth!
And travellers of that rare tribe,
Who've seen the countries they describe!
Who study'd there, so strange their plan,
Not plants, nor herbs alone, but man.

Ladies who point, nor think me partial,
An Epigram as well as MARTIAL;
Yet in all female worth succeed,
As well as those who cannot read.

Once Faithful Memory! heave a sigh,
Here ROSCIUS[1] gladden'd every eye.

Why comes not MARO[2]? Far from town
He rears the Urn to Taste and BROWN;[3]
Plants Cypress round the Tomb of GRAY,
Or decks his English Garden gay;
Whose mingled sweets exhale perfume,
And promise a perennial bloom.
Here, rigid CATO,[4] awful Sage!
Bold Censor of a thoughtless age,
Once dealt his pointed moral round,
And, not unheeded, fell the sound;
The Muse his honour'd memory weeps,
For CATO now with ROSCIUS sleeps!
Here once HORTENSIUS[5] lov'd to sit,
Apostate now from social wit:
Ah! why in wrangling senates waste
The noblest parts, the happiest taste?
Why Democratic Thunders wield,
And quit the Muse's calmer field?
Taste thou the gentler joys they give,
With HORACE[6] and with LELIUS[7] live.

Hail, CONVERSATION, soothing Power,
Sweet Goddess of the social hour!
Not with more heart felt warmth, at least,
Does LELIUS bend, the true High Priest!
Than I, the lowest of thy train,
These field flowers bring to deck thy fane!
Who to thy shrine like him can haste,
With warmer zeal, or purer taste?
Oh may thy worship long prevail,
And thy true votaries never fail!
Long may thy polish'd altars blare
With wax lights' undiminish'd rays!
Still be thy nightly offerings paid,
Libations large of Lemonade!
On silver vases, loaded, rise
The biscuits' ample sacrifice!
Nor be the milk white streams forgot
Of thirst assuaging, cool orgeat!

1 Garrick. 2 Mason. 3 'Capability' Brown. 4 Dr Johnson. 5 Edmund Burke. 6 Horace Walpole. 7 Sir W. W. Pepys.

> Rise, incense from fragrant Tea,
> Delicious incense, worthy Thee!
> … … …

Elizabeth Vesey continued to give her parties even when in later years she became extremely deaf. Madame D'Arblay describes the result:

> But what most contributed to render the scenes of her social circle nearly dramatic in comic effect was her deafness. She had commonly two or three or more ear trumpets hanging to her wrists, or slung about her neck, or tost upon the chimney-piece or table. The instant that any earnestness of countenance or animation of gesture struck her eye, she darted forward, trumpet in hand, to inquire what was going on, but almost always arrived at the speaker at the moment, that he was become, in his turn, the hearer.[10]

When Elizabeth Vesey's husband died in 1785 he left her financially less well-provided-for than his long standing mistress much to the fury of Elizabeth Montagu and Elizabeth Carter. Fortunately her husband's nephew stepped into the breach and made sure that she was able to continue living a comfortable life. However, she was inconsolable in her grief and Elizabeth Montagu reports her as 'weeping continuously.' Her mental health declined rapidly to the point she no longer recognised her faithful and loving friends.

Part Four

A Model of Conduct for Young Ladies

LETTERS

ON THE

IMPROVEMENT OF THE MIND.

ADDRESSED TO A LADY

BY MRS. CHAPONE.

WITH

THE LIFE OF THE AUTHOR.

I consider an human Soul without Education, like marble in the Quarry, which shows none of its inherent Beauties till the Skill of the Polisher fetches out the colours, makes the surface shine, and discovers every ornamental Cloud, Spot, and Vein that runs through the Body of it. Education, after the same Manner, when it works upon a noble Mind, draws out to view every latent Virtue and Perfection, which without such Helps are never able to make their Appearance. ADDISON.

A New Edition.

LONDON:

PRINTED FOR SCATCHERD AND LETTERMAN, AVE-MARIA LANE; LONGMAN, HURST, REES, ORME, AND BROWN; SHERWOOD, NEELY, AND JONES; LAW AND WHITTAKER; BALDWIN, CRADOCK, AND JOY; AND GALE, CURTIS, AND FENNER.

1815.

Title page of the 1815 edition of Letters on the Improvement of the Mind

Chapter 18

Letters on the Improvement of the Mind: Letters I to V

In 1773 Hester's conduct book *Letters on the Improvement of the Mind*[1] was published. Following in the already well-established tradition of conduct literature, the prescriptive advice she gives is so eminently sensible and written in so sympathetic a style that it is easily accessible. In it Hester sets out a model for a young gentlewoman's education which encompasses the key constructs for the eighteenth century ideal model of a woman: virtue, modesty and obedience. However, it also includes a rigorous programme of structured study of key subjects with an emphasis on encouraging a capacity for rational thought, something which many previous books in the genre had neglected. Hester has borrowed part of the title from an earlier work on education which did stress the importance of rational thought: Isaac Watts in his book *The Improvement of the Mind* (1741) sets out a scheme for the improvement of knowledge in young men.

Elizabeth Montagu had read parts of Hester's manuscript and offered criticism and advice. The high opinion in which Elizabeth Montagu held Hester, and Elizabeth's connections with the powerful and wealthy, together with her encouragement, were invaluable when it came to publishing it by subscription some six years after Hester began writing it for her eldest niece, Jane – or Jenny as she was referred to in the family. *Letters on the Improvement of the Mind* would establish Hester's literary reputation and influence in educating young women from the gentry. The popularity of the book would continue into the nineteenth century. It would also enable Hester to enjoy a more secure financial position and social standing as a widow who, unlike many of the Bluestocking circle, did not have great wealth to cushion her from the discomforts of life. For Hester the friendship and support which the Bluestocking movement gave her were invaluable in finding her voice once again after the tragedy which nearly took her life in 1761.

Hester was an excellent letter writer and could combine a lightness of touch with a more serious tone. It is no surprise that she wrote the book in the epistolary form so beloved by Richardson who had given Hester encouragement in her writing in the early days and had perhaps even more importantly given her the confidence to set down her thoughts on paper. By employing the structure of the letter form Hester is able to create an intimate tone when addressing her niece, yet as her aunt she is also able to be fairly prescriptive in tone when advising her on not only suitable subjects of study but also on matters of personal development and entry into adult society.

The book is dedicated to Mrs Montagu who, with Elizabeth Carter, read it in manuscript form, suggested alterations and offered encouragement to the seemingly somewhat diffident Hester on having it published by subscription.

TO
MRS MONTAGU

MADAM,

I BELIEVE you are persuaded that I never entertained a thought of appearing in public, when the desire of being useful to one dear child, in whom I take the tenderest interest, induced me to write the following Letters:– perhaps it was the partiality of friendship, which so far biassed [sic] your judgment as to make you think them capable of being more extensively useful, and warmly to recommend the publication of them. Though this partiality could alone prevent your judgment from being considered as decisive in favour of the work, it is more flattering to the writer than any literary fame; if, however, you will allow me to add, that some strokes of your elegant pen have corrected these Letters, I may hope, they will be received with an attention, which will insure a candid judgment from the reader, and perhaps will enable them to make some useful impression on those, to whom they are now particularly offered.

They only, who know how your hours are employed, and of what important value they are to the good and happiness of individuals, as well as to the delight and improvement of the public, can justly estimate my obligation to you for the time and consideration you have bestowed on this little work. As *you* have drawn it forth, I may claim a sort of right to the ornament and protection of your name, and to the privilege of publicly professing myself, with the highest esteem,

MADAM,
Your much obliged friend,
and most obedient,
humble servant,
HESTER CHAPONE.

Letters on the Improvement of the Mind, originally produced in two volumes, is divided into ten letters, each covering a different aspect of conduct which Hester deemed important for her young niece to master if she is to take her place as a useful member of eighteenth century society. Hester sums up her aim which is to create a suitable model 'for the direction of your conduct through life.' The niece, to whom the letters are addressed, was the eldest daughter of her second brother, John, and his wife, Jane. In 1765 Hester had spent several months at the parsonage at Thornhill and during her stay she became particularly attached to Jenny. Hester, realising only too well the limitations in the education she herself had received by comparison with her brothers, and no doubt aware of her brother John's dismissal of academic education for girls, set about devising a model which would encourage her niece's intellectual development. In the six years between 1766 and 1772 she put together her model. Religion forms the cornerstone of her philosophy of education for young women. It is Hester's firmly held belief that by espousing the tenets of Christianity her niece will achieve virtue and happiness which will enable her to govern her temper and manners and so become not only a useful but also an agreeable member of society.

Hester sets a warm and intimate style with the salutation 'MY DEAREST NIECE' in Letters I, III, VII, IX and X. The remaining five letters are bare of salutations. Instead Hester goes straight into the main text of her letters but does refer to Jenny in the body of the text variously as:

> 'My Dearest Child, my beloved niece,' and 'my dearest girl.'

She signs herself variously:

> Your faithful friend and most, affectionate AUNT;
>
> How earnestly I wish you this happiness, you can never know, unless you could read the heart of Your truly affectionate;
>
> I am, my dearest Niece, Your ever affectionate;
>
> Your most affectionate;

and:

> Adieu, my dear child! – I am, with the tenderest affection, Ever your's [sic].

Each letter covers a particular subject area:

I	*On the first Principles of Religion;*
II	*On the Study of Holy Scriptures;*
III	*The Same Subject continued;*
IV	*On the Regulation of the Heart and Affections;*
V	*The Same Subject continued;*
VI	*On the Government of the Temper;*
VII	*On Economy;*
VIII	*On Politeness and Accomplishments;*
IX	*On Geography and Chronology;*
X	*On the Manner and Course of reading History.*

The letters vary in length: the opening letter is the shortest comprising just fourteen pages while the longest – *On the Regulation of the Heart and Affections* – runs to forty-seven pages: a subject with which Hester wanted her niece to be fully conversant. Well aware of the possible pitfalls and dangers for a young girl when dealing with the charms of the opposite sex and the risk posed to her beloved niece's virtue Hester tackles the subject by dividing her strictures between letters IV and V. The remaining letters each number twenty-two pages, apart from letters II *On the Study of the Holy Scriptures*, thirty-six pages, and letter IX *On Geography and Chronology*, only sixteen pages in length. The brevity may be explained by Hester's opinion of the subject at the beginning of the letter: 'In Geography – the easiest of all sciences, and the best adapted to the capacity of children …'

The concept of tying virtue with happiness is central to Hester's advice. It is through careful study of certain sections of the Bible that her niece will come to a deeper understanding of true Christian virtue which will affect all aspects of her life. Although recommending close study of the Bible she wisely recognises that her niece is still young and offers sensible advice which is to read 'the Historical Books of the Old Testament – provided you read them as an history, and keep the thread of it in your mind, as you go on.' She ends this first letter:

> Adieu, my beloved Niece! If the feelings of your heart, whilst you read my letters, correspond with those of mine, whilst I write them, I shall not be without the advantage of your partial affection, to give weight to my advice; for, believe me, my own dear girl, my heart and eyes overflow with tenderness while I tell you, with how warm and earnest prayers for your happiness here, and hereafter, I subscribe myself
> Your faithful friend,
> And most affectionate AUNT.

Hester devotes the second letter to close study of the Old Testament, working her way chronologically from Genesis to Esther, which she regards as the 'last of the canonical books that is properly historical' having dismissed en route Leviticus and the first eight chapters of Numbers as affording 'no great instruction to us now.' Again she advises skipping whole sections which she regards as of being of little interest to her niece at her age and is succinct in her summary of other books opining that: '*The Song of Solomon* is a fine poem – but its mystical reference to religion lies too deep for a common understanding; if you read it therefore, it will be rather as a matter of curiosity than of edification.' She has practical hints to help her niece get the historical perspective by recommending the use of the index before moving on to the New Testament in the third letter.

She starts: 'We come now to that part of scripture, which is the most important of all; and which you must make your constant study.' She emphasises that with regard to the four Gospels 'you must make yourself perfectly mistress of them all.' She describes St Paul: 'He was a man of extraordinary eloquence ... He seems to have been of an uncommon warm temper, and zealous in whatever religion he professed' and points out that he was an educated man and a Roman citizen enjoying the privileges which were denied to most of the other disciples but most importantly was the seeker of truth. From reading and studying St Paul her niece will learn not to despise anyone for their beliefs as 'there are wise and worthy men among all sects of Christians' but rather show benevolence to everyone. Hester recognises that parts of the Epistles are too difficult for her niece to fully comprehend at her age and further aligns herself with her pupil by declaring: 'and many of them beyond my abilities to state clearly.' She places the book of Revelations in the same category, commenting: 'but, I think, it is yet too soon for you to study this part of scripture.' Her advice and methodology are eminently practical and sensible for a fifteen-year-old who, living under her father's roof, would presumably already be reasonably well versed in Bible study. Her father, John Mulso, was by then Prebendary at both Winchester and Salisbury Cathedrals.

It is in her fourth letter *On the Regulation of the Heart and Affections* that Hester reveals her own views on young women in polite society. Although Hester's advice reflects the eighteenth century view of the subservient young woman she espouses her Bluestocking values which sought to push forward the boundaries for women who wanted to achieve a greater parity with men when it came to intellectual thought and freedom. However, she is caught by the dichotomy of praising intellectual rigour while at the same time counselling against openly revealing by argument too much when in the society of men – many of whom will not admire a young woman who can argue rationally. She is only too well aware that men were suspicious and in some cases antagonistic towards intelligent women who voiced their opinions in company. Some male writers belittled women. Lord Chesterfield held:

> Women are only children of larger growth. They have entertaining tattle, sometimes wit, but for solid reasoning, and good sense, I never in my life knew one who had it, or who acted or reasoned in consequence of it, for four and twenty hours together. A man of sense only trifles with them, as he does with an engaging child; but he neither consults them, nor trusts them in serious matter.[2]

A view which in many male circles would have been echoed. Hester attacks this male construct of women still prevalent at the time as being the result of lack of education and opportunity to widen horizons beyond those laid down by male dominated society. She censures:

> Pride and vanity, the vices opposite to humility, are the sources of almost all the worst faults, both of men and women. The latter are particularly accused – and not without reason – of vanity, the vice of little minds, chiefly conversant with trifling subjects.

Hester has harsh words on 'timid minds' and pours scorn on women who are constantly dissatisfied with their looks and appearance and seek to effect change by affectation which she argues implies 'a mean opinion of one's own real form, or character, while we strive against nature to alter ourselves by ridiculous contortions of the body, or by feigned sentiments and unnatural manners.' She exhorts her niece to have a bold and confident mind and, rather than courting admiration, command it. A withering condemnation of her sex for their lack of ambition follows:

> Whilst men are proud of power, of wealth, dignity, learning, or abilities, young women are usually ambitious of nothing more than to be admired for their persons, their dress, or their most trivial accomplishments. The homage of men is their grand object; but they only desire them to be in love with their persons, careless how despicable their minds appear, even to these their pretended adorers. I have known a woman so vain as to boast of the most disgraceful addresses; being contented to be thought meanly of, in points the most interesting to her honour, for the sake of having it known, that her person was attractive enough to make a man transgress the bounds of respect due to her character, which was not a vicious one, if you except this intemperate vanity.

In eighteenth century polite society assemblies, balls, masquerades, ridottos, theatre, opera, Vauxhall and Ranelagh pleasure gardens could offer a suitable setting for attracting the eye of a possible suitor in the London season: similarly at spa towns such as Bath and Tunbridge Wells. Mary Delany considered it of prime importance to introduce her young niece, Mary Dawes, into the public sphere although she drew the line at her attending masquerades which presented too high a risk for one so young. Propriety in public places had to be safeguarded for the unwary young woman who might well fall victim to an unwelcome admirer. Fanny Boscawen recounts in 1748 the dangers of venturing into the dark walks of Vauxhall Gardens without gentlemen. This resulted in three gentlewomen allegedly being chased and kissed by six or seven men and being whipped by them. Fortunately the account proved to be false. It turned out that the women had been mistaken for prostitutes by some drunken apprentices who had pursued them. Still as Fanny pragmatically points out: 'I pity the poor young women and blame 'em too, for all three of 'em go often enough to Vauxhall, to know the dark walks at 12 at night are for other purposes than for three women of fashion to wander in.'[3] The dangers facing the unwary young woman were only too familiar to parents and their daughters and one which Fanny Burney's hugely successful novel *Evelina: or The History of a Young Lady's Entrance into the World* would have as its central theme. Happily for the heroine she wins the hand of Lord Orville.

Hester's scathing attack on women reflects her contempt for the social world she herself eschewed once her own mother had died. Later in this letter she argues that if a young woman is presented with a model of femininity in which specific qualities such as tenderness, softness, weakness and timidity are lauded then she will adopt them and even take them to extremes by weeping for a fly, starting at a feather and being so weak that:

> ... the smallest accident quite overpowers her. Her fondness and affection become fulsome and ridiculous; her compassion grows contemptible weakness; and her apprehensiveness the most abject cowardice: for, when once she quits the direction of Nature, she knows not where to stop, and continually exposes herself by the most absurd extremes.

One wonders at the reaction of Hester's niece to this advice and, if given her aunt's authoritative permission to adopt a more robust and rational outlook on life, whether she embraced it. Hester is made of stern stuff when she tells her niece that she must keep her emotions in check and not become emotionally self-indulgent. This she can achieve by embracing situations which demand self-control and selflessness. She continues that a woman must have patience and fortitude, presence of mind and 'a calm resignation in danger.'

Was she perhaps thinking of the dangers of childbirth which a woman in the eighteenth century would have to face without the panacea of anaesthesia or skilled medical intervention? The many pregnancies faced by women such as Hester Thrale, who bore twelve children of whom four survived to adulthood, needed to be borne with a sense of fortitude. Difficult pregnancies, births and the dangers of infection in early infancy were only too common. Frances Boscawen during her third pregnancy writes to Edward, her husband, on May 18, 1747, just after the news had arrived of the victory in the First Battle of Finisterre against the French in which ten French ships had been captured. Edward had distinguished himself aboard his ship, *Namur*, but had been injured by a musket ball. Because of Fanny's condition the news was initially kept from her but by May 18 she had been told in case she should hear of it through other channels. She reports that a week ago:

> I was taken ill in the afternoon and continued in pain all night, so that at 5.a.m. I sent for Mrs Chapman (who had appointed to come the evening of that day) and, at noon, I informed the doctor how I was – but without desiring of his assistance, for I did not think it was time enough for that. And I judged right, for I have continued much in the same way ever since; sometimes in pain so that I think the execution is at hand; sometimes quite easy, much as I was with the boy … But I don't believe this will be so long. I have appointed it as next Wednesday, which completes the 39th week. I have been miserably terrified with the thoughts of it – such horrors and tremblings as were indeed dreadful. But now, since Saturday, I think nothing of it – I think of you and you only.[4]

Happily for the couple Edward returned on May 27 and their second daughter, Elizabeth, was born the next day. Fanny went on to bear two more children one of whom was stillborn in 1754 after which she herself was seriously ill. Maternal mortality was a real fear: Fanny's own mother had died giving birth to her.

Hester had helped nurse her niece's mother after Jenny's birth when both mother and child almost died. John Mulso confided his fears about his wife's pregnancies in 1764 to Gilbert White after his second son George died that year aged one and his second daughter, Hester was born. He admits that he is thinking that he will 'cease to enlarge his family'. In fact another son, William, was born in March

1765 bringing the total to four surviving children.

There were not only the risks entailed in childbirth but also the risk in winter of epidemics of the dreaded smallpox, measles, scarlet fever, typhoid, diphtheria and whooping cough. Infant mortality was high and features in women's letters, diaries and journals of this period. For Frances Boscawen the health of her beloved children was a constant anxiety about which she writes to her husband. Lady Mary Wortley Montagu, the brilliant writer and poet who herself had had smallpox in Turkey, introduced the first smallpox inoculation when she returned to London in 1718. She was the wife of the British Consul in Constantinople and had had her four-year-old son inoculated in 1717 while there and her daughter in 1721 in London. She also arranged the inoculation of the King's children. Servants who had had smallpox were favoured over those who had not. Fanny recounts with some triumph how in August 1748 she managed to keep secret the fact that a servant, Daniel, had contracted smallpox: she arranged to smuggle him out of the house: 'I shall never forget that hour, nor the terror it threw me into. My three children and my cousin! I recollected how solemnly Daniel told me he had had it.'[5] She would later have her second son, Billy, inoculated against it in 1755. Inoculation carried some risk and was accompanied by purging and blood letting.

Hester believes that a woman must not allow her emotions to subsume her reason and must therefore learn to control them and display fortitude in difficult situations or circumstances – something which she herself had learnt in bitter circumstances when John Chapone died so suddenly. This letter ends with practical advice on the thin line between vicious envy and virtuous emulation. Hester illustrates her point by asking her niece to imagine a situation in which her sister is commended when she is not and to examine her feelings. If she can honestly say that she is happy for her sister then she is truly benevolent.

In her fifth letter Hester continues the very important subject for a young woman: *On The Regulation Of The Heart and Affections*. She starts:

> The attachments of the heart, on which almost all the happiness or misery of life depends, are most interesting objects of our consideration. I shall give my dear niece the observations which experience has enabled me to draw from real life, and not from what others have said or written, however great their authority.

Hester turns her attention to the importance of choosing one's friends. She warns her niece against having friendships with girls of her own age commenting:

> The grand cement of this kind of friendship is telling secrets, which they call confidence: and I verily believe that the desire of having secrets to tell, has often helped to draw silly girls into very unhappy adventures.

She advises instead to seek friendships with a young women eight to ten years older than her who will offer advice and guidance: a role which Elizabeth Carter fulfilled for Hester. Hester admits that she herself made mistakes in forming friendships before she fully understood the true meaning of the term. She defines friendship as being based on the following: first, as might be expected, she places a shared respect for religion and its precepts on morality, reasoning that anyone who treats the matter light-heartedly will not be a true friend; next she places reputation, warning her niece to avoid indiscrete women who lack modesty and prudence. She must seek out friends who have a rational way of thinking and have good common sense, as well as possessing a good temper. She advises her niece to observe her friends in their relations within the family: with their servants, with children and with animals. She comments somewhat scathingly of her sex:

> Compassion, for instance, was not impressed upon the human heart, only to adorn the face with tears, and to give an agreeable languor to the eyes; it was designed to execute our utmost endeavours to relieve the sufferer. ... Women are in general very liable to ill health, which must necessarily make them in some measure troublesome and disagreeable to those they live with.

Hester herself had been seriously ill after the death of her husband in 1761 but by all accounts had shown great gratitude for the love and care she received from family and friends, especially the devoted Burrows sisters who looked after Hester with such compassion both then and later. But Hester may have been only too painfully aware that she herself had been found wanting when it came to tending her dying husband. She was banished from seeing him in his final days: her presence in the sickroom being judged as injurious.

Having established that religion, discretion, good sense and good temper are essential qualities in the true friend she turns her attention to keeping 'the best company, and to be worthy of such society, you will probably meet with some one among them deserving your affection, to whom you may be equally agreeable.' She defines the best company not as people of high rank and fortune but rather those who are worthy and sensible, admitting, however, that by mixing with those socially superior her niece will be enabled to learn valuable social skills deemed so essential for polite society in the eighteenth century: 'It is very important to a young woman to be introduced to life on a respectable footing, and to converse with those whose manners and style of life may polish her behaviour and give her consequence.' Hester herself was only too well aware of the benefit her correspondence and friendship with Richardson and Elizabeth Carter had brought. Richardson had written to her in September 1751 on the subject of friendship: 'Friendship is the perfection of love, and superior to love; it is love purified, exalted, proved by experience and a consent of minds. Love, Madam, may, and love does, often stop short of friendship.' Later as a friend of the egregious Elizabeth Montagu she is clearly mindful of the advantages friendship bestowed on her. Certainly she found great joy and strength in her friendships which became even more important after she was widowed so tragically and so early in her marriage.

Hester's views on those of low birth and education are firm: 'Above all things avoid intimacy with those of low birth and education!' – a view shared by Mary Delany. Her reasoning is that such people will be servile and use flattery which will corrupt her beloved niece. Instead she advises treating them with caution while being civil and kind but never trusting them with secrets which could ensnare her. Instead she must seek her friends according to the qualities she has already described and having found them keep the friendship in good repair by being a good and faithful friend herself. But if her friend should 'engage in any unlawful pursuit – if, for instance, she should intend to carry on an affair of love, unknown to her parents' then she must refuse to be a party to the secret and even inform her friend's parents.

For Hester the companionate marriage was the ideal in which husband and wife enjoyed a marital relationship underpinned by friendship. Marriage in which the woman was regarded as a commodity to be exchanged for land and superior social rank, as is so painfully illustrated in Mary Delany's first marriage to Pendarves, and was so often at the behest of the tyrannical father, as Richardson had described in *Clarissa*, and which Hester had argued against so vehemently and with such passion when in her early twenties, was not the model to which Hester wanted her niece to conform. She writes:

> The highest kind of friendship is indeed confined to one;– I mean the conjugal – which in its perfection, is so entire and absolute an union, of interest, will and affection, as no other connection can stand in competition with.

She denounces:

> a married woman, who encourages or tolerates the addresses of a

> lover. May no such person be ever called a friend of your's [sic] but if ever one whom, when innocent, you had loved should fall into so fatal an error, I can only say that, after proper remonstrances, you must immediately withdraw from all intimacy and confidence with her.

It could be argued that Hester was not best qualified when it came to advising on marriage as her own had been short-lived and allegedly had been deemed by some to be an unhappy one although her relations subsequently stoutly denied this. But it was a subject which she had written about copiously. She does sound a note of extreme caution when she advises:

> If there is danger in making an improper choice of friends, my dear child, how much more fatal would it be to mistake in a stronger kind of attachment – in that which leads to an irrevocable engagement for life! Yet so much more is the understanding blinded, when once the fancy is captivated, that it seems a desperate undertaking to convince a girl in love that she has mistaken the character of the man she prefers.

She adds:

> But young women know so little of the world, especially of the other sex, and such pains are usually taken to deceive them, that they are every way unqualified to choose for themselves, upon their own judgement.

A somewhat surprising comment when she had chosen John Chapone in spite of her father's opposition. She warns against romantic notions. Instead she argues that the happiest marriages are based on rational grounds:

> – on suitableness of character, degree, fortune – on mutual esteem, and the prospect of a real and permanent friendship. Far be it from me to advise you to marry where you do not love;– a mercenary marriage is a detestable prostitution:– But on the other hand, an union formed on mere personal liking, without the requisite foundation of esteem, without the sanction of parental approbation, and, consequently, without the blessing of God, can be productive of nothing but misery and shame.

Hester emphasises the importance of parental blessing, painting a grim scenario of those who enter into an engagement without it which will lead to misery for everyone. Certainly Hester's own marriage was based on love and friendship. Hester describes the companionate marriage as 'the best blessings this world can afford, in a faithful and virtuous union with a worthy man, who may direct your steps in safety and

Frances (Fanny), Mrs Boscawen, famed for her manners

honour through his life ...' thus upholding the eighteenth century view of the wife as being subservient to her husband. Fanny Boscawen certainly regarded herself as subservient to Edward, her husband, and described herself as her husband's 'faithful Penelope.' Fanny also encapsulated another eighteenth century view of the ideal wife: she must seek to lead a virtuous life. Fanny wrote to Edward, her husband: ''tis not that I prefer you to solitude, but that I prefer you to all the world.'[6] Hester emphasises to her niece that both subservience and virtue will be second nature for a wife if her choice of husband is a rational one based on mutual friendship and love rather than intemperate passion or economic pressure from her family. The guidance but not the tyranny of parents is to be respected. Ultimately the young woman should enjoy the liberty of freedom of choice when it came to marriage – something denied to Mary Granville and to many other young women.

Of course Hester had already expounded her views on marriage governed by the tyranny of a father in her letters to Richardson on *Filial Obedience* and *A Matrimonial Creed*. The latter sought to soften her views as at that time Hester herself was in the marriage market. After the circulation of her letters on *Filial Obedience*, comments, from those who had read her views, no doubt brought her to the realisation that she might have dug her own grave by expressing her views so forcibly in spite of the fact that she had flattered Richardson, whom she addressed as her second father, thus creating an epistolary relationship in which she portrayed herself as seeking correction from Richardson in order that she might learn and thereby improve herself. In fact her logical argument, which she underpinned so effectively by quoting John Locke in response to Richardson's demand of unwavering filial duty in the face of parental tyranny, led her to express her views on marriage so effectively that it meant she was on a collision course with the patriarchal views which in the early 1750s still often bound women in unhappy marriages. By 1773 Hester was forty six, had been married, widowed and was childless. She had had ample opportunity to observe the marriages which were fulfilling and happy ones.

She was a friend of Mary Delany, who remained Pendarves's widow from 1724 until 1743. Mary, who was still very attractive and attracted suitors, determined that she would marry only when she found a man with whom she fell in love and could have a close friendship. She found that man in Patrick Delany. They enjoyed a companionate marriage and found the happiness which had eluded her in her first forced marriage to Pendarves. For Hester Thrale however, when she fell in love with an Italian music teacher after the death of her husband, there was outright social condemnation. Elizabeth Montagu never remarried after the death of Edward. Instead she enjoyed the flirtatious attention of men. Perhaps Hester was right that when she commented: 'Mrs Montagu, êntre nous, is an ignoramus on this subject.'[7] She went on to claim that she was a better judge on the subject than either Elizabeth Montagu or Elizabeth Carter.

For a woman not to marry was often a cause for pity and speculation as to how she had failed in the marriage stakes. However, some women, like the educated Elizabeth Carter, preferred the single life, and retired from society to protect their virtue. A woman who turned down prospective suitors, especially when she, like Elizabeth, did not possess a fortune, was often viewed with suspicion: Elizabeth had not been without suitors. She was advised by her father to retire to Deal if she had set her mind against marriage. This she did and was accepted as a highly educated woman whose very modesty belied this fact. Her intellectual rigour made her one of the most admired members of the

Bluestocking circle during its heyday in the mid 1770s to the mid 1780s. Perhaps observing the freedom which Elizabeth Carter had guarded so assiduously led Hester at the end of this very frank and spirited letter to recommend a single life as preferable to an unhappy marriage if her niece fails to find a worthy man with whom she may enjoy a faithful and virtuous union. Hester describes how close friends can supply the single woman with esteem and affection which is far better than an unhappy union with a man unworthy of her. Certainly Hester found great happiness in her friendships with other members of the Bluestockings especially with Elizabeth Carter, Elizabeth Montagu, Mary Delany, Fanny Boscawen, William Pepys, and Fanny Burney. The support they offered underpinned her sense of worth in society which she might otherwise well have lacked after the death of her husband.

Chapter 19

Letters VI to VIII

Richardson referred to Hester as 'little spitfire.' It was a trait in her character well recognised by her friends, family and herself. Hester was not a physically attractive woman particularly in later life. But what she lacked in beauty as a young woman she made up for with a self-confidence, assertiveness and open intelligence so Letter VI is especially interesting. *On the Government of the Temper* opens:

> The next great point of importance to your future happiness, my dear, is what your parents have, doubtless, been continually attentive to from your infancy, as it is impossible to undertake it too early – I mean the due Regulation of your Temper. Though you are in great measure indebted to their forming hands for whatever is good in it, you are sensible, no doubt, as every human creature is, of propensities to some infirmity of temper, which it must now be *your own* to correct and to subdue.

She continues that constant diligence is necessary to avoid a relapse into former faults. Hester places an amiable disposition as a central tenet of religious duty for a woman 'placed above the reach of want, and out of the way of sordid or scandalous vices.' Hester accepts that the greatest sphere of influence a woman has in her life is within the family. She emphasises to her niece that it is by governing her temper that the greater happiness of the family will be achieved and in turn society will benefit. She condemns passion, peevishness and obstinacy as injurious to the harmony of society, likening passion to intoxication. Instead she advocates gentleness, meekness, and patience as the peculiar distinctions of women, sternly advising: 'when you find yourself heated so far as to desire to say what you know would be provoking and wounding to another, you should immediately resolve either to be silent, or to quit the room.' Yet Hester enjoyed the cut and thrust of intellectual argument and at times was provocative. She warns her niece against becoming obsessed with the minutiae of everyday life which will pass unnoticed by her husband whose mind is engaged with more interesting matters. Therefore she advises, especially in old age, but beginning with a foundation in youth, reading, rational conversation, reflection and religion which will allay any petty anxieties. She picks up the theme of peevishness by sketching a vividly amusing picture of a self-conscious young woman going out into society:

> How often have I seen a girl, preparing for a ball, or for some other public appearance – unable to satisfy her own vanity – fret over every ornament she put on, quarrel with her maid, with her clothes, her hair: and growing still more unlovely as she grew more cross, be ready to fight with her looking-glass for not making her as handsome as she wished to be! She did not consider that the traces of this ill-humour on her countenance would be a greater disadvantage to her appearance than any defect in her dress – or even the plainest features enlivened by joy and good-humour.

A scenario which a girl in her teens like Jenny would find amusing if not familiar.

In this insightful letter she tackles sullenness and obstinacy: two emotions which her young female readers would doubtless recognise! She advises that by embracing honesty and accepting blame or criticism her niece will learn principles on which to base future attitudes and actions. Girls who fail to learn this will be governed by caprice and so make a marriage with a husband who indulges it, which she warns 'seldom fails to reduce women to the miserable condition of a humoured child.' Hester emphasises the importance of learning the art of conversation, reading widely and discussion. Above all she stresses that the art of conversation is to bring pleasure to others and advises her niece against becoming combative in argument. Hester herself loved argument and, as illustrated by her letters to Richardson, could more than hold her own but was aware that in many circles her views however rationally put were not popular especially when voiced by a young woman. Hester is treading a very fine line here between the accepted view of polite behaviour for young women entering the public sphere, who were expected to show a sweet submission to men, and promoting a more rigorous intellectual and rational model for her young niece.

Hester ends this letter by advising her niece in the popular eighteenth century pastime of reading aloud to entertain and give pleasure to others. Like letters, novels were read aloud and discussed endlessly. The lure to discussion was further promoted by the growth in the number of periodicals to meet the demand of the market. Elizabeth

Montagu and many other women refer to this pastime as one of the most pleasurable social activities. Hester does not neglect private reading which she commends as bringing pleasure from the subsequent discussion between friends. In Hester's correspondence with Elizabeth Carter there is much reference and criticism on what they are currently reading as well as suggestions and recommendations on further reading matter. Elizabeth Montagu refers to Fanny Burney's novels as her travelling companions on her long journeys north from Bulstrode to Denton.

Finally Hester stresses the importance of learning music, painting or some other skill which will give social pleasure but she warns against vanity. The point of performing for others is not to draw praise from others but to give the close family pleasure 'by studying to promote the happiness of others, in every instance, small as well as great.' Hester's beautiful singing voice was a social asset and clearly much appreciated by her family and fellow guests.

Domestic Economy is the subject of Letter VII. This topic was central to conduct books which emphasised its importance and centrality once a woman was married. Training in this sphere of life was to begin while the young woman was still living at home and so had her mother as a model. This was the role in which most married women had real authority. In a large household her duties would be demanding and Hester places great emphasis on the smooth running of the household which she holds as central to the happiness of the woman in her role as wife and mother pointing out that not only is managing the everyday life of the household an art, but also a virtue. She recognises that many young women lack any experience in running a household and warns of the pitfalls awaiting a young bride where it has been woefully neglected in her education. She paints a bleak picture of the newly-wed who:

> ... is sent from her father's house to govern a family, without the least degree of that knowledge which should qualify her for it: this is the source of much inconvenience; for though experience and attention may supply, by degrees, the want of instruction, yet this requires time – the family in the meantime may get into habits, which are very difficult to alter; and what is worse, the husband's opinion of his wife's incapacity may be fixed too strongly to suffer him ever to think justly of her gradual improvements.

To avoid this she suggests her niece start jotting down practical points on household management while still in her parents' home and to ask her mother to let her actively participate as 'whilst you are under her eye, you cannot do much harm.' While Hester was still in her teens she had assumed responsibility for the running of her parental home when her mother began to suffer increasingly ill health and then on her death had remained at King's Court until her marriage in 1760.

In order to help women run their homes efficiently pocket memorandum books were popular. Here could be recorded all the minutiae of the day-to-day running of the house such as payments due to tradesmen, servants' wages, running repairs on linen, as well as useful check lists of printed rates for payments for services, important dates in the calendar, and on a lighter note, songs, and pictures of the current fashions for women. Hester advises:

> Make use of every opportunity you can find, for the laying in some store of knowledge on this subject, before you are called upon to the practice; by observing what passes before you – by consulting prudent and experienced mistresses of families – and by entering in a book memorandum of every new piece of intelligence you acquire.

Hester sets out an outline for domestic economy to help her niece. She starts with invaluable advice – namely to live within her means. Hester had first hand experience of this both during her ten month marriage and then after she was widowed when she suffered a drop in income. She points out:

> 'Perhaps it may be said, that the settling the general scheme of expences is seldom the wife's province, and that many men do not choose even to acquaint her with the real state of their affairs. Where this is the case, a woman can be answerable for no more than is entrusted to her.'

She refers then to husbands who are not open with their wives on their financial affairs, advising her niece to set about earning the confidence of her husband so that she can play a fuller role in the finances of the family because she understands them. Certainly Hester was faced with debts after John Chapone died and may in fact have been unaware of his true financial standing. Frances Boscawen had to manage the financial affairs because of her husband's long absences at sea. She displays her knowledge of their finances in her letters to her husband when she writes detailed accounts as to how his money is being spent. After Edward Montagu's death in 1775 Elizabeth assumed responsibility for overseeing the collieries in the north as well as their farms and estates. She proved herself extremely able.

Hester starts by outlining fixed and regular expenses such as clothes, pocket money, donations to charity and gifts to friends. Next she moves to the settling of bills. Housekeeping bills should be paid each week but 'all other tradesmen should be paid, at furthest, once a year.' She does point out that it is better to pay them on a more regular basis, recognising that many tradesmen suffer undue hardship and ruin because of deferred payments.

Next she passes swiftly over the art of learning the prices and true value of things before moving on to achieving propriety in her dress and her table, warning her niece that: 'To go beyond your sphere, in either dress or in the appearance of your table, indicates a greater fault in your character than to be too much within it.' Her advice to guard against an ostentatious show of wealth is very similar to the advice in *The Young Lady's Companion; Or, Beauty's Looking Glass ... in a letter of advice from a father to his daughter ... written by a person of quality* and published thirty-three years earlier in 1740. Elizabeth Montagu loved displaying her wealth both in the way she dressed and in the sumptuous decoration of her homes. She oversaw the building and decoration of Montagu House and led guided tours when it was nearing completion. However, many other Bluestocking gatherings were held in much less opulent surroundings. Hester's gatherings reflected a simplicity in entertaining commensurate with her financial position. Elizabeth Carter lived very simply indeed and abhorred ostentation.

Something which Hester and Elizabeth Carter did not share was skill with the needle. Elizabeth could turn her hand to making shirts and mending clothes and linen for her father's second family when he remarried. Hester reveals that it is not a skill she herself values highly although she admits: 'yet, in a middling rank, and with a moderate fortune, it is a necessary part of a woman's duty, and a considerable article of expense is saved by it,' adding that many young ladies 'make almost *every thing* they wear.' Hester clearly does not approve of this as a few lines later she states that she would prefer to see her niece spend less time on needlework and more time devoted to exercise and reading even though it would mean she was less well-dressed.

As she views idleness as inexcusable every moment of the day is to be constructively filled for the young wife with her day starting early so that it may be organised efficiently and productively. This is in order that husband and guests may relax without disruption. Conduct books invariably emphasised the comfort of the husband as paramount. Hester has no time for maintaining excessive neatness in the house scathingly commenting that 'it gives a lady the air of a housemaid, and makes her excessively troublesome to every body, and particularly to her husband.' Instead she praises women who achieve an aura of ease and elegance in their homes. A very different view from that of Jane

Collier, who was part of Richardson's circle, and openly and ironically attacks the conventions followed by conduct books. Written in 1753 her *Essay on the Art of Ingeniously Tormenting; with Proper Rules for the Exercise of that Pleasant Art* encourages the wife to openly vent her frustration on the accepted subservience of the wife:

> Carefully study your husband's temper, and find out what he likes, in order never to do any one thing that will please him.
>
> If he expresses his approbation of the domestic qualities of a wife; such as family oeconomy, [sic] and that old fashioned female employment, the needle; neglect your family as much as ever his temper will bear; and always have your white gloves on your hands. Tell him, that every woman of spirit ought to hate and despise a man who could insist on his wife's being a family drudge; and declare, that you will not submit to be a cook and semstress to any man. But if he loves company, and chearful parties of pleasure, and would willingly have you always with him, nose him with your great love of needle-work and housewifery.

Hester's admonitions to her niece are based not on satire but on her ambition to offer young women greater and more equal opportunity to realise a fuller intellectual potential but within the parameters of female propriety. Mary Wollstonecraft would further develop a stronger feminist argument in *A Vindication of the Rights of Woman*.

Within the kind of household which Hester is describing, that of the gentry, servants played an important part. She regards them as integral to the smooth running of the household and its happiness, likening their roles to deputies who enforce directions from above. Great care must therefore be taken when selecting servants who have power over the more lowly and she warns: 'the mistress of the family must be ever watchful over their conduct – at the same time that she must carefully avoid every appearance of suspicion, which whilst it wounds and hinders 'a worthy servant, only excites the artifice and cunning of an unjust one.' Her views on the treatment of servants reveal a sensitivity about their lives. She attacks thoughtless and selfish members of the gentry who fail to recognise the needs and rights of servants or consider the kind of life they must of necessity lead without asking whether it is conducive to their health, their morals, their religion and their general enjoyment of life. Servants are people and must be treated as such with due care and respect. She illustrates this with the following scenario:

> I have heard the most insolent contempt of the whole class expressed at a table, whilst five or six of them attended behind the chairs, who the company seemed to think were without senses, without under-

> standing, or the natural feelings of resentment: these are cruel injuries, and will be retorted in some way or other.

She exhorts her niece when she becomes head of a household to treat the servants with courtesy which will bring her their respect and affection, adding that due praise is important. However, her niece must guard against having a favourite among her servants as it will lead to envy and possibly lead the favourite into abusing her position. Hester regards servants like children: their welfare both moral and economic is the woman's responsibility and this must continue into old age when they are no longer useful to the household. By giving charity to the poor and needy, money, which otherwise might be spent on trifles, will bring much needed relief. Generosity and management of the household economy 'which will be the grace and crown of all your attainments' are thus held up to be two of the most important attributes for a young woman if she is to fulfil her role as a successful wife and mother.

Having covered household management Hester turns to the social skills which her niece will need. Letter VIII is devoted to *Politeness and Accomplishments*. She defines them as follows:

> Politeness of behaviour, and the attainment of such branches of knowledge and such arts and accomplishments as are proper to your sex, capacity, and station, will prove so valuable to yourself through life, and will make you so desirable a companion, that the neglect of them may be reasonably deemed a neglect of duty. ... To be perfectly polite, one must have *great presence of mind*, with a delicate and quick *sense of propriety*; or in other words, one should be able to form an instantaneous judgement of what is fittest to be said or done, on every occasion as it offers.

The importance Hester places on propriety reflects its centrality in the eighteenth century ideal of a young woman in polite society. Hester admits that some people are born with this ability but for most it has to be observed, learnt and practised by mixing in what she describes as good company. In order to become an agreeable member of polite company she declares that her niece must learn not to outshine other people by displaying her talents at the cost of others. Conversation is a social skill: she must not push her point to the detriment of others leaving them nowhere to retreat but aim rather at creating an ease in the exchange of ideas. Polite conversation must be pleasurable not combative argument. Hester recognises that her niece will not be able at first to participate easily in conversation because of her lack of educational opportunity. Hester advises her that instead of merely answering 'yes' or 'no' to questions she should play a proactive role and initiate questions herself and, if she is silent – here Hester admits that some think very young women cannot be too silent and reserved in company – then she should look interested. What she must avoid at all cost is to chatter and giggle with other young women about other members of the company. Poking fun at the infirmity of the old is sternly condemned.

When it comes to dealing with the opposite sex Hester cautions: 'In a young lady's behaviour towards gentlemen, great delicacy is certainly required: yet I believe, women oftener err from too great a consciousness of the supposed views of men.' She continues that her niece is at the moment rather too young to need rules on this subject but warns very sternly against men of loose morals or impertinent behaviour. She advises that if she should find herself in their company she should keep them at a distance with a cold civility. In conversing with men of whom her parents approve she should take it as an exchange between two rational people not an opportunity for engaging in coquetry or prudery. Men who indulge in idle gallantry must be treated with due contempt whereas those who treat her with esteem and love must be taken seriously but not given encouragement unless it is sincere and meets with parental approval.

Hester recognises that a young gentlewoman's sphere up to her fifteenth year has been largely confined to the domestic. However, now that she is on the cusp of entering into the public sphere of society with assemblies, balls, pleasure gardens, theatres and all the other public entertainments so enticingly beckoning in the eighteenth century this is no excuse for not following a fairly rigorous plan of education. Hester places great importance on reading books, which must be properly chosen and regulated; dancing, which will be useful in helping better deportment; French, which will improve the mind and afford the opportunity of reading 'books of female literature' thus protecting her from any mortification in company if she has not read them, and Italian, which although Hester does not see as necessary for her niece's 'station in life' will be easy to learn after mastering French.

Next come writing legibly and the ability to understand arithmetic which she regards as indispensable. Both will have practical applications in a century when letter writing was the vogue and the ability to manage and keep the household accounts a necessity. Music and drawing are regarded as offering 'innocent amusement' with the bonus of filling up empty hours, 'which too often hang heavily on the hands of a woman, if her lot be cast in a retired situation' and there must have been many women for whom this was true. Hester sees their real value as leading to a deeper appreciation of music and drawing which will not get in the way of 'a rational scheme of life, nor lead you into dissipation, with all its attendant evils of vanity and luxury.'

Perhaps somewhat surprisingly she does not advocate her niece's learning Latin or Greek. Her reason being not only that the amount of time and work involved is 'generally incompatible with our natures and proper employment' but books can be read in translation in English or French. This is somewhat surprising for a woman who so admired Elizabeth Carter. She goes further by warning:

> The danger of pedantry and presumption in a woman – of her exciting the envy in one sex and jealousy in the other – of her exchanging the graces of imagination for the severity and preciseness of the scholar, would be, I own, sufficient to frighten me from the ambition of seeing my girl remarkable for learning. Such objections are perhaps still stronger for the abstruse sciences.

Hester is no revolutionary when it comes to educating her niece and would have been only too aware of the male censure from some quarters with which women like Elizabeth Carter had to contend. Instead Hester recommends the study of history as a key subject in developing a critical mind capable of forming independent opinions and promises that she will explain further in a future letter. Her emphasis on developing a young woman's critical faculties and independence of mind reflects a key shift in her attitude to female education of the time. However, when Hester examines the benefits of studying poetry she is treading well-known and safer ground: 'The faculty, in which women usually most excel, is that of imagination; and, when properly cultivated, it becomes the source of all that is most charming in society.' She recommends Shakespeare, and Elizabeth Montagu's *Essay on Shakespeare*. Milton, Homer and Virgil are listed as well as a recommendation to read mythology.[1] By reading mythology her niece will more fully understand allegorical references which as Hester points out: 'Boys, in their school-learning, have this kind of knowledge impressed on their minds by a variety of books, but women, who do not go through the same course of instruction, are very apt to forget what little they read or hear on the subject.' A reminder of the limited and limiting educational opportunities open to women at the time.

It is no surprise that Hester includes Natural Philosophy in her scheme for educating her niece. She first met Gilbert White, the celebrated naturalist when she was eighteen. Her lyricism in her description here of natural beauty and creation could not have failed to enthuse her niece to study nature more closely:

> But, if from the earth, and from these minute wonders, the philosophic eye is raised towards the heavens, what a stupendous scene there opens to its view! – those brilliant lights that sparkle to the eye of ignorance as gems adorning the sky, or as lamps to guide the traveller by night, assume an importance that amazes the understanding – they appear to be worlds, formed like ours for a variety of inhabitants – or suns, enlightening numberless other worlds too distant for our discovery! – I shall ever remember the astonishment and rapture with which my mind received this idea, when I was about your age.

This is Hester at her best!

When it comes to studying Moral Philosophy she wisely recognises that many concepts are beyond her niece at fifteen. Therefore she suggests reading periodicals such as '*The Spectators, Guardians, Ramblers and Adventurers*' because they will introduce her niece to many different subjects and ideas. After dismissing books on criticism and taste as being too difficult at the moment she turns her attention to fiction:

> I think the greatest care should be taken in the choice of these fictitious stories that so enchant the mind – most of which tend to inflame the passions of youth, whilst the chief purpose of education should be to moderate and restrain them. Add to this, that both the writing and sentiments of most novels and romances are such as are only to vitiate your style, and to mislead your heart and understanding. The expectations of extraordinary adventures – which seldom ever happen to the sober and prudent part of mankind – and the admiration of extravagant passions, and absurd conduct, are some of the usual fruits of this kind of reading; which when a young woman makes it her chief amusement, generally render her ridiculous in conversation, and miserably wrong-headed in her pursuits and behaviour. There are however works of this class in which excellent morality is joined with the most lively pictures of the human mind, and with all that entertain the imagination and interest the heart. But, I must repeatedly exhort you, never to read anything of the sentimental kind without taking the judgement of your best friends in the choice; for, I am persuaded, that the indiscriminate reading of such kind of books corrupts more female hearts than any other cause whatsoever–.

This outburst is against the endless novels which her mother had encouraged her to read in her youth, but did this proscribing of the novel which was such a popular form merely encourage her niece to indulge in an illicit pleasure?

Chapter 20

Letters IX and X

The final two letters, IX and X, are devoted to *Geography and Chronology*, and *On the Manner and Course of Reading of History*. Hester regards Geography as 'the easiest of all sciences and the best adapted to the capacity of children.' She presumes that her niece has already learnt the basics but if not then only two or three lessons are necessary before moving on to studying maps and using her memory to fix places and names. She emphasises that what is essential is knowing the boundaries of European countries, adding that as for the rest of the world she need only know where there are European settlements. From a historical perspective she should memorize some facts about the country such as identifying Egypt as 'the nurse and parent of arts and superstition' whereas Greece is identified with 'freedom and genius.' Hester then begins a chronological canter through ancient history, starting with Noah and the flood, and finishing with classical Greece and Rome. She strongly advises going over the chronology of events a second time so that her niece can commit it to memory. Moving on she covers the birth of Christ to Charlemagne, taking in the Saracen Empire en route before arriving at modern history which she dismisses: 'I shall spare you and myself all trouble about at present; for if you follow the course of reading which I recommend, it will be some years before you reach modern history.' At the end of this thirteen page letter she suggests some books to her niece to help her get a good chronological appreciation of historical events, ending with the withering comment:

> 'Indeed, my dear, a woman makes a poor figure who affects, as I have heard some ladies do, to disclaim all knowledge of times and dates: the strange confusion they make of events, which happened in different periods, and the state of ignorance when such are referred to as are commonly known, are sufficiently pitiable: but the highest mark of folly is to be proud of such ignorance – a resource, in which some of our sex find great consolation.'

Her final letter concentrates on the methodology of reading history in order to retain a chronological overview. Although she recommends interspersing her niece's reading with other activities such as poetry she must adhere to the chronological plan she has set out if she is not to become confused. She suggests that the most natural way of fixing events in her mind is by discussing either by letter or in conversation what she has read. Hester recommends several books which she thinks will appeal to her niece in the study of ancient history before moving on to the study of modern history. She appears to have forgotten that earlier she had recommended modern history was to be left to one side for future study and begins by examining Britain's role in the world which at that time was buoyant, powerful and expanding: 'You may pass to every quarter of the earth, and find yourself still in the British dominion: this island in which we live, is the least portion of it; and, if we were to adopt the style of ancient conquerors, we might call it the throne, from which we rule the world.' Her niece will necessarily need to know about the British Empire, especially the East and West Indies. When she comes to America, she condemns the cruelty to and suffering of the indigenous people. In 1773, the same year her book is published to such acclaim, the Boston Tea Party took place: an indicator of independence which would come soon.[1] She justifies Britain's presence in the Americas as being established by just means praising the colonies on the east coast of America.

Hester is at her best when describing the plight of the Aztecs in Mexico:

> At first indeed the invaders appeared supernatural beings, who came upon them, flying over the ocean, on the wings of the wind, and who mounted on fiery animals, unknown in that country, attacked them with thunder and lightning in their hand – for such the fire-arms of the Spaniards appeared to this astonished people.

She regards the British colonisation of India as beneficial to the local populace where previously rulers were beset by local wars, jealousy and the vice of overwhelming luxury. Her view of India is naturally Eurocentric when she describes the fate of the Indians: 'with astonishment they saw the intrepid leaders of brave, free Britons, boldly oppose and repeatedly put to flight millions of these effeminate Indian slaves – and in a short time, raised for them an Empire much larger than their mother country.'

Her final recommendations form a reading list of suggested authors on British and European history: Shakespeare for English history; Robertson for Scottish history (Hester had met the author in

Edinburgh on her trip to Scotland in 1770); Mezerai and Voltaire for French history. She considers France the most important of European countries to study because of its similarity in thought and manners and literature which 'make them peculiarly interesting to us; and we cannot but find our curiosity excited to know their story, and to be intimately acquainted with the character, genius, and sentiments of this nation.' The rest of European history is to be covered by reading a series of tracts and is dismissed quickly giving one the impression that Hester was on somewhat shaky ground.

Letters on the Improvement of the Mind ends with Hester's issuing dire warnings to her niece should she fail to observe her aunt's advice.

> As I cannot, with certainty, foresee what degree of application or genius for such pursuits you will be mistress of, I shall leave deficiencies of this collection to be supplied by the suggestions of more informed friends – who, if you explain to them how far you wish to extend your knowledge, will direct you to the proper books.
>
> But if, instead of an eager desire for this kind of knowledge, you should happen to feel that distaste for it, which is too common in ladies who have been indulged in reading only works of mere amusement, you will perhaps rather think that I want mercy in offering you so large a plan, than that there needs an apology for the deficiencies of it: but, comfort yourself with the assurance that a taste for history will grow and improve by reading: that as you get acquainted with one period or nation, your curiosity cannot fail to be awakened for what concerns those immediately connected with it: and thus you will insensibly be led on from one degree of knowledge to another.
>
> If you waste in trivial amusement the next three or four years of your life, which are the prime season of improvement, believe me you will hereafter bitterly regret their loss: when you come to feel yourself inferior in knowledge to almost every one you converse with – and, above all, if you should ever be a mother, when you feel your own inability to direct and assist the pursuits of your children – you will then find ignorance a severe mortification and a real evil. Let this, my dear, animate your industry – and let not a modest opinion of your own capacity be a discouragement to your endeavours after knowledge; a moderate understanding, with diligent and well-directed application, will go much further than a more lively genius, if attended with that impatience and inattention, which too often accompanies quick parts. It is not from want of capacity that so many women are such trifling insipid companions – so ill qualified for the friendship and conversation of a sensible man – or for the task of governing and instructing a family: it much oftener from the neglect of exercising the talents which they really have, and from omitting to cultivate a taste for intellectual improvement; by this neglect, they lose the sincerest of pleasures; a pleasure which would remain when almost every other forsakes them – which neither fortune nor age can deprive them of – and which would be a comfort and resource in

almost every possible situation of life.

If I can but inspire you, my dear child, with the desire of making the most of your time and abilities, my end is answered; the means of knowledge will easily be found by those who diligently seek them – and they will find their labours abundantly rewarded.

And now, my dear, I think it is time to finish this long correspondence – which, though in some parts it may have been tedious to you, will not, I hope, be found entirely useless in any. I have laid before you all that my maturest reflections could enable me to suggest, for the direction of your conduct through life. My love for you, my dearest child, extends its views beyond this frail and transitory existence; it considers you as a candidate for immortality – as entering the lists for the prize of your high calling – as contending for a crown of unfading glory. It sees, with anxious solicitude, the dangers that surround you, and the everlasting shame that must follow, if you do not exert all your strength in the conflict. Religion therefore has been the basis of my plan – the principle to which every other pursuit is ultimately referred. Here then I have endeavoured to guide your researches; and to assist you in forming just notions on a subject of such infinite importance, I have shown you the necessity of regulating your heart and temper, according to the genuine spirit of that religion which I have so earnestly recommended as the great rule of your life. To the same principle I would refer your attention to domestic duties – and, even that refinement and, elegance of manners, and those graces and accomplishments, which will set your virtues in the fairest light, and will engage the affection and respect of all who converse with you. – Endeared to society by these amiable qualities, your influence in it will be more extensive, and your capacity of being useful proportionably enlarged.

The studies, which I have recommended to you, must be likewise subservient to the same views; the pursuit of knowledge, when it is guided and controlled by the principles I have established, will conduce to many valuable ends; the habit of industry, it will give you – the nobler kind of friendships, for which it will qualify you, and its tendency to promote a candid and liberal way of thinking, are obvious advantages. I might add, that a mind well informed in the various pursuits which interest mankind, and the influence of such pursuits on their happiness, will embrace with a clearer choice, and will more steadily adhere to, those principles of Virtue and Religion which the judgment must ever approve, in proportion as it becomes enlightened.

May those delightful hopes be answered which have animated my heart, while with diligent attention I have endeavoured to apply to your advantage all that my own experience and best observation could furnish. With what joy should I see my dearest girl shine forth a bright example of every thing that is amiable and praiseworthy;– and how sweet would be the reflection that I had, in any degree, contributed to make her so! – My heart expands with the affecting thought, and pours forth in this adieu the most ardent wishes for your perfection! If the tender solicitude expressed for your welfare by this 'labour of love'

> can engage your gratitude, you will always remember how deeply your conduct interests the happiness of
>
> Your most affectionate
>
> AUNT.
>
> FINIS.

These sentiments reflect how deeply Hester loved her niece and how concerned and interested she was in her future development. Hester had eloquently expressed her feelings about children to Elizabeth Carter:

> I am not of your opinion that children are not a reasonable object of our wishes, as far as we are permitted to wish for any temporal good. The sensations of parental fondness are, I suppose, the most delightful of any our nature is capable of, except the conjugal; and those mutually assist each other and complete domestic happiness. The dangers and sorrows which this affection often brings with it, seem to me to shew the value of its blessings, and are no more than the common conditions on which we enjoy every advantage relative to this world.[2]

Although Hester did not experience the joys of motherhood she would experience such sorrows as a result of her great affection for her beloved niece many years later.

Chapter 21

'ye great Harvest of her Fame'

Hester received £50 for the two volumes of *Letters on the Improvement of the Mind*. The publisher made considerably more: about £500. Such was the success of the book that a second edition was published the same year. John reports to Gilbert White on the success of the book on July 5:

> I have not seen her since ye great Harvest of her Fame; she is much gratified by ye Praises that resound on all Sides; & indeed I fairly think She deserves them! The critical Reviewers have confined their Plaudit chiefly to ye religious Turn of the Book, wherein indeed it shines, but I wonder that they took no Notice of some elegant & very judicious Observations in it, that are very much out of ye Common way of Writing.

However, he adds that one reason for its success must lie in the fact that the letters were written to a real person and so were animated with true love and affection which would have been lacking had the niece been an imaginary one and not his daughter, Jenny. Hester writes to Elizabeth Carter from Farnham Castle, her uncle's residence, where she is staying:

> I am much obliged by the kind interest you take in the success of my publication, which has indeed been far beyond my expectation. The bookseller is preparing the second edition with all haste, the whole of the first being gone out of his hands; which considering that he printed off fifteen hundred at first, is an extraordinary quick sale. I attribute this success principally to Mrs Montagu's name and patronage, and secondly to the world's being so fond of being educated, that every book on that subject is well. My friends all fret and scold at me for having sold my copy, and grudge poor Waller his profits. But for my own part I do not begrudge what I have done, as I am persuaded the book would not have prospered so well in any hands as in his. Though I love money reasonably well, yet I fear I have more vanity than avarice, and am therefore very happy in the approbation the let-

> ters meet with, though my profits are not the heavier. I have had within these few days a very kind long letter from Mrs Montagu.[2]

Her friends and family were delighted with her success. Many friends held strong views on the education of young women including Mary Delany who had written to her sister, Anne Dewes, in 1752:

> I *cannot* think it necessary to the accomplishment of a young lady that she should be *early* and *frequently* produced in public, and I should rather see a little awkward bashfulness, than a *daring and forward genteelness*! Good company and good conversation I should wish to have my niece introduced into as soon as she can speak and understand, but for all public places till *after fifteen* (except a play or oratorio) she should not know what they are and then *very rarely*, and only with her mother or aunt. I believe you and I are perfectly well agreed on these points. And I am sure the general behaviour of young people will not encourage us to alter this scheme.[2]

Mary was enthusiastic in her praise of Hester's work when she wrote to the Reverend John Dewes on May 25, 1773:

> There are two little volumes come out on 'the improvement of the mind,' addressed to a little girl of fifteen (from Mrs Chapone to her niece), that I will send my brother at the first opportunity; they appear to be upon the best plan I have ever met on the subject. It is plain truth in an easy and elegant style, and the sentiments natural and delicate. I have just finish'd it which has insensibly lead [sic] me to give my opinion of it, which I did not intend doing, but as it has given me pleasure and edification I cannot forbear sending it the first opportunity. It *sells prodigiously*. One should hope from that, tho, there are many corrupted minds, there are also many *ready to listen to the voice of the charmer*. Adieu.[3]

She was proved right in her judgment on the book.

Further editions ran to more than sixteen during Hester's lifetime. Almost twenty years later Mary Wollstonecraft in *A Vindication of the Rights of Woman* attacked the deficiencies of eighteenth century education for women but comments in Chapter V: 'Mrs Chapone's Letters are written with such good sense, and unaffected humility, and contain so many useful observations, that I only mention them to pay the worthy writer this tribute of respect. I cannot, it is true, always coincide in opinion with her; but I always respect her.' Hester comments to Elizabeth Carter in 1794:

> I have seen nothing of Mrs Wolstonecroft's [sic] except her Rights of Women; in which I discerned some strong sense, amidst many absurdities, improprieties, and odious indelicacies. The desire of dis-

tinction is, I believe, the grand spring that sets so many pens at work, to shake and overturn every principle of order and happiness, and makes so many foolish people depart from the good they have been taught, to become their disciples, and affect a libertinism which their hearts disavow. Humility is indeed our great preservative: Mrs Wolstonecroft is so good as to attribute it to *me*; and I have at least enough to be not ashamed of it, and earnestly to wish I had more.[4]

Hester's influence in the education of young women continued into Austen's time when the book was often bound with other conduct manuals to form a larger work for the improvement of young women. Its influence is apparent in *Mansfield Park* (1814) in which Fanny Price embraces filial duty, is a good listener, reads voraciously to assuage her loneliness, disapproves of flattery and ostentation, values true friendship, respects and understands natural forces. She accepts Edmund, her cousin, who has been to Eton and Oxford, as her mentor:

> Kept back by everybody else, his single support could not bring her forward, but his attentions were otherwise of the highest importance in assisting the improvement of her mind, and extending its pleasures. He knew her to be clever, to have a quick apprehension as well as good sense, and a fondness for reading, which properly directed, must be an education in itself. Miss Lee taught her French, and heard her read the daily portion of History; but he recommended the books which charmed her leisure hours, he encouraged her taste, and corrected her judgement; he made reading useful by talking to her of what she read, and heightened its attraction by judicious praise.

The young Fanny loves him and happily by the end of the novel her mentor, who has moulded her, falls in love with her.

The success of *Letters on the Improvement of the Mind* brought Hester public recognition as an authority on the education of young women. More importantly for Hester it established her position in the Bluestocking circle as a woman who could achieve outstanding success through publication. Furthermore, she had put her name to the work. Gone were the days when her outlook on life was coloured by a feeling of being insignificant and intellectually inferior to her mentors. Her views on the education of young women were respected and she was now much in demand for first hand advice on how to educate young women. She had pushed forward the boundaries of their education by designing a curriculum which followed much of the established curriculum for boys and sought to encourage rational thought in young women. But she had also worked within the acceptable eighteenth century boundaries by advocating the key qualities for the role of wife – propriety, virtue and obedience. The shift was subtle: a marriageable

Mary Wollstonecraft, early feminist

young woman could both be educated and an obedient daughter and wife.

Her concern for the well-being of her niece combined with her lightness of touch create an intimacy between writer and reader. Hester, in adopting a conversational tone, avoids being heavily didactic which would not appeal to a fifteen year old girl. It is not surprising that friends had earlier urged her to become a governess. Hester had refused, realising, like Elizabeth Carter, that her independence would have been limited within an aristocratic household, something which Fanny Burney rued and wrote so movingly about when appointed to court in 1786.

Part Five

Fame, Family and Friends

William Weller Pepys, close friend of Hester Chapone in later life

Chapter 22

Miscellanies in Prose and Verse and William Weller Pepys

Hester continued her habit of spending the winters in London where she stayed in lodgings. Here she saw friends, especially her beloved Burrows family whose friendship she valued so highly and who would show her such love and compassion in her later years; seeing her brother Thomas and his family in London; and both attending Bluestocking assemblies and hosting somewhat serious small parties at her lodgings. Once the finer weather arrived in spring she would go off on her customary jaunts further afield. Her uncle, Bishop Thomas, and aunt valued her company at Farnham Castle as did her brother John, who was now rector of Meonstoke and lived at Winton near Winchester. Her friendship with Elizabeth Carter and Elizabeth Montagu continued to flourish and it was they who encouraged her to collect earlier pieces of her writing and to produce new work for publication. Hester had been working on this project since before the publication of *Letters on the Improvement of the Mind*. However, she found it much more difficult to produce. Instead of writing letters of advice to her niece which she was then encouraged to publish she was now writing with a commercial end in view.

She turned to her friend William Weller Pepys[1] for help. Pepys was also a writer, widely read, and a member of the Bluestocking circle. Described by Horace Walpole as: 'as long as his nose,' a reference to his short stature, he was a popular member of the Bluestockings and was a close confidant of Hannah More. It was Pepys' wife who transcribed More's celebration of polite conversation in *Le Bas Bleu* before its publication in 1786 in order to safeguard Hannah's anonymity. William was particularly delighted to be referred to as Lelius[2] in the poem and ensured that it circulated widely in manuscript form. Such was its popularity that George III asked for a copy in Hannah's handwriting. Pepys was a great conversationalist, could recite poems at length, was charming and well-mannered, unlike his adversary Johnson who could wound with a cruel remark and offend with his appalling table manners. Pepys enjoyed fashion and could entertain on a lighter level with amusing anecdotes. He could also take on a heavy-weight like Johnson in more serious discussions and arguments, although unlike Johnson he did not always seek to be victorious. He organised his own Bluestocking parties into small groups and would wander among them before settling his attention on the group which he found the most interesting and stimulating. Both Elizabeth Montagu and Lord Lyttelton were great friends of his. It was he who sent Hester a moving account of George, Lord Lyttelton's death in August 1773 causing Hester grave concern over Elizabeth Montagu's health.

When Johnson attacked Elizabeth Montagu's *An Essay on the Writings and Genius of Shakespear* (1769) which she wrote in response to Voltaire's criticism of England's greatest dramatist, with the damning: 'It does her honour, but it would do no one else honour,' William Pepys sprang to her defence. He was after all referred to as her prime minister in relation to her position as 'Queen of the Blues'. It is hardly surprising then that when Johnson finally published the six volumes of *The Lives of the English Poets* in 1781 Elizabeth Montagu objected to his comments on Lyttelton, whom she admired and who had been such a close friend. Johnson was fully aware of Elizabeth's devotion to Lyttelton and that Pepys would support her view.

It was probably through Elizabeth Montagu that Hester began her acquaintance with Pepys which blossomed into a close and lasting friendship for the rest of her life. In 1770 Hester refers to his kind attention to her before teasing William about falling in love. He has been staying at Hagley in the company of Elizabeth Montagu and 'amongst the Young, the Beautiful, the Great and the Witty.'[3] Elizabeth Montagu was at this time making suggestions and corrections on *Letters on the Improvement of the Mind*. At the end of the letter Hester refers to her late husband, John Chapone's sister, Sarah Sandford, whose husband, Dr Sandford, has just died leaving her to bring up four sons, of whom the eldest was only five. The Sandfords had only just moved into their new home having been living with Patrick and Mary Delany who regarded them as family.

Hester admired Pepys's knowledge of literature and his ease with words and by July 1771 after some discussion with him as to his willingness to participate had invited him to contribute essays for her next book. She is finding it difficult to produce work as the following reveals:

> You cannot do a more friendly or charitable deed than by lending me a pennyworth of sense, without which I fear I can never make a penny of my poor little Stock of Poetry, as the Vol. must be eked out, and I find that sitting down with *malice prepense* to write to the public, is death & destruction to every idea I have in the World. I have hammer'd out two or three sheets upon *Conversation* but I don't much like it – if anything occurs to you on the subject pray let me have it, and I will contrive to weave it in somehow or other. I should like to have your thoughts on Affection & Simplicity or on Enthusiasm and Indifference – or in short whatever you will. If they suit my own manner of thinking, I can cool them down to my own manner of writing, for we must not have a hotch potch of Stiles, and if for any reason I should not be able to make use of them, *you* will still have the benefit of having written them, and may peaceably possess your own property; but if I take them, remember I am to have the whole right in them, fame & all, and that when you shall hear it said that the only admirable part of my book is that which you know yourself the Author, you must suppress every conscious look, smile, or shrug; & tamely submit to see me swallow down the praise. If you think you are capable of such a strain of Generosity, sit down at the first Inn, & instead of muzzing over past vexations, forget yourself and all the World, but me, – and pour out your lubrications on paper.[4]

Perhaps unsurprisingly the terms did not appeal to Pepys and he demurred. Undeterred, Hester tries to engage his interest in her next letter, answering his doubts about the scheme and her own desperation: 'if anything good, bad, or indifferent does come into your head, I beg you will set it down for me in rude outlines or finished compositions, which you please; for I cannot fix on any subject that pleases me, nor hit upon any thought that I do not reject.'[5]

When Hester met William he was unmarried but actively seeking a wife. Hester was a sympathetic and practical matrimonial adviser. The problem for William was that when he liked a woman she did not reciprocate his feelings and conversely when the woman liked him he felt no attraction. In 1771 William is having no luck in the matrimonial stakes. Hester comments on 'the affair which has distres't us so much,' but continues by saying that the ending of it is in his best interests. In her letters to William she is quite open about her own character and warns him that she is prone to share perhaps too frankly her opinions and feelings where her friends are involved. Hester is delighted by this friendship and describes it 'as infinitely more valuable than all the Gold of Peru, I feel myself a much richer Woman since I could flatter myself that I had gained a little snug settlement in a warm corner of your heart.'

During this period Hester is spending much of her time staying at Hadley in Middlesex with the Culling Smiths who were also friends of

William. Mary Smith was the Burrows's eldest daughter. She was equally eager to see this fashionable and charming young man find a suitable wife. In October1773 while at Millhill, staying with friends, having just returned from a trip to Winchester, Hester writes a sympathetic letter consoling William about another failed relationship because of some obstacle which Mary Smith will not divulge. Both Hester, who advised proceeding with caution, and the Smiths, who in joining the search and giving advice on finding what William referred to as the 'essential requisite,' may well have begun to wonder by this time whether he was a confirmed bachelor who had become too set in his way of life to marry. In spite of Pepys's refusal to collaborate on Hester's latest literary endeavour their friendship flourished. Hester offers advice on personal matters and discusses their mutual friends, Elizabeth Montagu, the Smiths, the Burrows and her new friendship with Fanny Boscawen.

Hester was introduced to Fanny by Mary Smith. Fanny has recently bought a country home in nearby Colney Hatch, relatively close to Hadley, having sold Hatchlands in 1770. Like her previous country retreat at Enfield she has named it Glan Villa, after her mother's family name, Glanville. Here Fanny can escape from the noise and dust of the building boom in London and indulge her love of plants and gardens. Hester reports to Mary Delany that she is 'charmed by her affable friendly manner, as well as her good sense.' Mary Delany had met Fanny in 1769 and in spite of the nineteen year age difference between them they became good friends. All Fanny's friends remark on her agreeable manners and conversation. James Boswell in his *The Life of Samuel Johnson LL.D.* (1791) paid her the following accolade: 'If it be not presumptuous of me to praise her, I would say that her manners are the most agreeable and her conversation the best of any lady with whom I ever had the happiness to be acquainted.' Unlike Elizabeth Montagu she did not seek to dazzle but rather to engage. Her smaller and more serious Bluestocking parties which she hosted at her London home at 14 South Audley Street reflected her character just as those thrown by Elizabeth Montagu and Elizabeth Vesey did theirs.

Hester's second book *Miscellanies in Prose and Verse* was published in 1775. The preface is dated January 20, 1775 and addressed from her lodgings in Wardour Street. The book is dedicated to Elizabeth Carter. Her literary reputation now meant that she was able to command a much higher payment of £250. However, *Miscellanies in Prose and Verse* did not receive the same acclaim as *Letters on the Improvement of the Mind*. In a letter dated January 31, 1775 to Gilbert White her brother gives his view on it:

> My Sister Chapone's Vol. is come forth under ye Conduct of the alert Mr Dilly. She made her Bargain for this, & it is as good as the former was bad; she secures £250. So that calculating thye [sic]) 3 Voll. at £100 each She is well off. We all abuse her this time for cheating the Public; when her Work was inestimable, She was ill-used. However, the Work has not ye Merit indeed of general Use, yet there is Merit in it. She has a slap at Ld. Chesterfield, & has managed it happily & appositely to her Subject. It is well my Lord is not alive; he would begin to complain with Lewis [sic] ye 14th, that the Ladies armed against him.

The collection opens with three essays. The first entitled *On Affectation and Simplicity* contains a strong condemnation of Lord Chesterfield's advice in *Letters to his Son* which was not intended for publication but published posthumously by his son's widow in 1774. The son, who was illegitimate, had died in 1768 aged thirty and the advice which Chesterfield offers is the antithesis of Hester's advice to her niece in 1773. Not surprisingly she is critical although not as damningly so as Johnson who described Chesterfield's letters as displaying 'the morals of a whore, and the manners of a dancing master.' Johnson never forgave Chesterfield, a noted patron of the arts, for his belated offer of patronage. He wrote the following stinging response on February 7, 1755:

> To The Right Honourable The Earl Of Chesterfield
>
> My Lord, I have been lately informed, by the proprietor of The World, that two papers, in which my Dictionary is recommended to the public, were written by your lordship. To be so distinguished is an honour which, being very little accustomed to favours from the great, I know not well how to receive, or in what terms to acknowledge.
>
> When, upon some slight encouragement, I first visited your lordship, I was overpowered, like the rest of mankind, by the enchantment of your address, and could not forbear to wish that I might boast myself Le vainqueur du vainqueur de la terre;– that I might obtain that regard for which I saw the world contending; but I found my attendance so little encouraged, that neither pride nor modesty would suffer me to continue it. When I had once addressed your Lordship in public, I had exhausted all the art of pleasing which a retired and uncourtly scholar can possess. I had done all that I could; and no man is well pleased to have his all neglected, be it ever so little.
>
> Seven years, my lord, have now passed, since I waited in your outward rooms, or was repulsed from your door; during which time I have been pushing on my work through difficulties, of which it is useless to complain, and have brought it, at last, to the verge of publication, without one act of assistance, one word of encouragement, or one smile of favour. Such treatment I did not expect, for I never had a patron before.
>
> The shepherd in Virgil grew at last acquainted with Love, and

> found him a native of the rocks.
>
> Is not a patron my lord, one who looks with unconcern on a man struggling for life in the water, and, when he has reached ground, encumbers him with help? The notice which you have been pleased to take of my labours, had it been early, had been kind; but it has been delayed till I am indifferent, and cannot enjoy it: till I am solitary, and cannot impart it; till I am known, and do not want it. I hope it is no very cynical asperity not to confess obligations where no benefit has been received, or to be unwilling that the public should consider me as owing that to a patron, which providence has enabled me to do for myself.
>
> Having carried on my work thus far with so little obligation to any favourer of learning, I shall not be disappointed though I should conclude it, if less be possible, with less; for I have been long wakened from that dream of hope, in which I once boasted myself with so much exultation,
>
> My Lord, Your lordship's most humble, most obedient servant,
> Sam. JOHNSON.[6]

Although Hester did not employ such biting language in her attack on the dissimulation and affectation, which Chesterfield recommends to his son in order to get on in society, she is contemptuous of his views. She opens the essay with: 'If I were asked, which of all the qualities that constitute an amiable character, would singly go farthest in gaining my love and admiration, I should answer, without hesitation, Simplicity.' Those who seek admiration fall into affectation which Hester condemns as disgusting because it is not pleasing to others. She illustrates among particular affectations which annoy her: giggling in young women; ostentatious show of generosity and goodness; being stern to cover tenderness; debauchery and boasting in order to gain acceptance into male company; vanity and false humility. Citing particular letters, but not in chronological order,[220, 221, 40, 207, 151, 129, 242] of Chesterfield to his son Hester condemns his advice because, she argues, it goes against the true nature of a person and therefore is a social artifice, a charade. She dismisses the ambition of Chesterfield for his son that the world be his bubble by seeking to progress his own advantage at all times with: 'a hypocrite under the age of twenty has very little chance of making " the world his bubble."' She ends her letter with a scathing attack on Letters 129 and 242 which reflect Chesterfield's view of women as lacking any rational judgment. She condemns on moral grounds Chesterfield's advice to his son to keep a married woman of fashion rather than an 'opera girl' as deserving only of ridicule and corrupting the youth of the nation and society.

Hester's second essay is on one of her favourite topics – the art of conversation: 'I have always considered the universal practice of card-playing as particularly pernicious in this respect, that, whilst it keeps people perpetually in company, it excludes conversation.' This championing of conversation over card playing is hardly surprising for someone of such Bluestocking outlook and it is a subject which Hester has already written about with passion before. Here she warns against adopting French fashions in conversation which do not sit well with the dry and reserved temper of the English, and the constant need to be gay in company which again she argues goes against the natural English temperament. Idle gossip and hypocrisy have no part in good conversation which can so easily become debased and turn into pure malice. Hester recommends that good conversation is based on a genuine concern for the feelings of others especially towards those who are new to society and unused to having their views ridiculed for the amusement of others. Hester ends this essay by stressing the importance of the choice of the company one keeps.

The third essay *On Enthusiasm and Indifference in Religion* opens with Hester recalling her enthusiasm when she was about fifteen for 'The Mystics'. However, as rational thought replaced romantic idealism she realised that her feelings had been based on her imagination. She cautions that the same danger may be encountered concerning God and that our true understanding must be based on reason. Furthermore she argues that it is all too easy for a person of fashion to neglect the true precepts of Christian belief. She paints a picture of the vacuous woman who is a follower of fashion where self-indulgence is paramount. The thumb-nail sketch gives a fascinating insight into the lives which so many women of the period led:

> If a modern lady of fashion were to be called to account for the disposition of her time, I imagine her defence would run in this style:– "I can't, you know, be out of the world, nor act differently from every body in it. The hours are every where late – consequently I rise late. I have scarce breakfasted before morning visits begin – or 'tis time to go to an auction, or a concert – or to take a little exercise for my health. Dressing my hair is a long operation – but one can't appear with a head unlike every body else. One must sometimes go to a play, or an opera; though I own it hurries one to death. Then what with necessary visits – the perpetual engagements to card-parties at private houses – and attendance on the public assemblies, to which all people of fashion subscribe, the evenings, you see, are fully disposed of. What time, then, can I possibly have for what you call domestic duties? – You talk of the offices and enjoyments of friendship – alas! I have no time left for friends! I must see them in a crowd or not at all. As to cultivating the friendship of my husband, we are very civil when we meet; but we are both too much engaged to spend much time with each other. With regard to my daughters, I have given them a French governess and

> proper masters – I can do no more for them. You tell me, I should instruct my servants – but I have no time to inform myself, much less can I undertake any thing of that sort for them, or even be able to guess what they do with themselves the greatest part of the twenty-four hours. I go to church, if possible, once on a Sunday, and then some of my servants attend me; and if they will not mind what the preacher says, how can I help it? The management of our fortune, as far as I am concerned, I must leave to the steward and the house-keeper; for I find I can barely snatch a quarter of an hour to look over the bill of fare when I am to have company, that they may not send up any thing frightful or old-fashioned. – As to the Christian duty of charity, I assure you I am not ill-natured; and (considering that the great expense of being always dressed for company, with losses at cards, subscriptions, and public spectacles, leave me very little to dispose of) I am ready enough to give my money when I meet with a miserable object. You say I should enquire out such, inform myself thoroughly of their cases, make an acquaintance with the poor of my neighbourhood in the country, and plan out the best methods of relieving the unfortunate, and assisting the industrious. But this supposes much more time, and much more money, than I have to bestow. – I have had hopes, indeed, that my summers would have afforded me more leisure, but we stay pretty late in town; then we generally pass several weeks at one or other of the water-drinking places, where every moment is spent in public; and for the few months in which we reside at our own seat, our house is always full, with a succession of company, to whose amusement one is obliged to dedicate every hour of the day.

All the rules which Hester laid down for her niece are ignored by this fictitious lady of fashion yet she was based on women whom Hester observed, no doubt with a jaundiced eye. She contrasts this selfish and vacuous life with the life led by Sir Charles and Lady Worthy who espouse a rational and virtuous outlook on life and organise their lives accordingly to the benefit of family and society.

The three essays show Hester in fine form arguing her points with great conviction and yet with a lightness of touch which is entertaining without becoming overly didactic in tone. The essays are followed by *Fidelia* which had already seen publication in *The Adventurer*, Issues 77, 78, 79 in 1753, and in contrast to the preceding three essays emphasises Hester's juvenile style some twenty years earlier. The collection of poems include her first poem *To Peace*, written about 1747 in response to the Jacobite rebellion of 1745; the ode prefixed to Elizabeth Carter's *Epictetus*; and the ode *To Aspasia* written to her by her friend Susanna Highmore, now Mrs Duncombe, who had been part of Richardson's coterie at North-End, in response to Hester's ode *To Stella*. However, poetry was not Hester's real *métier* and some of the works which are included are less than memorable.

Chapter 23

'That one talent which is death to hide'

Hester is now forty-eight and although *Miscellanies in Prose and Verse* did not meet with such critical success as *Letters on the Improvement of the Mind* it did further establish Hester's position as a writer in the society in which she moved. Furthermore, Elizabeth Montagu helped her financially by giving her an annuity of £100 after Edward's death in May 1775. Her social life at this time is varied and stimulating. In May, 1776 she reports attending a *fête champêtre* with Mrs Ogle, near Winchester which, in spite of the inclement weather ruining plans for breakfasting outside and the haymakers' being forced to don cloaks, she had enjoyed although she is suffering from grumbling teeth and jaws. However, Hester did not let these discomforts prevent her from dining at Lord Bateman's the following day. The same month sees her and Fanny Boscawen visiting friends where Hester enjoyed a lively debate on a book about which she and her uncle had differed in their views.

It is while visiting her uncle, Bishop Thomas, in August 1776 that Hester first meets George III and Queen Charlotte and her pleasure and sense of self-worth are palpable:

> Yes, my dearest – "simple as I sit here," I have been in company with the King and Queen; have enjoyed "the sweet aspect of princes;" been complimented over and over by royal lips about my book; been exhorted to write more; my niece inquired about; my place of abode; my address in London asked; and in short "as great honours done me as shall be desired, look you, on a summer's day." But I was still more gratified by the cordial esteem and kindness testified to my dear uncle and aunt by their royal guests, and by the joy which beamed in their countenances, and will gladden their hearts as often as they recollect this visit.

Hester continues by saying that she is writing to her brother to describe the event and: 'nothing could exceed the good humour, the ease, the kindness, I may say friendliness, of the royal guests.' The King

Queen Charlotte, wife of George III, friend of Mrs Delany

during a walk in the park had enquired about the bishop's family and:

> The King remembered me as Miss Mulso, but did not before know that my name was Chapone; and the Queen (before I appeared) expressed her surprise to find that the author of the letters she admired was the bishop's niece. She said she had asked several people but could never learn who Mrs Chapone was. This accounts for her having never mentioned the book to the bishop, which I had rather wondered at, having been told by Dr. M. that she liked it and had read it more than once (which she herself confirmed here).

Hester describes how nervous her aunt was about meeting the Queen. Hester opines:

> I am certain the queen was much more pleased with my aunt than she expected to be with an old lady, whom she had never seen at court, and whom, therefore, she probably considered as long disused to the world.

Much to Hester's amusement the people who lined the streets to see the Queen were disappointed by her appearance. They had expected her to be wearing a crown, not a black hat and plain blue greatcoat. The letter ends with Hester commenting on the effect this visit has had on her uncle:

> These honours to the bishop in his old age are the more gratifying to him, as his love for the king is the strongest passion in his soul.'[1]

In spite of the recognition and respect she was now held in, she values the company and views of her old friends which enable her to express her true self. She writes in a letter to Mr Burrows who is in Dublin:

> I, who live upon the love of my friends, can soon surfeit on the most delicate feats of mutual flattery, which seems to me to be too much the kind of intercourse among my new acquaintances, and in which they find me terribly deficient, and consequently terribly insipid. Our jarring society, as Mrs. B. calls it, is much more suited to my nature, and nothing can ever make me amends for that luxurious ease and security, in the kindness of all around me, which enables me to wrangle, abuse, and dispute, till I am black in the face, without the least apprehension of any harm ensuing; but life would be too happy if I were always to spend it with my brother and your family.[2]

She writes movingly to Elizabeth Carter about her feelings in a letter in which she thanks Elizabeth for her approbation of her 'little publications' and continues:

> the hope which you confirm, of their doing some good, has indeed afforded me an inexpressible satisfaction, which, as I know my own heart, is not founded in vanity. It appeases in some measure, that uneasy sense of helplessness and insignificance in society, which has often depressed and afflicted me; and gives me some comfort with respect to the poor account I can give of 'That one talent which is death to hide.'
>
> The testimony of a friend, and particularly such a friend, is far more precious than that of the public voice, had it been even as universal as you partially suppose; and is ever laid up in the choicest cabinet of my heart, along with every other endearing proof of your friendship and goodness to me.[3]

This sense of insignificance and dejection had been expressed by Hester earlier, before the publication of *Letters on the Improvement of the Mind*. The little publication Hester refers to is her last published work: *A Letter to a New-Married Lady* (1777). It is addressed to a young friend who has sought Hester's advice on her new position in society as a wife and the duties which will be expected of her. Hester plunges straight in with the admonition that the young woman, who has not been brought up on modish principles and who will shortly leave her own family for the hustle and bustle of London to which she is unaccustomed, must be obedient to her husband and accept this subjection willingly and happily. Temptation will lie in wait for the young wife which, if she succumbs, will be her undoing. The husband, referred to as Mr B. is wealthy, and the marriage is based on love rather than any financial benefit the marriage might bring to the husband: 'I, who know the disinterestedness of your nature, and the perfect freedom of rejection which your parents have always allowed you, have not the least doubt that your preference of him was the genuine effect of a real attachment, without any bias from his riches.' However, the young bride must show her husband that this is so by expressing her preference for his company and showing her affection for him.

She refers to the advice book by Dr John Gregory, whom Hester had met while accompanying Elizabeth Montagu to Scotland. She describes Gregory as: 'An amiable author, of much more delicacy than the Dean [Jonathan Swift].'[4] Gregory's *A Father's Legacy to his Daughters* and Hester's *Letters on the Improvement of the Mind* had displaced the hugely popular and successful *Advice to a Daughter* by Lord Halifax. However, Hester attacks Dr Gregory's advice that a young woman should never show the extent of her love for her husband: 'a precept which does no honour to his own sex, and which would take from ours its sweetest charms, simplicity and artless tenderness.' She admits that Swift in *A Letter to a Very Young Lady, on her Marriage Written in the Year 1723*[5] albeit 'in his coarse way,' has some very sensible advice on the subject before she mounts an attack not only on him but adds '(and almost every male writer on the subject)' who hold that passion is destroyed by possession and therefore cannot be sustained in marriage. Hester has pragmatic advice to offer: as passion subsides affection for one's spouse should succeed and a durable friendship will ensue. However, it is up to the wife to do everything in her power to safeguard and promote the enjoyment and happiness of her husband in her company and in his home. His interests and pursuits must therefore necessarily be hers and moreover she can learn from him and thereby improve herself.

Hester moves next to the complexities of the new wife's relationship with her mother-in-law. She pragmatically acknowledges that a newly married woman's husband has been a good son. She must respect this fact by not coming between son and mother. However, Hester points out that the woman in question is fortunate in that her husband has declined to have his mother live with them, something which Hester was spared in her short marriage. The new wife must avoid both any argument with her mother-in-law and any criticism of her. However, when it comes to any interference by her mother-in-law in domestic matters the young wife must be polite but act according to her own principles. Hester also recognises the problems which might arise between the two newly related families and recommends cultivating friendship with her new family while remaining a loving member of her own family.

Her next piece of advice is:

> Whatever may be said of the quarrels of lovers, believe me those of married people have always dreadful consequences, especially if they are not short and very slight. If they are suffered to produce bitter or contemptuous expressions, or betray an habitual dislike in one party of any thing in the person or mind of the other, such wounds can scarcely ever be thoroughly healed ... The painful recollection of what is past will often intrude upon the tenderest hours, and every trifle will awaken and renew it.

She paints a grim picture of how a petty jealousy can lead to an argument and warns her friend against demanding more affection than her husband can give. Instead she cautions that the wife must match her own feelings to those of her husband for her: 'for it is your part rather modestly to follow as he leads, than make him feel the uneasiness of not being able to keep pace with you.' Was the strong-minded young Hester able to do this in her marriage? It was Hester who was attracted to John Chapone at first meeting while he took a little longer to return her feelings. Fully aware that many husbands, such as Henry Thrale[6] and Agmondesham Vesey, were often tempted to look elsewhere Hester advises her friend if this should be the case to seek solace in religion and duty. By showing her patience and understanding she can earn her husband's affection once more. Children, which Hester did not produce in her short marriage, are seen by her as a source of comfort and joy and 'for their sakes, life will still be valuable to you, and entertained with chearfulness.'[sic].

Finally Hester once again turns her attention to Swift's advice to young women not to make friendships with members of her own sex. Hester points out that in society of the day, if they were to follow his advice, then the young woman would be without any friends for the rules of society discourage friendship with the opposite sex with very good reason. She dismisses Swift's advice succinctly:

> The reasons the Dean gives for this preposterous advice, if ever founded in truth, are certainly so no longer. You may find advantage in the conversation of many ladies, if not the equal to those which men are qualified to give, yet equal at least to what you, as a female are capable of receiving. Yet in one point the Dean and I agree; in recommending your husband to be your first and dearest friend, and his judgement to be consulted in the choice of every new one you may hereafter make.

Hester published nothing further. She was now in a position of no longer needing to publish her work for financial reasons.

Chapter 24

'belonging to the flying squadron'

In July 1775 Hester had written to her friend William Pepys from Farnham Castle offering her congratulations on his having been made Master in Chancery (an officer in the Court of Chancery). She presciently points out:

> As your income will now be such as even you will allow may maintain a family genteelly enough, your Field of Choice will be more ample; &, if you should ever gain that domestic happiness which you seem so peculiarly form'd to enjoy, you will now have leisure to taste it; which you could never be whilst you were toiling up to the eminence or toiling still more on the Summit. You may now be a Companion to your wife & a Preceptor to your children.[1]

Hester is still at Farnham Castle in December where she is nursing her ailing aunt. However she admits that she misses London and the opportunities to meet interesting people commenting: 'Mrs Barbauld in particular I regret, as the opportunities of cultivating her acquaintance are so scarce and valuable … and think her a prize not to be neglected.' In the same letter she refers to the pleasure she has in the company of John, her brother, 'and sad the separation in which we live.'[2]

William finally married in 1777 much to his, and Hester's delight and relief! Both are happy with the match. William describes his bride, Elizabeth Dowdeswell, as 'tall and beautifully shaped, and her countenance, without beauty, is expressive of goodness.' Perhaps even more important was her lack of affectation, something which both William and Hester abhorred. It proved to be an extremely happy marriage and Hester would share their happiness and joy in their growing family. Such was William's gratitude to Hester for all the support and advice she had offered in his search for a suitable partner that he offered her an apartment in their house. This would have given her a fixed address when she was in London instead of having the uncertainty of moving lodgings. Hester described herself as 'belonging to the flying squadron,' a reference to her ready generosity in giving her friends, and of course her family, the benefit of her practical assistance in times of illness and need. She writes from Farnham Castle to Pepys explaining her position:

> I was in hopes by this time to have been able to tell my dear Mr Pepys the day I meant to take possession of the apartment he has so kindly allotted me in his House. But alas, I am obliged to undergo the mortification of telling him that I fear it will not be at all in my power to avail myself of his, and Mrs Pepys kind invitation; my Friends here, whose wishes are commands, have desired that I will not leave them, but that I will accompany them to Chelsea on the 28th of this Month, and stay with them there some time, as they are to have none of their family with them, and will want me at that time more than ever. As I make it a rule to myself to suffer no engagement of pleasure, nor any inclination of my own, to interfere with my attendance on my Uncle & Aunt when they require it, you will not, I am sure, add to my disappointment, by taking this unkindly. I can with truth assure you that it is a sacrifice to duty that costs me very real regret, not only on account of the pleasure I had promised myself in such a free enjoyment of your conversation, which is always peculiarly agreeable to me, but more particularly as it deprives me of so happy an opportunity of cultivating an intimacy with Mrs Pepys.[3]

Family ties and familial duty now ruled Hester's life. She is fifty years old and although suffering from headaches and incipient asthma is far too valuable to her family as companion, nurse and confidante to lose to two relatively young and healthy friends. She clearly adores her two nieces and reports to William that she feels a maternal love towards them and believes they love her. At the end of this letter she reveals her disappointment with friendship: 'a world where there is so little real friendship, & where those intimacies which go by that name are usually connected by no stronger bonds than those of interest, or amusement, or vanity.' But rejoices: 'How inestimable are those Friends which have been tried in the fire and prove full weight, without alloy!' She is in good spirits and is enjoying the intellectual stimulus on which she thrived. During the more clement weather in spring and summer, she visits her brother John and his family in Hampshire and stays for quite lengthy periods with her aunt and uncle nearby in Winchester where she is visited by her beloved niece, Jenny. Her love of the countryside and walking remain undiminished as does her love of reading. She reports to Elizabeth Carter[4] that en route to Hampshire in 1777 she read *Pamela* aloud to her aunt: a journey which took three times as long and necessitated their breaking the journey overnight because her aunt had insisted on travelling by hired chariot. A further downside to reading the novel to her aunt, who was by now deaf, was that she had to scream it into her ear. In spite of this she still regards it as displaying Richardson's genius. However, she feels no such approbation for the Abbé Reynal whose views on the benefits of prostitution she condemns unsurprisingly as immoral and 'belongs to French philosophy to point.'

Somewhat surprisingly therefore, in view of this condemnation, Hester is intrigued and flattered when Fanny Boscawen invites her to meet Abbé Reynal. Reynal,[5] a French philosopher of the Enlightenment, was creating quite a stir among the Bluestockings in London. The Portugese Ambassador, a friend of Fanny's, is bringing him down from London to visit her. Hester reports that he is amazing and irritating in equal measure to those who meet him. When Elizabeth Vesey had introduced Reynal to Dr Johnson he responded that he had read Reynal's book, *Histoire Philosophique et Politique, Des Éstablissements & du Commerce des Européens dans les deux Indes* and had nothing to say to him. In a letter to Elizabeth Carter from Hadley, where she is staying, Hester describes her meeting with Reynal after she has commented on the inclement summer weather:

> The Abbé Reynal dined at Mrs Boscawen's at Glanvilla, [sic] about ten days ago, and she was so obliging to ask Mrs A. Burrows and me to meet him in the afternoon. I was exceedingly entertained, and not a little amazed, (not withstanding all I had heard about him) by the unceasing torrent of wit and stories, not unmixed with good sense, which flow from him; he had held on at the same rate from one at noon, (when he arrived at Glanvilla) and we heard that he went the same evening to Mrs Montagu's, in Hill Street, and kept on his speed till one in the morning. In the hour and a half I was in his company, he uttered as much as would have made him an agreeable companion for a week, had he allowed time for answers. You see such a person can only be pleasing as a thing to wonder at once or twice. His conversation was, however, perfectly inoffensive, which is more than his writings promise; his vivacity, and the vehemence of his action, (which, however, had not any visible connexion with his discourse) were amusing to me, who am little accustomed to foreigners. Mrs Boscawen is a very good neighbour to us here, and a most delightful companion every where. I never knew her in finer spirits than of late. One could not but make a comparison much to her advantage, between the overwhelming display of the abbé's talents, and that natural, polite, and easy flow of wit and humour which enlivens her conversation.[6]

The French Parliament later banned the book and Reynal was exiled for six years because of his attack on religion and French political tendencies. However, his works were read avidly by the young Napoleon.

Hester remained in lodgings having turned down Pepys' offer of an apartment in his house after his marriage. Here she entertained members of the Bluestocking circle on a somewhat frugal scale compared with the grandiose setting of Elizabeth Montagu and the fey Elizabeth Vesey. The much younger Fanny Burney records visits to Hester in her lodgings during the winter and accompanying her to other Bluestocking gatherings. She describes how each hostess created a different ambience:

> While to Mrs Vesey the Bas Bleu Society owed its origin and its epithet, the meetings at Mrs Montagu's were soon more popularly known by that denomination, for, though they could not be more fashionable, they were far more splendid ... But while the same bas bleu appellation was given to these two houses of rendezvous, neither that nor even the same associates could render them similar. Their grandeur or their simplicity, their magnitude or their diminutiveness, were by no means the principal cause of this difference; it was far more attributable to the presidents than their abodes; for though they instilled not their characters into their visitors, their characters bore so large a share in their visitors' reception and accommodation, as to influence materially the turn of the discourse.
>
> At Mrs Montagu's, the semi-circle that faced the fire retained during the whole evening its unbroken form, with a precision that it seemed described by a Brobdignagian compass. The lady of the castle commonly placed herself at the upper end of the room, near the commencement of the curve, so as to be courteously visible to all her guests; having the person of the highest rank or consequence properly on one side, and the person the most eminent for talents, sagaciously, on the other side, or as near to her chair and her converse as her favouring eye and a complacent bow of the head could invite him to that distinction.[7]

Other members entertained on a much more simple scale. Hannah More, one of the new generation of Bluestockings, had visited London for the first time with her sisters in the winter of 1774 where she was introduced to David Garrick and his circle. The patronage of David Garrick, the famous actor, theatre manager and producer, who introduced her to the London literary scene, brought enormous benefit for a brilliant young woman like Hannah with ambitions to be a dramatist. She had written plays for performance at the Mores' boarding school for girls in Bristol where she taught. Her writing ambitions were furthered as a result of deep personal unhappiness: at the age of 22 she had become engaged to a wealthy landowner near Bristol. William Turner

David Garrick, actor, and his Austrian wife, Eva, friends of Hannah More

was twenty years her senior but kept postponing the wedding. In order to end the engagement and extricate himself from the situation he settled an annuity of £200 on Hannah. This financial independence enabled her to pursue her interest in becoming a dramatist.[8]

From 1776 Hannah lived with the Garricks at their home in the Adelphi when she was in London on her annual visit. She describes offering cakes and tea there to Mrs Boscawen, Miss Reynolds, Dr Johnson – with whom she was a great favourite, Dean Tucker and the Garricks. She recounts how the meeting began at seven and ended at eleven with Garrick and Johnson exchanging anecdotes. Charles Burney and Elizabeth Carter were also part of the Garrick's circle. After Garrick's death in 1779 Hannah deserted writing for the stage. Instead she became involved in setting up Sunday schools in the Cheddar area, wrote on education and produced religious tracts. Her connection with the Garricks remained as she became Eva's companion when she was in London.

Fanny Boscawen held much more serious meetings where the lack of levity was in contrast to the foregoing description. Hannah More, in a letter home, describes the scene in 1775:

> I have been at Mrs Boscawen's. Mrs Montagu, Mrs Carter, Mrs Chapone and myself only were admitted. We spent the time not as wits, but as reasonable creatures; better characters I trow. The conversation was sprightly but serious. I have not enjoyed an afternoon so much since I have been in town. There was much sterling sense, and they are all ladies of high character for piety, of which, however, I do not think their visiting on Sundays any proof; for though their conversation is edifying their example is bad.[9]

Hester held meetings at her lodgings which were necessarily simple and according to Fanny Burney rather humdrum. She records how on the evening of December 30 1782:

> I went by appointment to Mrs Chapone's, where I met Mr and Mrs Pepys, Mr and Mrs Thomas Mulso, and Mr Burrows and his old maiden sister. We had rather a *hum-drum* evening. I cannot bring myself to be well enough acquainted with this set to try at enlivening it, because I cannot help being half afraid of them; otherwise a little rattling would prodigiously mend matters, and though they might stare a little, I am sure they would like it.[10]

Chapter 25

Hester Thrale and Fanny Burney

After the publication of her first novel *Evelina* to almost universal critical acclaim in 1778 Fanny Burney was drawn into both the Streatham set, over which Hester Thrale presided, and Elizabeth Montagu's set, over which Elizabeth ruled aided by her ever loyal prime minister, William Pepys. Some, like William Pepys and Johnson, who was much in demand, belonged to both sets. However, Johnson would be dropped by Elizabeth Montagu after the publication of *The Lives of the English Poets* (1779-81) because of his wounding comments on the *Dialogues of the Dead* by her great friend Lord Lyttelton:

> When they were first published, they were very kindly commended by the Critical Reviewers; and, Poor Lyttelton, with humble gratitude, returned, in a note which I have read, acknowledgements which can never be proper, for they must be paid either for flattery or for justice.

In March 1781 Johnson summed up the social situation between himself and Mrs Montagu with the aphorism:

> Mrs Montagu has dropt me. Now, Sir, there are people whom one should like very well to drop, but would not wish to be dropped by.[1]

Hester Thrale, who had no pretensions about her intellectual capacity, although she was clever, thrived on her capacity to offer generous hospitality to her friends and presided over Bluestocking gatherings at Streatham Park, her country estate in Streatham. She had brought a small fortune of £10,000, from Thomas Salusbury, her mother's brother-in-law, to her marriage in 1763, when she was twenty-two. Her husband, Henry, seventeen years her senior, was the son of a wealthy brewer, who owned the Anchor Brewery in Southwark. Their marriage cannot be described as based on romance but rather based on the practicalities of producing children – Hester bore twelve of whom four daughters survived to adulthood – and maintaining a social posi-

Hester, Mrs Thrale, later Mrs Piozzi, great friend of Dr Johnson

tion. Henry was elected MP for Southwark in 1765 where they lived at Brewery House. He held firm ideas on what a wife should and should not do, banning Hester from any involvement in all culinary matters and also banning her from riding which he deemed as being too masculine. He himself loved hunting and kept a pack of foxhounds near Croydon. He also had an eye for women and kept mistresses one of whom was the young and beautiful Sophy Streatfield,[2] who was famed for her ability to weep on command and still look beautiful much to the envy of women and the admiration of men. Sophy also had some knowledge of Greek. Classical languages were not usually studied by young women of the time and, if they were, then Latin was a more usual choice than Greek. Dr Johnson made the observation on Sophy: 'Taking away her Greek, she is as ignorant as a butterfly.' Hester Thrale comments on the relationship in *Thraliana*, a collection of her observations and anecdotes which she began in 1776 and which formed the basis for her *Anecdotes of the Late Samuel Johnson* (1786). This entry was written in 1779:

> Mr Thrale has fallen in love, really and seriously with Sophy Streatfield, but there is no wonder in that; she is very pretty, very gentle, soft and insinuating; hangs about him, dances round him, cries when she parts from him, squeezes his hand silly, and with her sweet eyes full of tears looks so fondly in his face – and all for love of me, as

> she pretends, that I can hardly help laughing in her face. A man must not be a man but an *it* to resist such artillery.

In 1765 Johnson was introduced to the Thrales by Arthur Murphy, one of Henry's closest friends. Murphy was a barrister, actor and playwright. And so began a friendship which was reciprocal in the benefits it brought to Hester and Johnson. She was lively, intelligent, possessed great charm, loved gossip and had what Johnson described as a wicked tongue. Moreover, she was not overawed by the great man. Johnson was given his own rooms when he increasingly spent more time at Streatham Park although he still retained his own rooms at 7, Johnson Court, off the north side of Fleet Street, and latterly at 8 Bolt Court where he moved in 1776. For Hester Thrale this close tie with Johnson brought with it the added kudos of having such a literary giant as an almost permanent member of the household. Johnson enjoyed the companionship and the comforts of living on the very pleasant country estate with its hundred acres where cattle grazed. He loved eating the fresh fruit from the large kitchen garden. Henry Thrale, who loved adding improvements to the estate, built a fine library, much loved by both Johnson and Fanny Burney, and in 1777 created a lake.

Here was a family into which he had been made welcome in spite of his demands on Hester and his less than socially attractive appearance and habits: his dress was often slovenly, his table manners appalling and he suffered from physical twitches of an alarming nature which made his progress in public places a spectacle for bystanders who would gather to stare. In spite of this he grew particularly close to Queeney, the Thrale's eldest daughter. Not noted for his manners Johnson was punctilious in showing due courtesy to his host Henry Thrale, donning a freshly powdered wig which was handed to him before he entered the dining room. Johnson's view of his host was: 'I know of no man who is more master of his wife, and family, than Thrale, if he but hold up a finger, he is obeyed.' Increasingly Johnson spent more of his time at Streatham Park rather than his home in Johnson's Court. The attraction of Streatham Park for Johnson are clear: here he had the admiring care and attention of the young Hester, who helped keep his melancholy at bay, good food and company and a ready audience. For Hester it brought male companionship, flattery and conversation all of which she lacked from her husband. Johnson did not regard Hester as an intellectual, referring to her learning 'as that of a schoolboy in one of the lower forms' in spite of her having received a good education for a young girl of her time from Dr Collier, who also interestingly was tutor later to Sophy Streatfield.

Thrale Place, later Streatham Park, where Dr Johnson loved to stay with the Thrales

It was in 1778 that Fanny Burney first met Johnson, by then a somewhat irascible man in his sixty-ninth year. He could be vicious in his criticism of others especially those with literary pretensions. Fanny had been 'scribbling', as she called her love of writing, since the age of ten. Now she was sheltering behind the cloak of anonymity, which she had gone to great lengths to safeguard, when her first novel, *Evelina*, was published that year and was apprehensive that the identity of the author might be discovered. Her father, Dr Burney, visited the Thrales' home regularly to give Queeney, the Thrale's eldest and somewhat difficult daughter in her teens, music lessons and had been admitted to the Streatham circle which included not only Johnson, William Pepys and Hester Chapone but also James Boswell, David Garrick, and Joshua Reynolds, a close friend of Johnson. After the publication anonymously of *Evelina*, for which Fanny received thirty guineas for the three volumes, Dr Burney invited Hester Thrale, Queeney, and Dr Johnson to visit his home en route to dine at Mrs Montagu's. Both Hester Thrale, then thirty-seven, and Johnson took to Fanny who was twenty-six. Hester invited her to stay at Streatham Park in August where the newly published *Evelina* was much discussed and applauded by Johnson, who had been lent a copy by Hester in July. It was at Streatham that Fanny's cover of anonymity, which her father Charles

Frances (Fanny) Burney, later Madame d'Arblay, Mrs Thrale's protégée

Burney had insisted on to protect her, was blown. Fanny describes it:

> A bustle with the dog Presto – Mrs Thrale's favourite – at the entrance of these ladies into the library, prevented any formal reception; but as soon as Mrs Montagu heard my name, she enquired very civilly after my father, and made many speeches concerning a volume of "Linguet," which she has lost; but she hopes soon to replace it. I am sure he is very high in her favour, because she did me the honour of addressing herself to me three or four times.
>
> But my ease and tranquillity were soon disturbed: for she had not been in the room more than ten minutes, ere, turning to Mrs Thrale, she said–
>
> "Oh, ma'am – but your Evelina – I have not yet got it – I sent for it but the bookseller had it not. However, I will certainly have it."
>
> "Ay, I hope so," answered Mrs Thrale, "and I hope you will like it too; for 'tis a book to be liked."
>
> I began now a vehement nose-blowing, for the benefit of handkerchiefing my face.

"I hope though," said Mrs Montagu drily, "it is not in verse? I can read anything in prose, but I have a great dread of a long story in verse."

"No, ma'am, no; 'tis all in prose, I assure you. 'Tis a novel; and an exceeding – but it does nothing good to be praised too much, so I will say nothing more about it; only this, that Mr Burke sat up all night to read it."

"Indeed? Well, I propose myself great pleasure from it; and I am gratified by hearing it is written by a woman."

"And Sir Joshua Reynolds," continued Mrs Thrale, "has been offering fifty pounds to know the author."

"Well, I will have it to read on my journey; I am going to Berkshire, and it shall be my travelling book."

"No, ma'am, if you please you shall have it now. Queeny, do look for it for Mrs Montagu, and let it be put in her carriage, and go to town with her."

Miss Thrale rose to look for it, and involuntarily I rose too, intending to walk off, for my situation was inexpressibly awkward; but then I recollected that if I went away, it might seem like giving Mrs Thrale leave and opportunity to tell my tale, and therefore I stopped at a distant window, where I busied myself in contemplating the poultry.

"And Dr. Johnson, ma'am," added my kind puffer, "says Fielding never wrote so well – never wrote equal to this book; he says it is a better picture of life and manners than is to be found anywhere in Fielding."

"Indeed?" cried Mrs Montagu surprised; "that I did not expect, for I have been informed it is the work of a young lady, and therefore, though I expected a very pretty book, I supposed it to be a work of mere imagination, and the name I thought attractive; but life and manners, I never dreamt of finding."

"Well, ma'am, what I tell you is literally true; and for my part, I am never better pleased than when good girls write clever books – and that this is clever – But all this time we are killing Miss Burney, who wrote the book herself."[3]

Hester Thrale has triumphed over her rival. The discomforted Fanny rushes out of the room amidst the gasps of Elizabeth Montagu and her attractive companion Dorothea Gregory, the daughter of Dr Gregory and now Elizabeth's companion. Fanny stays out of sight in her room until dinner time, by which time Johnson has joined the party. Much to her surprise, at Johnson's instigation, she is invited to Elizabeth Montagu's new house for a house warming on next Easter day. She is even more delighted when Johnson praises her book to the assembled company.

Fanny was now much in demand among other hostesses although the honour went to Hester Thrale as having been the first of the circle to have read the novel. However, Fanny sometimes grumbles about having to put in an appearance at Hester Thrale's Bluestocking parties. She reports having gone with her father rather late in the evening but:

> ... early enough, however, for me, as I was not in cue for a mixed party of Praters. I respect and esteem them, but they require an exertion to which I am not always inclined. The company was Mrs Montagu, Mrs Garrick, Miss More, Mr and Mrs Pepys, Mrs Chapone, and two or three less eminent.[4]

Hester Chapone praised *Evelina* for its representation of pure and elegant love on the part of the aristocratic lovers, Lord Orville and Evelina. She declares herself fond of Fanny Burney and likes her writing. Fanny for her part grew increasingly fond of Hester. It was Hester who took Fanny to Mr Burrows's home to meet Mr and Mrs Barbauld soon after she had introduced Fanny to Mrs Delany:

> I went afterwards, by long appointment, to Mr Burrows, to meet Mr. and Mrs. Barbauld. Mrs Chapone carried me. Mrs Chapone herself is the most superiorly unaffected creature you can conceive, and full of agrémens from good sense, talents and conversational powers, in defiance of age, infirmities and uncommon ugliness. I really love as well as admire and esteem her.[5]

Hester was fifty-two when Burney gave this unflattering view of her physical appearance but as beauty had never been Hester's to enjoy it was her mind and lively conversation which her friends valued. Certainly Hester had no time for vanity and was highly suspicious of any form of flattery. Her love of argument and intelligent conversation had not diminished over the years.

Chapter 26

'such a here and thereian'

England would once again be at war with France in 1778 bringing the constant threat of French invasion. However, the next decade was to bring several events which would shake members of the Bluestocking circle. Times were changing politically and the security and growth of Britain as an Empire nation was being threatened by the American War of Independence and then by The French Revolution. The English navy had been weakened through corruption and neglect making it fully stretched defending its colonies. France had sided with the Americans in the American War of Independence, a war in which Fanny Boscawen's only surviving son, George, fought, not in the navy like his father, but in the army. Not surprisingly Fanny wanted peace with America. In the West Indies, St Vincent and Grenada fell to the French in 1779 – although the British would recover them in 1783 – and Spain became an ally of France. The sense of national confidence and pride was threatened. Liberal views would be replaced: women who expressed their ideas too radically were seen as a threat. The Bluestocking movement which had done so much to encourage women to find their voice went into decline.

Hester had spent long periods at Farnham Castle in both 1777 and 1778. From here she wrote a marvellous description of another royal visit to her uncle, Bishop of Winchester, who was celebrating his eighty-first birthday. When told of the forthcoming event the King announced:

> 'Then', said he 'I will go and wish him joy.' 'And I,' said the Queen, 'will go too.' Mr B. then dropped a hint of the additional pleasure it would give the Bishop if he could see the princes. '*That*,' said the King 'requires contrivance; but if I can manage it we will *all* go'. ... and a little after eleven, came the King and Queen in their phaeton, three coaches and six, and one coach and four, with a large retinue of servants.

Hester then lists everyone before continuing:

> They were all conducted into the great drawing room by Mr. and Mrs. Buller, [Mrs Buller is the bishop's daughter] where, after paying their compliments to the Bishop and Mrs. T—, those of the first column remained there to breakfast; those of the second column left the room, and were led by Mrs. T— to the dressing-room, where Mrs.— and I were, and where I made tea for them. ... After our breakfast was over, as well as that of the upper house, the royal guests came to visit us in the dressing room. The King sent the princes in to pay their compliments to Mrs Chapone. Himself, he said, was an old acquaintance. Whilst the princes were speaking to me, Mr Arnold, (the sub-preceptor), said, 'These gentlemen are well acquainted with a certain Ode prefixed to Mrs Carter's Epictetus, if you know any thing of it.' Afterwards the King came and spoke to us, and the Queen led the Princess Royal to me, saying, 'This is a young lady, who, I hope has profited much by your instructions. She has read them once and will read them oftener;' and the princess assented to the praise which followed with a very modest air.[1]

Hester continues this delightful description with comments on the royal children: the Prince of Wales, who was sixteen, his brother Prince Frederick, Duke of York, fifteen and their younger brother Prince William, Duke of Clarence, thirteen. Hester notes that Prince William is small for his age but sensible and so engaging that the bishop was especially taken with him. William, she reports, stayed with the bishop while the rest of the children ran about the house. The two daughters she mentions are the Princess Royal, who was fourteen and her younger sister, Princess Augusta, aged ten. Hester is much amused by the comments of the youngest of the Buller's daughters who was present. She describes her: '(a comical natural little creature, between eight and nine) says she thinks it hard the princes may not marry whom they please; and seems not without hopes, that, if it were not for this restriction, the Prince of Wales might prove a lover of her's.' Hester is moved by the King's obvious affection for her uncle and the latter's fondness for his royal pupil.

Hester remained at Farnham caring for her aunt and uncle and according to her brother, John, helping to enliven the atmosphere at the castle. Sadly for Hester her aunt Susanna died in November that year. Hester continues to look after her uncle and stays with him at Winchester House in Chelsea where Fanny Boscawen reports visiting her in December 1779. Two years later her uncle died. Much to Mary Delany's indignation he only provided an annuity of £30 which was added to the stipend of £20 he had given Hester during his lifetime from his income of £6,000 which seemed less than generous considering Hester's devotion to both him in his later years and to her aunt whom she had nursed so devotedly in her last illness. Visits to her aunt and uncle at Farnham Castle had given Hester an extremely pleasant setting in which to escape from the lodgings in London and these visits also provided her with the opportunity to indulge in her love of the countryside as well as meeting up with her brother John and his family. Fortunately for Hester her ties with Winchester and the Ogles were maintained and Hester still had a wide choice of family to stay with when out of London in the spring and summer.

She had good reason to be grateful that she could escape from London in 1780[2] when mobs ran riot. Hester very rarely refers to the political situation in England at the time but clearly the Gordon Riots shook her as this letter to William Weller Pepys reveals: it is written from the safety of the Reverend Burrows's home in Hadley:

> Many thanks to you both, my dear friends, for your kind Letter: it grieves me to find that Mr Pepys's eyes are again disordered, perhaps the Rioters are answerable for that, as well as for many other evils. I endured the terrors of Wednesday night without one moment's Sleep, better than I could have expected from such a frame of mine, and the kind invitation of my dear Friends to this place of quiet and of delightful Society the next day, gave me such a turn to my spirits, that after a couple of Nights I thought myself quite restored, but (whether from any latent effects of the past Horrors I know not) I was very ill Last Friday in my old nervous way. I am better again now, and do not *often* hear the distant shouts of the Platoon-firing after I am in bed. – I was rejoiced to hear that my Brother and Sister were to have the happiness of seeing you *both* to meet Mrs Barbauld on Thursday. I should have liked the party very much, but I own I am not yet reconciled to London to wish myself there. Mrs Barbauld was very fortunate in deferring her Journey till all was quiet. – I hope your street was remote enough from the grand Scenes of action to save you from immediate danger to your own person, the idea of general ruin was a sufficient distress even to those who fared best. I find you scorn'd to quit your Posts, and indeed you are so well guarded at present that you can have nothing to fear; but what will become of us hereafter – we may as well not think of; since we can do nothing in it. He who 'can still the waves and the madness of the People' will be our Guard if there are righteous men enough left to save the City. – pray let us hear a little how Thursday past (*went off* is the phrase here) and whether you are all in full song, or are all reduced to *croaking* by the badness of the times. Mrs Boscawen call'd here the day after I came, and look'd the image of horror and woe. But I have since had the pleasure of seeing her with a very cheerful countenance, full of the good news of Charleston being taken.[3]

She ends the letter with a reference to Hadley being full of refugees like herself.

In the mob rule which ensued, private houses were plundered and burnt, Newgate Prison set on fire and the prisoners released: it was finally ended when the King called out the militia. The news of the British victory at Charlestown in May 1780 was therefore welcome: General Clinton took 5,000 prisoners and 400 guns as well as capturing all the French and American ships in the harbour.[4]

★ ★ ★

In 1782 Hester is reading Fanny Burney's *Cecilia*, published that June, which had sold out almost at once. Hester is delighted with it as she is with all Fanny's works. Pepys is reported as being wild about it. He was not alone in his approval: Mary Delany recommended it to Queen Charlotte and her daughters. In November Hester asks Elizabeth Carter if she has read the book and reports that Elizabeth Montagu is warm in her commendation of it. However, she comments that Elizabeth Montagu had not liked *Evelina* which portrayed:

> ... the just and natural picture of the purest and most elegant love. Lord Orville and Evelina are lovers after my own heart. Mrs Montagu, êntre nous, is an ignoramus on this subject, as I have observed on many occasions, nor are you quite adept. It is the only subject in the world of which I think myself a better judge than either of you.[5]

She confides how fond she is of Fanny and commends her for the morality underlying the novels. She allows that in *Cecilia* the satire on society and its ways is entertaining but finds the pathos too much for her and feels that perhaps there are too many characters although she allows that they are well drawn. She is also reading the posthumous works of Rousseau and delights in his imagination which allows him in solitude to create his ideal society. Hester herself spent much of her time in London alone in her lodgings and she admits she escapes from unhappiness through her imagination when real happiness is denied her.

The following January it is Hester who introduces Fanny to Mary Delany. Fanny describes the meeting in her diary on Sunday, Jan. 19, 1783:

> And now for Mrs Delany. I spent one hour with Mrs Thrale, and then called for Mrs Chapone, and we proceeded to St James's Place. Mrs Delany was alone in her drawing-room, which is entirely hung with pictures of her own painting, and ornaments of her own designing.[6]

Sadly, Mary's eyesight is failing and as a result she can no longer continue to produce her flower mosaics for which she had grown so famous. In the previous year, 1782, she had written a poignant poem entitled *A Farewell* to her art which she had loved so much and which had been so central to her life after her husband's death:

The time is come! I can no more
The vegetable world explore;
No more with rapture cull each flower
That paints the mead or twines the bower;
No more with admiration see
Its beauteous form and symmetry!
No more attempt with hope elate
Its lovely hues to imitate!
Farewell! to all those friendly powers
That blest my solitary hour;
Alas! farewell! but shall I mourn
As one who is of hope forlorn?
Ah no! my mind with rapture feels
The promise which thy Word reveals.
Come Holy Spirit, on thy wing
Thy sacred consolation bring.
Teach me to contemplate that grace
Which hath so long sustained my race;
Which various blessings still bestows,
And pours in balm to all my woes!
O sanctify the pointed dart
That at this moment rends my heart;
Teach me, submissive to resign
When summoned by thy Will Divine.[7]

By now Mary Delany is eighty-three yet Fanny is charmed by her gentleness and sweetness of manner which reminds her of her own grandmother, Frances Sleepe. Mrs Delany has requested to meet Fanny because of the pleasure which her books have given her. Over a simple dinner which is elegantly presented and served Fanny and Mary discover that they both know the Crisp family. Fanny referred to Mr Samuel Crisp[8] as 'Daddy Crisp' and as 'other daddy'. Crisp had known Charles Burney since 1747. A highly cultured man with a private income he lived in retirement in Chesington (now spelt Chessington) at Chesington Hall two miles from Epsom where Fanny Burney often stayed. The Duchess of Portland, who visited her old friend Mary most days when she was in London, joins the party. The conversation

Mary, Mrs Delany, famed for her paper flower mosaics

turns to *Cecilia*. The duchess announces she has read all five volumes three times. She remembers that at first she was reluctant to read the novel because she had found both *Clarissa* and *Sir Charles Grandison* so tedious that in fact she never read them fully. Hester Chapone springs to defend both novels immediately but the duchess is not to be persuaded. She continues with praise of *Cecilia* for its construction which, she argues, keeps off that 'heavy depression given by Richardson' because there was also something to laugh about. Hester responds that she was caused such agitation by the plot and eagerness to know the ending that she could not cry or sleep. The three women continue to discuss the novel praising it for its moral worth. This panegyric on her writing both delighted and embarrassed Fanny: delighted her because it came from three women whom Fanny deemed to be 'so respectable, so moral, and so aged.'

1782 also brought Hester great sorrow. Edward, or Ned, her younger brother of whom she was so fond died suddenly and totally unexpectedly. He was a popular member of social circles with a ready wit and would soon have the company roaring with laughter at one of his anecdotes. He had been the brother with whom she shared most closely her love of music and who had accompanied her on violin when she sang. Richardson referred to him in a letter to Hester in those happy days when she was so much a part of Richardson's coterie at North-End: 'Had we had Mr Mulso's violin and the voice of his beloved sister we should have had still greater reason to rejoice in our concert.'

Ned's death is a great blow and Hester's health suffers. She is further distressed by the death of her old friend, Mary Smith. Hester's brother, John, is worried about her health and also, as he reports to Gilbert White, her itinerant lifestyle for she is constantly moving her lodgings. Without a permanent home in London it meant that every autumn, usually at the end of October, when she returned, having vacated her lodging in the spring, she had the problem of finding new lodgings. She reports the situation to William Pepys in 1783.[9] She describes how on her return from Southampton, where she has been with Mrs Ogle, she stayed with Mr Burrows in Great Russell Street because she had no lodgings arranged. Fortunately she fixes on lodgings at a Mr White's, a grocer in Dean Street. She has hopes of it being a comfortable home because of the landlady's character and it has another recommendation: 'the Drawing-room is rather better than any I have had.' Hester comments to William Pepys that she is 'such a here and thereian' that it is best to send letters to her brother's address. Hester is still far from well and has suffered a violent nose bleed which has weakened her. In April 1784 John is directing letters to his brother Thomas in Charlotte Street near Bedford Square because Hester is on the move once again. He reports again to Gilbert on April 17 that Hester is still not well and is now lodging at a Mrs North's in Stephen Street, Rathbone Place. In August she receives a further blow: her close friend Mrs Burrows dies. She bequeaths Hester an annuity of £10. Hester uproots herself again and settles in lodgings in Wardour Street where at last her health takes a turn for the better.

Hester Chapone has lost none of her intellectual sharpness and in spite of her declining health and uncertain accommodation retains her sense of humour as well as her warmth and sincerity that her friends valued so much. She has a high opinion of Fanny Burney who reciprocates her opinion by describing Hester's as 'the best' of her visits.

Chapter 27

'such mighty overbearing Passions are not natural in a Matron's bones'

In 1778 Hester Thrale had met Gabriel Piozzi[1] while on a visit in the company of Samuel Johnson to Dr Burney's house in St Martin's Street. Hester became restive with the evening: the other guests were in awe of Johnson who had remained silent. Deciding to enliven the atmosphere she crept up behind the singer and began to imitate him much to the consternation and displeasure of Charles Burney who remonstrated with her for her lack of musical appreciation shown by her mimicry of Piozzi which was spoiling the enjoyment of the others. Hester took the reprimand well and rejoined the rest of the group, trying to listen attentively. It would not have seemed from this somewhat inauspicious introduction to Piozzi that she would fall so completely in love with him and ignore all the warnings of her friends and children. She wrote in *Thraliana*: 'I have picked up Piozzi here, the great Italian singer. He is amazingly like my father. He shall teach Hester [Queeney].' Hester Chapone, like so many of the Bluestocking circle, is shocked by Hester Thrale's infatuation with Signor Piozzi: a foreigner, a Roman Catholic and not from the same social standing as Hester.

The following year Henry Thrale suffered a stroke and in the early autumn his wife, in the company of Fanny, took her husband to recuperate at Brighthelmstone, (Brighton) where the Thrales had a large house. A year later he had another stroke and this time was taken to Bath where Elizabeth Montagu was also in residence. They then moved on to Brighton where Hester bumped into Piozzi and asked him to give her daughter, Queeney, some lessons. He refused. However, in 1780 he relented and was appointed Queeney's singing teacher which brought him into regular contact not only with his pupil but also her mother. It was also in 1780 that Henry Thrale lost his seat in Parliament. His health was further declining partially due to his

Gabriel Piozzi, Italian second husband of Hester Thrale

inability to stop eating and drinking so much. There were also considerable anxieties over the financial state of the brewery. His wife meanwhile was planning to move to her grand new home in Grosvenor Square where she planned to throw a party on April 4, 1781 at which Piozzi would sing. It was not to be. Fanny Burney records: 'on the morning of a day on which half the fashion of London had been invited to an intended assembly at Grosvenor-square ...' Henry, who had been so hospitable and kind to both Johnson and Burney, died and the party was cancelled.

Hester Thrale was in her early forties, newly widowed, wealthy and very much besotted with Piozzi. However, in spite of her infatuation with him her name was being linked by many to Johnson who had enjoyed seventeen happy years in her household. But Hester, if she did remarry, was determined to marry for love. Her whole attitude changed towards Johnson. Where formerly she had indulged his eccentricities: his often shambolic appearance, his twitches and his terrible table manners, his uncalled for rudeness and demands on her time – she had sat up in the night with him as he hated to be alone and had a pathological fear of death – now he became a burden to have in the house and much to Johnson's distress she began to cold-shoulder him even though he was one of the four executors of her husband's will.

Johnson's behaviour was at times very difficult especially when he became embroiled in an argument on literary or political matters. While Henry Thrale was alive Johnson took care not to offend him. In May,1781, shortly after Henry's death and having met the executors of the will and the eventual buyer of the brewery, a Mr David Barclay, Hester was forced to intervene when Johnson and Pepys became embroiled in an argument at dinner over Johnson's *Life of Lyttelton*. Pepys, who like Elizabeth Montagu had been a friend of Lyttelton, had no wish to enter into an argument with Johnson and confided his reluctance to Fanny. But Johnson engaged in battle all guns blazing at the unfortunate Pepys whom he harangued unmercifully. Fanny describes the scene at Mrs Thrale's table:

> We had a terrible noisy day. Mr and Mrs Cator [Cator was an executor of Henry Thrale's will] came to dinner, and brought with them Miss Collison, a niece. Mrs Nesbitt was also here, and Mr Pepys. The long war which has been proclaimed among the wits concerning Lord Lyttelton's "Life," by Dr. Johnson, and which a whole tribe of blues with Mrs Montagu at their head, have vowed to execrate and revenge, now broke out with all the fury of the first actual hostilities, stimulated by long-concerted schemes and much spiteful information. Mr Pepys, Dr. Johnson well knew, was one of Mrs Montagu's steadiest abettors; and, therefore, as he had some time determined to defend himself with the first of them he met, this day he fell the sacrifice to his wrath.[2]

It was an encounter that Pepys had done his best to avoid but there was no such restraint on Johnson's part. The fiery encounter continued after the ladies had withdrawn with Johnson vehemently attacking Lyttelton. When the men joined the ladies in the drawing room and the argument threatened to continue over tea Mrs Thrale finally intervened and very firmly announced: 'here is too much about it, indeed, and I should be very glad to hear no more of it.' A sentiment no doubt shared by many of those present. Although the two men shook hands on Pepys's departure – it was a cold and formal farewell. Hester Thrale ostracized Johnson from then on. He lost the friendship of Elizabeth Montagu who never forgave him because of his intemperate expression of his opinion of Lyttelton. He was no longer a welcome guest at her house and was a much less welcome guest at Hester Thrale's home.

It was to Fanny Burney that Hester Thrale had confided her love for Piozzi. Fanny was horrified at the scandal which would ensue if, as Hester seemed determined to do, she married this man for whom she felt such passion. Queeney, by then eighteen, found the whole scenario distasteful in the extreme. The gossip and speculation were rife.

Elizabeth Montagu and Hester Chapone condemned the relationship. Hester Chapone was forceful when expressing her trenchant opinion to Pepys:

> ... there must be really some degree of *Insanity* in that case for such mighty overbearing Passions are not natural in a 'Matron's bones.' The 4 daughters render it a most frightful instance of human wretchedness indeed! It has given great occasion to the Enemy to blaspheme and to triumph over the Bas Bleu Ladies.[3]

But in spite of strong opposition from her daughter and open social disapproval Hester went ahead and married Piozzi on July 25, 1784. Hester appears to have found real happiness in her second marriage but, through following her heart, incurred the social disapproval of her Bluestocking friends. The circle at Streatham was no longer. Samuel Johnson suffered a stroke in 1783, losing his power of speech which terrified him. He recovered but other ailments conspired against him and on December 13, 1784 he died at Bolt Court. Death, of which he had been so terrified, had finally claimed him. Fanny attends a meeting at Hester Chapone's soon after Johnson's funeral and reports in her diary: 'How melancholy will all these circumstances render these once so pleasant meetings.' Hester Piozzi's relations with Fanny, who had enjoyed so many happy times at Streatham Park with its large grounds and its library, and the other Bluestocking members were either strained or broken. Queeney disowned her mother and decamped to Brighton with her two younger siblings. Hester Chapone's sense of propriety was not only outraged at the other Hester's passion at the age of forty-four but also that she should marry a man from such a different social background.

However, Mary Delany had always refused to meet and become friendly with either Hester Thrale or Johnson. In her opinion they did not as far as she was concerned belong to polite society.

The marriage was a happy one. On their nineteenth wedding anniversary on the 25th July, 1803 Hester wrote this charming poem to her husband:

Accept my Love this honest Lay
Upon your Twentieth Wedding Day:
I little hop'd our Lives would stay
To hail the Twentieth Wedding Day.
If you've grown Gouty – I grown Gray
Upon our Twentieth Wedding day –
'Tis no great Wonder;– Friends must say

"Why 'tis their Twentieth Wedding Day."[4]

They spent much of their time at Brynbella which they built in 1794 on Hester's estate in north Wales. Piozzi would die from gout on 26 March 1809. He left his wife £6,000.

In 1783 Hester Chapone, who is now fifty-six, has lost none of her impatience with matters which she feels are misguided or downright wrong. Nor has she lost her critical eye for literature. She is reading Gilbert White's poems which her brother John has passed on to her. As one might suspect the subject matter is drawn from nature and Hester is complimentary about his versification but likes *The Rainbow* the least of the three poems because she feels it was a poor imitation of Milton. Her correspondence with Elizabeth Carter continues and here reflects her long held views on love and conversation:

> I am persuaded there must be something very wrong and unnatural in the method of living in civilized countries; for it could never be the original nature of the animal man to be so perpetually infested by disease. Perhaps we ought not to have eat animal food; and perhaps all that contributes to cultivate our finer sensations, and even all that adorns and ennobles our minds, may tend to render our bodies delicate and liable to perpetual injury. Somebody was observing, t'other day, that love was of modern invention, and that no such thing existed in Homer's time. Nervous complaints, I dare say, came into fashion with love, and brought a great many more painful feelings in their train. However, I am better pleased to have been a sufferer from them, than to have been carrying a stinking seal, with a blanket skewered round me, into the woods after some lordly savage, perfectly unacquainted with the fashion of love or conversation.[5]

Hester in London was enjoying her friendships and attending the varied Bluestocking gatherings at the Pepys's, Elizabeth Montagu's, Elizabeth Vesey's and Fanny Boscawen's. She became friendly with the younger generation of Bluestockings who were making names for themselves including Fanny Burney, the former protégée of Hester Thrale, and Hannah More, the protégée of Elizabeth Montagu. Hester Chapone was a well-known and well-liked member of the group which included Laetitia Barbauld who had published a very successful book of poetry in 1773 when she was thirty. She went on to publish in various different genres including primers for children, politics, and in 1804 edited Samuel Richardson's correspondence. Hester Chapone was included, along with such luminaries as Johnson and Pope, in Barbauld's *The Female Speaker* (1811), a collection of essays and poetry for girls. Laetitia and her husband ran a very successful boys' school in

Suffolk which they left in 1785 as a result of her husband's weakening mental health which made teaching no longer congenial for him. In 1808 they separated after he assaulted her and he later committed suicide by drowning in the river.

Although she would publish nothing further Hester did continue to write poems to her friends in sonnet form. She wrote on subjects which were now pertinent to her heart. One such subject was insomnia from which she was suffering increasingly. Her invocation to sleep begins:

> In vain I close my weary lids,
> Some envious power all sleep forbids.
> Why must I endless vigils keep?
> I'm sure I never 'murder'd sleep,'
> But nurs'd-it with indulgence kind,
> By writing 'Letters on the Mind.'
> No air-drawn daggers scare my soul,
> Nor blood-stained hand, nor poison'd bow;
> No injur'd orphans haunt my bed,
> Nor demons hover round my head.
> Hold – There, perhaps, I say too much;
> For aught I know there may be such ...[6]

The poem continues with her trying the well-worn tricks to bring sleep – reciting poems, counting or remembering stories – all to no avail. Her efforts are further disturbed by the bells of St Paul's Cathedral and the shouts of night watchmen as they bang their clubs on her door. She is finally sent to sleep by her 'own dull verses.'

The summer sees her following her usual pattern of staying with her brother, John, in Hampshire at the end of August before moving on in September to stay with Dr Buller and his wife at Alresford, in Hampshire, after which she goes on to stay with Dr and Mrs Ogle at Winchester where he is Dean. It was with good reason that her brother John christened her 'the Wanderer'. The ill health, from which Hester increasingly suffers, is accompanied by periods of dejection which prevent her in the summer of 1784 from enjoying the social contact on which she thrives. She writes to Elizabeth Carter:

> You were very good, my dear Mrs Carter, to favour me with a letter so early; and upon the whole the account it brought me was as satisfactory as I could expect. I should have thanked you for it sooner but that I have been very much indisposed this last fortnight. A bad cold brought back my cough and low fever, with the addition of a sore

> throat. The dejection of spirits which attended the low fever is much the worst part of the disorder; and you will know that one symptom of it is a perfect listlessness and disinclination to set about any employment that can be omitted. I am better, but still far from well: however I have just enough power of exertion to resolve that I will no longer appear ungrateful to your kind attention. I do not expect to get rid of my complaints whilst this watery solstice continues. Sunshine is essential to my well being, and when to that is added country air, I flatter myself I shall be restored to my common state of health, which, I bless God, is such as affords me many enjoyments.
>
> ... Our enjoyments in this world seem to depend more on animal spirits than on the principles of right conduct; and a wicked man, with high health and spirits, shall laugh through the day, whilst an innocent and pious mind is drooping under the heaviest dejection, and more alarmed by mere human frailties, than the first is by shocking crimes.[7]

She continues by offering robust advice at the end of this letter on the subject of marriage; a subject still very dear to her heart. Having been told by Elizabeth Carter that an acquaintance, who is getting no younger, has lowered her sights in the marriage market and wants to marry an impecunious clergyman, she is brisk and pragmatic in her opinion on the matter: she should marry a man she likes so long as he has character and is a gentleman. Instead of criticising her, her friends and mother should support her decision which is a pragmatic decision when she has failed for so long to find a suitable husband.

Chapter 28

'I shall be good and happy': The Bluestockings in Decline

When Mary Delany's close friend the Dowager Duchess of Portland died in 1785 it was Fanny Burney who became her chief comforter. She goes to stay at St James's Place. Mary, who is by now eighty-five, with failing eyesight, and Fanny set about sorting through her long correspondence with the duchess. Her death was a great loss to Mary for the two women had been friends for almost fifty years and summers at Bulstrode had been a regular part of Mary's life. The King and Queen, who visited Bulstrode, were great admirers of her art and treated her as a much loved friend. Much to Fanny's relief the highly solicitous King George and Queen Charlotte, realising that Mary's financial situation was severely strained insist that she remove to a grace-and-favour home at Windsor, which she does in September. In fact the King was waiting to greet her when she arrived and the Queen sent this warm and loving letter:

> My Dearest Mrs Delany
> If coming to me will not fatigue your spirits too much I shall receive you with open arms, and am
> Your affectionate friend
> CHARLOTTE[1]

Hester comments to Pepys:

> … the Queen desired she would suggest whatever could conduce to Mrs Delany's comfort so that she might have no occasion to bring anything besides Cloaths. All kinds of stores – such as Wine, Tea, sugar & were ready provided. What a refined attention in the Manner of obliging does this shew! I am quite in love with it! much more than the Duchess Dowr. Of Portland's giving £1200 for Sir William Hamilton's fine Vase.[2]

They also provided Mary with an annuity of £300. Surprisingly the Duchess of Portland had not remembered her old friend Mary in her will except for two snuff boxes and two pictures of mice. It was her son the new Duke, realising the paucity of the bequest, who invited Mary to take anything of his mother's she wanted. Typically the only thing Mary would accept was an African weaver bird as a living link with her dead friend. Fanny reports in her Diary on November 30 that year how she finds the bird dead in its cage. The Queen is informed and immediately substitutes one of her weaver birds in its place trusting that Mary with her poor eyesight will not spot the difference. Fanny is less sure! She decides the best course of action is to tell Mary: 'the tears came into her eyes, and she looked at it with great tenderness, and exclaimed, "Don't you, too die in my hands!"'

Through her friendship with Mary, Fanny is drawn more and more into the royal orbit and in 1786 is appointed 'dresser to the Queen' much to Mary's delight and that of Dr Burney. A somewhat reluctant Fanny accepted the position of Second Keeper of the Robes for which she received £200 per year. Fanny was thirty-four and unmarried. She had rejected a proposal in 1775 and in 1784 her romance with a young clergyman, George Cambridge, had ended. Sadly for Fanny it was a disastrous appointment: she had little time to write. Socially she was isolated: she spent interminably boring days waiting on the Queen in dark, cold corridors which affected her health. She also had to endure vicious backbiting from Madame Schwellenberg, one of the Queen's wardrobe women, who constantly complained about Fanny. Added to which the King's mental health was highly unstable causing grave concern. She was to remain in the royal household for five years until her parlous state of health enabled her to resign in 1791. She received a pension of £100 a year.

Hester Chapone by 1786 is fast approaching sixty. Increasingly she is suffering from ill health. She has been nursing Mrs Ogle and staying with John where she is to be found in the summer months until early autumn. The same year her great friend Reverend Burrows dies and is buried at Hadley. Many of the older generation of Bluestockings are either dead – Johnson, Richardson and David Garrick, or ageing – Sir Joshua Reynolds, Elizabeth Carter, Frances Boscawen, who has sold Glan Villa in Colney Hatch and bought a house between Richmond and Kew, Elizabeth Montagu, and the other-worldly Elizabeth Vesey. Mary Delany, the most senior member is eighty-six, almost blind and increasingly frail. Hester Piozzi has been cold-shouldered from polite gatherings and removed to Italy with her youngest daughter and new husband before returning in 1787, having published *Anecdotes of the late Samuel Johnson LL.D.* the previous year. In 1788, the year her beloved and gentle Mary Delany dies, Fanny Burney describes meeting Hester at an assembly given for Fanny by Mrs Ord on January 31. First she is greeted by Mrs Garrick and then by Pepys with whom she discusses Mrs Piozzi's publication of Johnson's letters which Pepys fears may represent him in a less than complimentary light. Sir Joshua Reynolds greets her and is shortly followed by Mrs Montagu:

> Then up came Mrs Chapone, and after most cordially shaking hands with me, "But I hope," she cried, "you are not always to appear only as a comet, to be stared at and then vanish? If you are, let me beg at least to be brushed by your tail, and not hear you have disappeared before my telescope is ready for looking at you![3]

Many of Hester's friends were attending the trial of Warren Hastings[4] who stood accused of misgoverning India. The trial began on February 13 1788, at Westminster Hall and competition for tickets was fierce. It was apparently better than attending the theatre: Edmund Burke,[5] one of the leading political thinkers and orators of the day, made a moving and eloquent speech for the prosecution, ably backed up by his allies: the playwright and MP, Sheridan,[6] and his friend the Whig politician, Charles James Fox.[7] Hannah More and Fanny Burney supported Hastings who would finally be acquitted on all the charges seven years later, in 1795. By November the same year the King, George III, was dangerously ill with a mental disorder and was being treated by Sir Lucas Pepys, the brother of Hester's great friend and confidant. He too was a member of the Bluestocking circle and a good friend of Fanny Burney and Hannah More. With the King unable to govern, a regency crisis was looming but was averted with the King's recovery at the end of the year. Worse was to follow in July 1789 when the Storming of the Bastille in Paris heralded the start of The French Revolution and divided public opinion in England. Fanny Boscawen supported the aristocracy and voiced: 'Licence, anarchy, injustice, robbery and oppression prevail!' as desperate refugees fled to England. Charles James Fox supported both the American and French Revolutions as did the English historian Catherine Macaulay[8] whose perceived scandalous behaviour in her private life so shocked society.

Apparently unshaken by political events Hester continues her 'jaunts' as her brother describes them and in August 1789, having been reassured by the doctor that her ill health is not caused by dropsy, sets off to spend August in Bath with a friend, Mrs Beavior, a widow. She asks John to enquire whether Gilbert White, whose *Natural History of*

Selborne is published that same year, has read Erasmus Darwin's *Loves of the Plants*.[9] When writing to Gilbert, John comments that although Hester admires the poetry 'ye Subject, ah pah! "with the Loves of Flowers," says she, "one might play with one's Fancy; but the Loves of Stamens & Pistills is too much for my strength." ' The following year John's wife, Jane, of whom Hester was so fond and had nursed during and after childbirth, dies and John himself becomes ill and unable to attend services at either the Cathedral or his parishes. He now describes Hester as an invalid 'but a chearful one.'

For Hester the death of her brother, John, in 1791 is an added blow coming so soon after the death of his wife but she remains a solicitous aunt to their four children, especially her eldest niece Jenny to whom she felt a special bond. Her visits to Winchester, where she now stayed with Mrs Ogle at the Deanery, continue. Winters see her back in London in a variety of lodgings. In December 1791 she is lodged at 17, Carlisle Street, Dean Street, from where she sends a charming invitation to Fanny Burney:

> Are you in town, my dear Miss Burney, and do you remember an old soul that used to love your company? If you will give it me next Thursday evening you will meet Pepys, Boscawen &c.; so you may put on your blue stockings. If you have got any boots to walk about in the mornings, I shall like you as well in them.
>
> I hope all the family are well. I need not say that Dr. Burney's company would be an additional pleasure on Thursday. I am, dear madam, your affectionate servant,
>
> H. Chapone.[10]

Fanny Burney was unable to go but came a few days later to a smaller party at which the Pepyses were the only other guests. Hester is delighted by the conversation which Fanny and Pepys engage in and comments to Elizabeth Carter: 'How seldom is it that one gets such a treat of conversation. I find I can still enjoy it when in perfection.' The party did not break up until eleven 'with regret on all sides.'[11]

Elizabeth Montagu continues to throw lavish parties. Fanny reports attending a breakfast party the following year at which four or five hundred people are present but the days of the Bluestocking gatherings for serious intellectual discussion were drawing to a close. Mrs Vesey, for whom Elizabeth Carter and Elizabeth Montagu had expressed such indignation when her second husband's mistress had in 1785 been left well-provided for, while she, his wife, had met with financial neglect, had died in 1791 having become a prisoner to depression and finally a form of dementia.

Meanwhile across the Channel the political situation was worsening with the French Revolution; in August 1792[12] the surrender of Louis XVI and the bloody September massacres sent shock waves across Europe. The King was tried and executed in January 1793 fulfilling the prophecies of Burke.[13] These were stormy times and opinion in England shifted from support for liberal and radical thought to disgust and fear of events across the Channel. At the beginning of February England was once again at war with France.

For Hester the year 1793 brought the death of one of her oldest friends – Gilbert White. Their friendship had initially been built on a light-hearted almost flirtatious tone and developed into a shared love of writing and poetry although Hester could never fully appreciate Gilbert's love of botanical detail. In spite of becoming increasingly frailer she still remained highly interested in having news from her friends – especially Elizabeth Carter who would outlive Hester and died aged eighty-nine in 1806. Elizabeth Montagu, of whom initially Hester had been in such awe, is suffering from failing eyesight which causes Hester to complain to Pepys that she never writes although she hears of her through friends. Elizabeth would die in August 1800, leaving her wealth to her nephew, Matthew Montagu, whom she had adopted and educated. Frances Boscawen, whose love of serious conversation and sensibility appealed to Hester; and William Weller Pepys, whom Hester had steered into marriage, would both outlive her: Fanny would die in 1805 and was reunited with her beloved husband in Cornwall at St Michael Penkival church; Pepys received a baronetcy in 1801 and died in 1825.

The younger Bluestocking members such as Fanny Burney, Hannah More and Laetitia Barbauld, were building on the groundwork laid by the older generation who had initiated a movement which enabled women to be taken more seriously as intellectual equals of men and by doing so enabled them to forge and voice an independent identity. In 1793 Fanny Burney married Alexandre D'Arblay, an impoverished artillery officer and French exile. She continued to be a published author. In 1796 her hugely successful novel *Camilla*, for which Fanny Boscawen had kept a book of subscribers, was published and from the proceeds she and her husband were enabled to build a house, Camilla Cottage, at West Humble, Surrey. She also continued to keep her diary and, when she developed breast cancer, she recorded its progress and her experience in 1811 of a mastectomy, without the benefit of anaesthesia, in all its horrendous detail. Her beloved father, to whose memory she was so loyal, died in 1814 and much later, in 1832, she published memoirs of him. Fanny died aged eighty-seven in

1840 and had seen major political and social changes during her long lifetime. She and Hester Thrale Piozzi, who died in 1821, never picked up their close friendship again.

Chapter 29

'Your irreparable loss'

Hester Chapone's health by 1794 is further declining. She finds the air in London in the heat of the summer suffocating and her strength sapped, making her feel faint. She berates herself for her idleness but much to her joy her niece, Jenny, has been staying with her at her lodgings in Francis street while on business in London for three weeks in June. Hester frets that she has not been able to offer many amusements. She reports to Elizabeth Carter on the noisy celebrations following Lord Howe's victory over the French naval force off Ushant on June 1:

> Her company helped me to support the *miseries* of *rejoicing*, which were really very great, notwithstanding the real joy I partook in Lord Howe's victory. I would willingly have given up one night's rest, but three was hard upon me; and the more so as I suffered a severe fright the first night, when, having heard not a word about rejoicing before I went to bed, I was waked at two o'clock by the most violent knocking, which fully persuaded me the house was on fire. My niece and I met on the stairs, *en chemise*, and by degrees learnt the truth, and saved our windows by hurrying up all the candles we could find. The two following nights we were regularly illuminated; and I, who can trust nobody where fire is to be feared, watched – and started every moment at cannon, guns, pistols, squibs, and crackers, to the no small torment of my unfortunate nerves.[1]

Fortunately for Hester she can still escape London and her lodgings. The summer sees her staying with Mrs Ogle. However, tragedy[2] hits the Ogle family with the news that their third and favourite son has died from yellow fever in the West Indies. It was Hester who broke the news to his mother. Unfortunately the Dean is away in the north and comes hurrying home to be with his wife. Both of them are shattered by his loss and Hester fears for their health. Her nephew, William, who has been made a lieutenant and has been waiting impatiently, finally joins Lord Howe and the fleet adding to Hester's anxieties about his safety whenever there is a heavy gale. The following year Hester confides to Elizabeth that her nights are full of anxieties:

> I have two souls ... I should be glad to know *who* the *two* are that so often disturb my rest with their contentions in the night, while one of them keeps calling the other "coward! idiot!" and I know not what vile names, for suffering the thoughts of fire, robbers, future contingencies, and past griefs to worry the brain, and make the heart beat.[3]

Her pleasure in the written word has not diminished for she and her brother, Thomas, have been exchanging poems for their mutual amusement. Hester has been writing a story for what she refers to as: 'Mrs H. Moore's cheap publications, who I thought must want assistance,' adding, 'but I find she has more composers than she knows what to do with; so I should grudge my trouble, were it not that I know I did it with good intention.' Hannah had by now abandoned writing plays. She was a member of The Clapham Sect which opposed slavery and came under the influence of William Wilberforce. In 1787 she started a programme of opening Sunday schools in the Cheddar area. In 1795 she started producing religious tracts and in 1799 wrote didactically on education.

Hester continues to visit Hadley. Here she delights in the company of Amy Burrows. She recounts enjoying an evening of amateur dramatics in the parlour which includes eighteen children in masquerade costumes and attracts fifty spectators; and she is still enjoying reading widely. Although much frailer she still manages to travel to Winchester and in a letter to Elizabeth Carter, who is now eighty, she reports that she has just returned from a two month long visit there where she had stayed with Mrs Ogle at the Deanery:

> But never was a summer and autumn in which one had so little reason to regret being surrounded with brick and tile; and my good friend carried me an airing every tolerable day, which helped my health, though I cannot boast of it much. I brought a bad cold with me to town, which the fogs and cold will not suffer to get well. Otherwise I think my general health is better than it was a few months ago, and indeed as well as I ought to expect, considering that with so many complaints I have attained the age of man.
>
> It was a great pleasure to me to receive a comfortable account from yourself, which has since been confirmed to me from different hands.

Hester then describes how while there:

> I had great satisfaction in seeing my darling niece established in the happiest manner at Winchester with a husband who seems in every respect calculated to make her happy. My younger niece was on a visit

> to Mrs Ogle the whole time I was there, and we travelled to London together. I found her in poor health and bad spirits; for the loss of her brother affected her so deeply that I almost feared she would sink under it. And it was long before she regained any degree of cheerfulness; but I bless God she is now recovered in health, and much mended in spirits.

The two nieces are of course Jenny, to whom she wrote *Letters on the Improvement of the Mind* more than twenty years previously, and Hester with whom she never had quite the same rapport but who would later prove to be so solicitous. Tragically their brother, William who was by 1797 captain of the sloop *Hermes* in the Royal Navy, was drowned with the entire crew, confirming Hester's worst fears for him. Hester continues:

> I was pleased to hear that you, as well as my dear Mrs Burrows, [Amy Burrows] were able to pursue the pleasant and healthful employment of a gardener. She worked very hard whilst I was with her, and though she cannot do the same this season, she assures me she has preserved a good share of health through all the bad weather. I was also well pleased to see that you were no longer reduced to seek amusement only in novels. I have surfeited on them and am 'supt full of horrors.' Can you tell me of something rather more rational without being too deep for a feeble brain? I suppose you have read (for everyone has) 'Pursuits of Literature;'[4] and have felt the same indignation I did at the author, for making a she dog of Mrs Montagu. And the same contempt for his taste, his spleen, envy, and nonsense in that line which displays them all. "Her yelp, though feeble, and her sandals blue."
>
> A she dog in sandals is not more absurd than a feeble yelp applied to one of the ablest as well as most ingenious criticisms that ever was written. Indisposed as I was against the author, by this and some other instances of ill nature, I cannot but acknowledge that some of his notes and prefaces testify a laudable zeal on the right side both in politics and religion, which should mollify his scurrility and indecency. – Poor Doctor Warton is severely dealt with: how far he deserves it I know not, for I have not seen his last publication, but should be grieved if he had disgraced his later years by any thing like what this coarse satirist alledges [sic]. I suppose nobody knows who he is. The secret seems well kept, and with reason, for he has great cause to dread the vengeance of so many wounded without provocation.
>
> My little world are gathering fast together; but alas in winter I am cooped up, and can seldom see them. I hope you will not fail us after Christmas, and that fate will be more propitious to our meetings than last year, but whether in presence or absence, I must be ever my dear Mrs Carter's affectionate and obliged friend,
>
> H. Chapone.[5]

Winchester is now more central to Hester: her great friend, her cousin,

Mrs Ogle is there with all her warm hospitality; her newly married niece, Jenny, is settled there with her husband, the Reverend Benjamin Jeffreys, a fellow of Winchester College, whom she married in 1797 when she was almost forty; and Hester's widowed brother, Thomas, joins the Ogles each autumn when Hester is also there. Hester is planning to settle in Winchester to be closer to Jenny who is expecting her first child in March 1799. But ill fortune strikes not once but twice. First her last remaining brother, Thomas, the eldest of her family and to whom she was deeply attached died suddenly in February 1799. He and his wife, Pressy, who had died the previous year had remained close to Hester when she was in London and had provided sanctuary when Hester became so ill after John Chapone's death. The following month her beloved niece, Jenny, died after suffering a stillbirth. For Hester it was a terrible blow. She had so looked forward to living close to Jenny and welcoming the next generation. To add to her woes the Dean and Mrs Ogle left Winchester and moved to their property, Kirkley Hall in Northumberland. Hester returned to lodgings in London once more. Fanny D'Arblay having heard the news of her niece's tragic death wrote to her on April 4 from Camilla Cottage at West Humble:

> It was from your own affecting account, my dear Madam, that I learned of your irreparable loss, though a letter by the same post from my sister Burney confirmed the melancholy intelligence. I will not attempt to say with what extreme concern I have felt it. Your "darling niece," though I must now be glad I had never seen, I always fancied I had known from the lively idea you had enabled me, in common with all others, to form of what she ought to be. If this second terrible trial, and the manner in which you have supported it, had not shown me my mistake, I should have feared the terrible expression on your countenance – which I cannot forget – in our last mournful interview, that the cup was already full! But it is not for nothing you have been gifted, – or that so early you were led to pray "the ill you might not shun to bear." Misfortunes of this accumulated – I had nearly said desolating – nature, always of late years sharpen to me the horrors of that part of the French revolution which, to lessen the dread of guilt, gives death to eternal sleep. What alleviation can there be for sufferers who have imbibed such doctrine? I want to disperse among them an animated translation of false principles, beautiful conviction, and final consolation of Fidelia. For since, in this nether sphere, with all our best hopes alive of times to come,
>
> Ev'n Virtue sighs, while poor Affection mourns
> The blasted comforts of the desert heart,

> what must sorrow be where calamity can see no opening to future light? And where friends, when separated, can mark no haven for a future reunion, but where all terminates for ever in the poor visible grave? – against which all our conceptions and perceptions so entirely revolt, that I, for one, can never divest the idea of annihilation from despair.
>
> I read with much more pleasure than surprise what you say of Mr Pepys: I should have been disappointed indeed had he proved a "summer friend." Yet I have found many more such, I confess, than I had dreamed of in my poor philosophy, since my retirement from the broad circle of life has drawn aside a veil which, till then, had made profession wear the same semblance as friendship. But few, I believe, escape some of these lessons, which are not, however, more mortifying in the expectations they destroy than gratifying in those they confirm. You will be sure, dear Madam, but I hope not angrily, of one honour I am here venturing to give myself.[6]

After initialling the letter 'F. D'A' Fanny adds: 'M. d'A entreats you accept his sincerest respects.'

Jenny's death was the final blow. It was too much for Hester to bear and sadly her health deteriorated rapidly. It was not only her physical health which was affected but also her mental state. She was seventy-two. It was decided by her family that she should live with her surviving niece, Hester, at Winchester. However, with her debility rapidly overtaking her, a further move to Hadley with her niece was made in the autumn of 1800. Here she was near to Amy Burrows who had been her friend for so many years and had been such a support, with her sister Mary, after the death of John Chapone. However, such was the rapid progress in Hester's physical and mental debility that she was largely confined to her room upstairs. Sadly at times she was lost to the outside world and failed to recognise her niece or Amy Burrows or Mr Cottrell, who had succeeded the Reverend Burrows at Hadley, and showed great solicitude for her, visiting regularly. By October 1801 she had become a total invalid and her lively and enquiring mind was now clouded. She continued to be cared for devotedly by her niece and Amy Burrows who brought what comfort they could to her other world. On Christmas Day 1801 she fell into a doze and, at eight o'clock that evening, died in the arms of her niece, with Amy Burrows beside her. She was seventy-four.

Chapter 30

'enlighten my understanding'

Hester was buried at Hadley. After her death this prayer was discovered in her writing:

> O Gracious Father of the universe! Behold thy creature humbly imploring thy forgiveness of her numerous past transgressions, and thy compassion for her present faulty dispositions, and her defects in all those virtues that must raise her to a better condition. Turn not from me, O my God, the light of thy countenance, nor take from me the blessed influence of thy spirit! – enlighten my understanding – strengthen my faith – purify and invigorate the desires of my heart towards that which is good. Save and deliver me from evil, O Lord God most holy! Most beneficent and merciful Creator! Consign me not to destruction – cast me not out from thy presence and the society of good spirits, – but grant me all the assistance I stand in need of, to become what I ought to be, and to make the best use of that short period of life, which may still remain for me in this world, after all the time I have wasted or misemployed. Thou knowest all my weaknesses and wants, and all the infirmities of my soul and body. Help me O my Father to obey thee and to love thee as I ought. Raise my dull spirit to such true reverence and adoration, – such gratitude for past benefits – and such hope in thy future mercies, as may best recommend the humble homage of my prayers and thanksgivings. And grant that the time may come when my heart shall be as sincere and warm in these affections as my frail nature is capable of. Imperfect as they are, may thy goodness however accept them, and, through the merits and mediation of my blessed redeemer, bring me to that state where I shall be good and happy, and praise thy glorious name for ever and ever. Amen![1]

An anonymous obituary appeared in *The Gentleman's Magazine* 71:

> At Hadley, in her 75th year, deserving a high rank on the roll of British literati, Mrs H. Chapone; to whom the literary world is indebted for many valuable works on education and elegant pieces of poetry. Her pen was always directed to moral purposes and virtue; far from shewing repulsive austerity, her representations were distinguished by

> endearing graces. Her publications, which are admirably calculated to form the infant mind to virtue and piety are, Letters on the Improvement of the Mind, addressed to a young Lady, 1773, 2 vols. 12mo. These very sensible letters were, soon after their publication, honoured with a very distinguished popularity. The subjects of them are, Religion; the study of the scriptures; the regulation of the heart; temper; oeconomy; accomplishments; geography; chronological and historical reading. They are eminently worthy the attention of the younger part of the fair sex, as the instructions which they offer tend to render them equally amiable and useful in every situation and circumstance of life.
>
> Miscellanies in Prose and Verse, 1775, 12mo. They contain observations on affection and simplicity; on conversation; and on enthusiasm and indifference in religion; the prose part concluding with the very instructive story of Fidelia, which first appeared in Dr Hawkesworth's Adventurer. The poems (except the translation from Metastatio's celebrated ode on Summer and an Italian sonnet) were the productions of early youth, and afford a very honourable testimony of that youth's cultivation. Among them the verses to Stella have peculiar merit.
>
> Letter to a new-married Lady, 1777, 12mo. This last publication gives plain and seasonable advice to newly-married ladies, and, by inculcating obedience to their husbands, was thought at the time of its appearance, by no means superfluous.
>
> Mrs C. is also supposed to have been a contributor to the Rambler, and particularly to have written the billets in No. X.
>
> This ingenious lady was one of the oldest friends of Mrs Carter, the amiable and learned translator of Epictetus, on which she addressed to her a poem characterized by a noble zeal of friendship, strength of imagination, and pious sublimity.
>
> Mrs Chapone was the daughter of Thomas Mulso, esq. of an antient [sic] family at Twywell, co. Northhampton, and sister of the late Thomas Mulso, esq. author of Calistus and Sophronius, who died of the stone, Feb.7, 1799, aged 78 (LXXIX. 254.), having married a sister of Gen. Prescott, and of John Mulso, M.A. of Oriel college, prebendary of Winchester, who died 1791, to whose son his uncle left his small paternal estate. She married, Dec. 30, 1760, Mr Chapone, attorney, of Clement's inn, who died Sept.17, 1761, leaving one daughter, Augusta, married, 1795, to Mr. Thresher, of the Strand.[2]

The attribution of a daughter to Hester and John appears nowhere else and must be mistaken.

Her reputation was firmly established as one of the early Bluestockings. Unlike Elizabeth Carter, who had the benefit of an excellent education for a young woman of her time, Hester was largely self-educated. She lived by her principles and had married for love. After the tragic loss of her husband so soon after their marriage, for which they had been made to wait for six long years until her father relented, she recovered her health and retained her independence refusing to become a governess. Her lively mind and intelligence brought her into the Bluestocking circle where she had contact with some of the leading literary figures and leading members of society of her day. With the support and encouragement from members of this circle and the patronage of Elizabeth Montagu she had published a best-selling book on the education of young women. *Letters on the Improvement of the Mind* moved forward the education of young women by encouraging rational thought as a key tenet in her system. But more than that she was loved as a person by her friends and family. Fanny D'Arblay wrote in 1832:

> But though the dignity of her mind demanded, as it deserved, the respect of some return to the visits which her love of society induced her to pay, it was téte-á-téte alone that gave pleasure to the intercourse with Mrs Chapone; her sound understanding, her sagacious observations, her turn to humour, and the candour of her affectionate nature, all then came into play without effort: and her ease of mind, when freed from the trammels of doing the honours of reception, seemed to soften off, even to herself, her corporeal infirmities. It was thus that she struck Dr Burney with the sense of her worth; and seemed portraying in herself the original example whence the precepts had been drawn, for forming the unsophisticated female character, that are displayed in the author's *Letters on the Improvement of the Mind*.[3]

Hester had made herself: not content to settle for the secondary role of the eighteenth century young woman she had set about building an education for herself by reading widely and systematically. She had taken on one of the great literary figures, Samuel Richardson, and argued her position well, earning his respect and had not been overawed by the mighty Johnson. Through her writing she established a position for herself in the Bluestocking circle. What attracted people to her was her lively intelligence which she so readily admitted made her love argument. She also possessed the gift of not taking herself too seriously as her correspondence with Elizabeth Carter and her light-hearted relationship with Gilbert White reveal. She was capable of strong emotional attachments, was a loyal and sympathetic friend and had strong principles on which she built her life especially after the tragic death of the man she had fallen so deeply and suddenly in love with. Her great gift of writing sympathetically in a highly readable style which reflected the popular epistolary form of the period brought her fame and financial independence. She helped pave the way for the second generation of the Bluestockings; a movement in which she represented the more serious and less flamboyant side. That she was much loved by her immediate family, whom she cared for with empathy, and, by those who knew her well, is abundantly shown in the letters which her brother John wrote to Gilbert White and by Fanny Burney's comments when she first met Hester Chapone.

Hester did not seek to break the system: rather she sought to bring improvement in the status and opportunity for women from within it. In this she succeeded admirably.

Part Six

Epilogue

The bluestocking is the most odious character in society … she sinks wherever she is placed, like the yolk of an egg, to the bottom, and carries the filth with her.

William Hazlitt[1]

THE

ANTI-CHAPONE,

OR

Grandmothers in the Wrong:

PROVED BY INCONTESTIBLE FACTS,

IN

A LETTER

FROM

AUNT LORINCIA, IN TOWN,

TO HER

YOUNG NIECE IN THE COUNTRY.

1810.

"Each Wit may praise it, for her own dear sake,
"And hint She wrote it, if the thing should take."

ADDISON.

PRINTED BY

BRODIE, DOWDING, AND LUXFORD,

SALISBURY.

Title page of The Anti-Chapone, *1810*

Chapter 31

The Backlash of Satire: The Anti-Chapone, or Grandmothers in the Wrong[1]

In 1798 the Reverend Richard Polwhele[2] published *The Unsex'd Females*. The poem attacks Mary Wollstonecraft's radical views on British society in *A Vindication of the Rights of Men* and in *A Vindication of the Rights of Woman*.[3] Wollstonecraft argues that women had been assigned a subordinate role to men, denied the benefits of education and thus the opportunity to develop rational thought. For a woman to enter onto the masculine stage of politics, history or radical criticism of British society was, at the end of the eighteenth century, regarded with hostility. The liberal views prevalent in Britain earlier in the century had been polarised, shaken by events in the last quarter of the eighteenth century. The American Declaration of Independence in 1776; the storming of the Bastille in July 1789 and the ongoing threat of a French invasion by Napoleon's troops made those of radical republican sympathies such as Mary Wollstonecraft and Catharine Macaulay suspect. Macaulay, like Wollstonecraft, had displayed an immodest disregard as to what was acceptable in her private life and had been shunned by polite society when she married at the age of forty-seven, William Graham, a relatively uneducated young man of twenty-one.

For Polwhele, Jacobin women who did not abide by Christian values of marriage, modesty and virtuous behaviour in society were beyond the pale. *The Unsex'd Females* invites the reader to:

> Survey with me, what ne'er our fathers saw,
> A female band despising NATURE'S law,
> As "proud defiance" flashes from their arms,

And vengeance smothers all their softer charms.
I shudder at the new unpictur'd scene,
Where unsex'd woman vaunts the imperious mien.

Unsurprisingly Wollstonecraft 'whom no decorum checks' is named in this category of excoriated women. Polwhele attacks her relationships with Henry Fuseli, the painter, who was married, and Gilbert Imlay, the American revolutionary, with whom she lived and whose child she bore. Also named and shamed are: Anna Letitia Barbauld, Mary Robinson, Charlotte Smith, Helen Maria Williams, Ann Yearsley, Mary Hays, and the artists Angelica Kauffman and Emma Crewe. Ranged against these women writers and artists he places exemplars of virtuous women writers who accepted their place and role in society and held Christian belief as central to their lives. Not surprisingly Hester Chapone and many of the Bluestocking women are included: Elizabeth Carter, Elizabeth Montagu, Hester Piozzi, Fanny Burney and Hannah More are all lauded:

Come, join, with wonted smiles, a kindred train,
Who, court, like you, the muse; nor court in vain.
Mark where the sex have oft, in ancient days,
To modest Virtue, claim'd a nation's praise;
Chas'd from the public scene the fiend of strife,
And shed a radiance o'er luxurious life;
In silken fetters bound the obedient throng
And soften'd despots by the power of song.

Polwhele in his notes on *The Unsex'd Females* pays tribute to Hester Chapone's *Letters on the Improvement of the Mind* as being: 'incontestable proofs of her ingenuity, and the goodness of her heart.' However, he cannot restrain himself from then waspishly commenting: 'But Mrs C. lately made an effort on the harp; an instrument which (she ought to have considered) requires gracefulness and ease. She was deficient in both: and her notes were weak and harsh. I was sorry to see so excellent an instructor of youth, expose herself by an affectation of things beyond her reach.'

It is the first category of women, castigated by Polwhele, that the anonymous author of *The Anti-Chapone, or Grandmothers in the Wrong* holds up as a model for education of young girls. Published in 1810, thirty-seven years after *Letters on the Improvement of the Mind*, it is written in the form of a letter from an Aunt Lorincia, in town, to her young niece Henrietta, in the country.

AN

INTRODUCTORY ADDRESS

TO MOTHERS.

IN sly disguise I here step forth,
And offer youth some chicken broth,
As if for infants fit;
Yet, mix'd with pepper and cayenne,
Quite strong enough for any man,
And deem it timely wit.

For tho' this broth is handed up
In trifling form of baby cup,
'Tis potent; and may prove
(If well digested) wholesome food,
And do infinity of good
To those you really love.

The **AUTHOR.**

"Increasing evils strongly me entice
"To laugh at follies or to lash at vice."

DRYDEN.

The Anti-Chapone: riddle for the name of the pseudonymous author, Aunt Lorincia

At the foot of the title page of the The Anti-Chapone is a couplet attributed to Addison. In fact the anonymous author has taken the liberty to change the gender of the pronouns from masculine in the original to feminine. It is taken from the prologue to *The Drummer, or The Haunted House* a comedy by Joseph Addison first performed at Drury Lane in 1713. It was published with a preface by Richard Steele in which he states: 'It had been some years in the hands of the author, and falling under my perusal, I thought so well of it, that I persuaded him to make some additions and alterations to it, and let it appear upon the stage.' However, Steele may possibly have contributed to it and some authorities doubt whether it was written by either Addison or Steele.

This is followed in *The Anti-Chapone* by 'An Introductory Address to Mothers' in the form of a riddle of twelve lines which conceals the author's true identity. At the foot of the address is a couplet attributed to Dryden: the second line is from Dryden's translation of *The Fifth Satire of Persius*. I have been unable to trace the provenance of the first line. 'In sly disguise' echoes Sly's strategy in *The Taming of the Shrew*.

The letter sets out to debunk the values espoused by Hester Chapone. It is addressed to Henrietta, aged just seven years old. It opens with an attack on the outmoded values of the old system which Henrietta's parents and grandparents still support. It continues:

> Your parents are very worthy people in their way, and *mean well* I have no doubt, but when they insist on virtue, morality, and decorum, &. to be necessary to your well doing in life, they only prove an ignorance of the world, and they inculcate false notions. O rather believe *me*, who know better, when I inform you such ideas will conduct you into the dark paths of error.

Aunt Lorincia's advice is based on moulding her niece's conduct so that she may be 'admired, caressed, and applauded; in short, to make a prosperous figure in life:' in short the antithesis of Hester Chapone's advice. The first step is for her niece to discount anything she has read in her Juvenile Library and ignore 'what any old woman may say or write, in the form of advice, built on the *old* principles.' These are identified as: being wise but not vain; content without 'panegyrists'; and to be useful rather than seeking celebrity. Lorincia continues that Henrietta's grandmother has also probably suggested that she should:

> … compare, to think, combine, methodise, and discriminate … She will probably remark, that you should study *truth*; "bring your imagination under proper dominion, and learn to reject what is dazzling, if it be not solid; and to prefer what is just to what is striking or new;" in short, recommend, with a celebrated authoress, that kind of knowledge "more fitted for home consumption than for foreign exportation."
>
> I GRANT that all these maxims were good in the days of your Great Grandmothers, but they are now *errors*; and you will find, as you grow up and look around you, that such sentiments are the very height of absurdity, and the truth of them contradicted every hour.

Instead Aunt Lorincia advocates:

> let your grand study be display. Let the decoration of your person, the well forming of your shape, the setting off every limb to advantage, be your daily toil. … No, let *display* be your object; it is not now sufficient to dance well and genteelly, to sing harmoniously, or to play agreeably, – No, you must strike the eye, astonish the ear, captivate the senses, and fascinate the soul!

Modesty in all things was one of Hester's key principles in moulding suitable conduct in her young niece prior to her entry into polite society. Aunt Lorincia is having none of it. In order to facilitate the development of this boldness in company, which Lorincia advocates for Henrietta, she prescribes a two stage plan:

> First, I would have you take every opportunity of mounting a coach-box before you are eight years old, and by early accustoming yourself to exhibit your legs in the ascendings and descendings, it will soon render you easy on that little point of delicacy.

Getting in and out of carriages with modesty was an important point of etiquette and one which was taught at the London boarding school for girls, known as the Ladies' Eton in Queen's Square, in the eighteenth century. To facilitate both ease and protection of modesty in this procedure 'with calmness and grace, and without any unnecessary display of their ankles,' the school used the body of a carriage: the young women could practice this all important and delicate art in relative privacy. Manners and deportment were given preference over academic subjects.[4] Advocating that Henrietta should display her legs in such an unseemly manner flouted convention and would have been guaranteed to shock.

In order for her niece to overcome any shyness and bashfulness the second stage of Lorincia's plan is for her niece to sit next to her father's coachman and talk to him. This, she argues, will enable her to develop unblushing effrontery and will also enable her to learn how to drive horses and in 'the process of time, be enabled to drive your own coachman, groom, or husband.' Many women did drive their chaises and report the exhilaration in doing so but they did not sit with a male coachman and engage him in conversation. Elizabeth Montagu loved being driven by her companion, Dorothea Gregory, in her one horse 'Whiskey' but she would have most certainly drawn the line at sitting with an unrelated male driver of such an inferior social class. Hester made a key distinction between modesty and bashfulness: the first was to be applauded but the latter was regarded as an awkwardness which needed to be conquered when in polite society. Needless to say it did not involve engaging the coachman in conversation or showing too much leg. By the time Henrietta is ten her aunt assumes she will have learnt the finer points of dancing and be able to contort her young body into various graceful attitudes and to play the piano, play the harp and sing 'like a Signora.' Lorincia also recommends that Henrietta be allowed to attend operas, plays and balls at the tender age of ten in order to:

> ... remove every atom of bashfulness, that awkward bane to polite life; and I will venture to hope, that by the time you attain twelve years complete, you will have much to boast over those children who are brought up, by mistaken parents, to be modest, diffident, gentle, feminine, and unassuming. Unfortunately! they will never succeed in life; but you, my dear HENRIETTA, will, through my means, I trust, steer clear of all this nonsense.

Mrs Delany would not have approved of one so young appearing in such a public domain.

Next Lorincia turns her attention to attacking what she argues are the outmoded ideas of Hester:

> Mrs Chapone, (in her Letters on Education,) will assure you, that a young person should not be careless of blame, nor indifferent to the esteem of the wise and prudent, – that the being so is a want of rectitude, and that *discretion* should be her guardian.

Letters on the Improvement of the Mind was still a popular conduct book in 1810 with two new editions appearing that year as well as an edition bound in with Gregory's *A Father's Legacy to his Daughters*. It continued to be published, often bound in with Gregory and Lady Pennington's *A Mother's Advice to her Absent Daughters* well into the middle of the nineteenth century. Chapone's ideas were clearly not outmoded and Aunt Lorincia's strictures are calculated to shock. But Lorincia goes further:

> Yes, my dear Niece, you will soon see, and will, I hope, hasten to imbibe the *true notion*, which is, to be daringly bold, – to speak fearlessly to the men, – to talk and laugh loud, nor ever encourage the least timidity, it is a very great inconvenience.

Thackeray's Becky Sharp would heartily agree. Hester cautioned her niece to show great delicacy in her behaviour towards the male of the species, warning her to avoid any contact with men of loose morals or impertinent behaviour who could besmirch her character and ruin her chances of a good marriage. Aunt Lorincia returns to this subject a little later in her letter after having given a brief run through the academic study that her niece is to follow.

The subjects to be studied are: Chemistry, Botany, Mathematics, Philosophy and Astronomy, Mineralogy, Mythology, Geology, Chronology, Physiology, Conchology, Nosology, Zoology, Ornithology, Ichthyology and Craniology. History, Religion and Geo-graphy are omitted, as is any mention of literature. Hester placed Religion as central to her scheme of education which, combined with a chronological study of major historical events, would give her niece a grasp of their significance. Hester also included learning French and Italian which Lorincia totally ignores. Instead Lorincia urges Henrietta not to skim over these subjects she has recommended for study but to dive into them and not to fear 'to utter "sonorous periods and cumbrous terms of science."' When it comes to the study of Botany Henrietta is not to limit herself to the learning of botanical terms: 'No, I would have you fearlessly dash into the whole system, and astonish your Grandmother with all the mysteries of that sublime subject.' This leads Lorincia on to the study of Anatomy as this will aid the study of modelling and drawing. The latter is not to be limited to merely drawing flowers and landscapes. Henrietta is exhorted to draw classical figures, especially the nude male form in all its beauty so that she can hold forth on the merits of classical figures to her, no doubt amazed and shocked, grandmothers.

Making a good marriage is central to Lorincia's grand scheme for Henrietta and with this in mind she proscribes Hester Chapone's rules for conduct and replaces them with her own:

> In a word, observe throughout your studies that your grand object be to strike, to fascinate, to display, to captivate. I could show you in this great metropolis the enviable effects of such conduct, and prove to you how far preferable to a modest and diffident one. Do not many of our noblemen and gentlemen take their wives from the Theatre, Sadler's Wells &c.? and they are men of education; they have every advantage in life "to know, to compare, to discern, to discriminate, and to understand;" they therefore must surely be competent to judge what is right, and they select such women because they display talents, (there can be no other reason); and these discriminating nobles overlook and reject quiet, modest women. Can your Grandmother deny that fact? – Certainly not;– and when you make your *debût* [sic] in Town, I will shew you, daily, women totally opposite to all what Mrs Chapone recommends young girls to be,-women who cannot boast, either by nature or by education, any of those qualities which that *supposed clever* lady wishes young creatures to find their happiness in the possession of, or to be studious in acquiring, and when acquired to be careful of preserving; and yet, I repeat it, I will shew you young women thus *deficient*, (as Hannah Moore [sic] would describe them,) who were chosen by men of rank,-yes, were preferred to modest women for wives.

She points out that, armed with these charms, women are able to lure away husbands, captivating 'Princes, Ministers, Generals, Admirals, and many more' and, goes on to say, that 'these seducing fair' benefited from fortunes which should rightfully have been bequeathed to the wives. Henrietta is not to worry about falling on hard times because even when she has lost her youth and beauty she will still have the tricks of the trade and be able to charm men to give her small fortunes. Display is everything. Times have changed since her grandmother's day. Men no longer seek a wife who is content to be subservient but prefer companions who display strength of mind. She urges Henrietta to chose a husband on the basis of wealth and rank and if 'otherwise suitable, nothing else need be so strictly attended to.' Parental advice on marital happiness is to be ignored especially when it concerns being a virtuous wife. Lorincia goes further:

> … there are many meek and amiable wives, abounding in modesty and good sense, whose manners are inspired by affection, but who are deserted for the profligate and violent tempered! Daily, may be seen *un*virtuous wives, who prove crowns to their husbands, gaining them fortunes by means of their infidelity.

She continues that nowadays men seek immoral women and 'prove by their conduct their preference of them, for sooner than marry a virtuous girl they take great pains to render such the reverse, and then marry her.'

Hester's views on the subject were the complete antithesis to those of the indomitable fictional Lorincia: Hester revered the institution and sanctity of marriage and condemned promiscuous behaviour. Lorincia reassures Henrietta:

> … that if after a season, you should ever be tempted to break the seventh commandment, do not therefore imagine, although your Grandmothers will make dreadful faces at your conduct, yet do not imagine that you will be scorned or rejected by all society, and be doomed to sigh in solitude severe,-O NO! those are the highly ridiculous ways of old.

She continues that if Henrietta is rich and titled then society will not ostracize her provided she gives balls, concerts and masquerades. There now follows a dire warning that if Henrietta should chose to follow a mode of conduct as recommended by her grandmother then Lorincia washes her hands of her. The result will be that her modesty and lack of dazzling display in society will consign her future to a life of retirement in a distant provincial town where she will 'mope out your days in blessed singleness and single blessedness, for such are not sought for here, believe me.' Henrietta is warned that modern young men are now 'more refined' in their taste. A view which Henrietta's grandmother would describe as being depraved and one which Hester

Chapone would most certainly have endorsed. This Lorincia ascribes to her grandmother's ignorance of 'phraseology, which knowledge, by the bye, I forgot to insert amidst the other "ologys."'

Having held up Hester Chapone's key elements in her rules of conduct to ridicule as being outmoded and misguided in the modern world Lorincia saves her most deadly salvo till last by attacking Hester's cornerstone: namely religion.

> If, indeed, it should so happen that, young as you are, you should have any idea of Religion (as may be the case), and if you are a candidate for another world, why, I confess, it puts a full stop to my *present-worldly advice*. ... ... *Even* this Letter will be deemed of no value, and its contents and sentiments be unheeded! For in that case I can have no hopes, and shall leave you to your fate, withdrawing all my meditated assistance in your progress through life; for you will thereby prove yourself, alas! too genuine a bud of the parent tree, too truly related to your Father and Mother, and quite unworthy this inestimable advice, offered you by your
>
> Well-meaning, and
>
> Affectionate Aunt,
>
> ***LORINCIA.***
>
> IRON-RAIL HOUSE
>
> 1810.

Just over twenty-nine pages in length the letter lampoons all the values so important in the polite society of Hester's day and the society for which Amelia Sedley has been prepared at Miss Pinkerton's Academy in Chiswick Mall. Thackeray's social satire *Vanity Fair* was published in monthly instalments in 1847-8, some thirty-seven years after the anonymous *The Anti-Chapone or Grandmothers in the Wrong* which debunks Hester Chapone's model of education for young women.

Satire flourished in the eighteenth century in literature, although for published women authors like Fanny Burney it was a genre that held high risks. She was advised by both 'Daddy' Crisp and her father not to continue with her satirical play *The Witlings*[5] which she was working on in 1778-79. In it Fanny had satirised the Bluestockings. Lady Smatter and her 'Esprit Club' and Mrs Sapient were based on Elizabeth Montagu and Mrs Thrale and were easily identifiable as such. As Fanny was now a member of the Bluestocking club and had their support, if she published she would have placed herself in an invidious position. Fanny bowed to their advice and the play in fact remained unpublished until 1995. In 1802 her comic play *The Woman-Hater* was completed, in which the tyrannised daughter rejects the improving books she is made to read with the cry: 'decamp, Mrs

Chapone!' Male writers like Sheridan satirised the manners of the time and women's education did not escape. Sheridan's play *The Rivals* (1775) has Sir Anthony Absolute questioning Mrs Malaprop as to what she would have 'a woman know'. She answers:

> Observe me, Sir Anthony – I would by no means wish a daughter of mine to be a progeny of learning; I don't think so much learning becomes a young woman; for instance – I would never let her meddle with Greek, or Hebrew, or Algebra, or Simony, – or Fluxions, or Paradoxes, or such inflammatory branches of learning – neither would it be necessary for her to handle any of your mathematical, astronomical, diabolical instruments; – But, Sir Anthony, I would send her at nine years old, to a boarding-school, in order to learn a little ingenuity and artifice – Then, Sir, she should have a supercilious knowledge in accounts; and as she grew up, I would have her instructed in geometry, that she might know something of the contagious countries ...

Sheridan has Lydia Languish, the romantic heroine in *The Rivals*, hiding her copies of the novelists Fielding and Smollett and pretending to read *Letters on the Improvement of the Mind* when her aunt, Mrs Malaprop, interrupts her. The opinion of writers in the nineteenth century was no kinder. Byron produced *The Blues: A Literary Eclogue* (1821) in which the character Lady Bluebottle is based on Elizabeth Montagu. Visual satire was merciless and women were open to attack on the political front and the social front. The Bluestockings did not escape the satirical eye of Rowlandson in his portrayal of the movement in 1815 entitled *Breaking up of the Blue Stocking Club* which depicts a scene of mayhem with overweight ladies attacking each other with whatever tea table utensils are at hand! The days of the Bluestockings were over.

But who was 'Aunt Lorincia?' Was the author male or female? The 'She/her' substitution might offer a clue. There are several women candidates but evidence is scant. Wollstonecraft was long dead; Fanny D'Arblay was living in France and suffering from cancer. Of the possible men, Hazlitt lived close to Salisbury, where the book was published, and was often visited by Lamb; Cobbett, in *Rural Rides* later railed against Brode, Dowding and Luxford, the Salisbury publishers of *The Anti-Chapone*; 'pepper and cayenne' might suggest the Anti-Jacobin writers Arthur Cayley and Richard Penn who had family in Salisbury.

I favour Richard Brinsley Sheridan: do she/her and 'in sly' point to his name? But most of my evidence is circumstantial. In addition to his reference to Chapone in *The Rivals*, Sheridan's mother, Frances, was a

Breaking up of the Blue Stocking Club: Thomas Rowlandson, 1815

literary contemporary of Hester Chapone, and his first wife, Elizabeth Linley, a singer, was also a Bluestocking. Chapone was close to the Ogle family with whom she often stayed in Winchester. Sheridan's 19-year-old second wife, whom he married in 1794, was Esther Jane Ogle, their daughter (1776-1817). Known as 'Hecca' by Sheridan theirs had been a rapid courtship which had not met with approval of her brother, Richard. Her father, Dr Newton Ogle, had misgivings about Sheridan's financial affairs and no doubt about Sheridan's reputation for philandering and drinking. Chapone, in 1793, when Esther and Sheridan, first met, was in reasonable health and may well have been privy to Ogle's concerns. The matter was resolved with 'the establishment of a trust for her, comprised of her £5,000 dowry and £15,000 in the 3 per cents raised by Sheridan'.[6] There are two further connections to Sheridan in the choice of the name 'Henrietta' in *The Anti-Chapone*. Thomas, Sheridan's son, by his first wife, married Caroline Henrietta Callender in 1805. Sheridan was delighted by this young woman and described her in glowing terms. Tantalisingly there is little information about a Louisa Henrietta Sheridan[7] who edited and wrote much of the annual, *The Comic Offering; or Ladies' Melange of Literary Mirth*, 1831-35. Could she have been the niece, 'Henrietta'?

Aunt Lorincia is in good satirical company: an anagram of LORINCIA is of course IRONICAL, perhaps an ironical taunt. Whether

Hester Chapone would have been amused had she been alive is doubtful. Her education system in *Letters on the Improvement of the Mind* for her beloved niece, Jenny, was based on the eighteenth century values of modesty, virtue and becoming a useful member of society: a far cry from the wanton behaviour which Aunt Lorincia encourages her niece, Henrietta, to espouse; far less radical in outlook than Mary Wollstonecraft's view that women's follies were the result of the tyranny of man: that once freed from this oppression they would then fully enjoy the rights which had been denied them for so long. What Hester did achieve was a shift in educational outlook: namely that women were capable of rational thought if given the opportunity and benefit of a more structured and wider education. Thus women could achieve a greater parity of opportunity and freedom of choice in a society which had been governed for too long by paternalism and hence the over-restriction of women. This greater equality need not preclude women from being good wives to husbands of their own choice nor of fulfilling their role as mothers to the next generation of more enlightened young girls.

Notes

Part One : Growing Up

Chapter 1: 'the admirable Mrs Chapone.'

1 William Makepeace Thackeray (1811-63) Writer, published *Vanity Fair* in serial parts starting in January 1847.
2 For an approximation of monetary value today I have used www.measuringworth.com which provides equivalent values as RPI (UK Retail Price Index) and Average Earnings in the UK: a cost of £100 in 1750 and 1800 would now be £14,400 and £5,400 respectively RPI; an annuity of £100 then would provide £150,000 and £80,000 a year respectively. Mrs Pinkerton's invoice for £93 4s 0d in her day would now be about £7,000 RPI.
3 Elizabeth Carter (1717-1806) Classicist, writer and member of the Bluestocking circle.
4 Samuel Richardson (1689-1761) Printer and writer. Three epistolary novels: *Pamela; or Virtue Rewarded* (1740-41), *Clarissa; or the History of a Young Lady* (1747-48), *The History of Sir Charles Grandison* (1753-54).
5 Richard 'Beau' Nash (1674-1762) Leader of fashion, Master of Ceremonies at both Bath and Tunbridge Wells.
6 Joseph Addison (1672-1719).
7 Trevelyan, G M: *History of England* (Longman Group, London 1973).
8 Elizabeth Montagu, née Robinson (1718-1800) Patron of the arts, hostess and leading figure in the Bluestocking Circle.
9 Admiral Edward Boscawen (1711-61) A Lord of Admiralty, Privy Councillor and MP.
10 James Cook (1728-79) Navigator and explorer, died in Hawaii on his third Pacific voyage.
11 Joseph Banks (1743-1820) Naturalist and explorer, President of the Royal Society (1778) and Director of the Royal Botanic Garden at Kew.
12 Robert Adam (1728-92) Made the grand tour in 1754, classical architect and leader of the Classical Revival.
13 Lancelot 'Capability' Brown (1716-83) Creator of English landscaped gardens, a major influence on landscape design.
14 Treaty of Paris (1763) ended the French and Indian wars, the Seven Years War.

Chapter 2: 'The desire to please polishes the intelligence'

1 *Journal of Charlotte Burney*: June 21, 1781. Moulton Library of Literary Criticism of English and American Authors (1901-05) 4:417.
2 Madeleine de Scudéry (1607-1701) French writer.
3 *Le Grand Cyrus* 10 volumes (1649-53).
4 Letter VI to Elizabeth Carter: July 31, 1750: *The Posthumous Works of Mrs Chapone* Vol. 1 (London.1807).
5 Essay III on Enthusiasm and Indifference in Religion: Hester Chapone: *Miscellanies* (1775) in *The Works of Mrs. Chapone* (1807).
6 Frances "Fanny" Boscawen née Glanville (1719-1805) Bluestocking, in 1742 married The Hon. (later Admiral) Edward Boscawen (1711-61).
7 Lady Mary Wortley Montagu (1689-1762) Poet, writer and traveller, promoted inoculation against smallpox on her return from Turkey in 1719.
8 Lady Margaret Cavendish Holles-Harley (1715-85) married the Duke of Portland.
9 Ridotto, popular 18th century entertainment with music and dancing, often with masquerade. Outdoors *al fresco* or indoors.
10 *fêtes champêtres*. Popular in 18th century, an elaborate garden party, often with an orchestra and fancy dress.

11 Mary Granville (1700-88) m. (1) aged 17 to Alexander Pendarves (2) 1743 to Dr Patrick Delany. Bluestocking, famous for her paper mosaic botanical collages.

Chapter 3: The Gilbert White Connection

1 Thomas Mulso (1719/20-99) m. 1760 Miss Prescott (Pressy) sister of General Prestcott.
2 John Mulso (1720/21?-91) m. Jane Young "Missy". Matriculated at Oriel College, Oxford, 1740. Became close friend of Gilbert White, matriculated at Oriel same year. Prebendary: Salisbury Cathedral, Prebend of Alton (1758-91), Rector: Sunbury (1747-60), Thornhill (1760-67), Witney (1767-71),Prebendary: Winchester Cathedral (1770-91), Rector: Meonstoke (1771-91), Easton (1776-91).
3 Dr John Thomas (1696-1781) Chaplain-in-Ordinary to King George II, 1742; Bishop of Peterborough,1747; Tutor to Prince of Wales, 1752; Bishop of Salisbury, 1757; Bishop of Winchester, 1761.
4 Named after 6th century BC Greek Lyric Poet, Anacreon: it numbered Johnson, Joshua Reynolds and James Boswell among its members.
5 Signora Frasi was a popular Italian singer.
6 Gilbert White (1720-93) Naturalist and ornithologist. *The Natural History and Antiquities of Selborne*: Gilbert White: published in December 1788 by his brother Benjamin but dated 1789 by the publishers.
7 Letter to Gilbert White, July 16, 1776 from Meonstoke: in Rashleigh Holt-White (ed.): *The Letters to Gilbert White of Selborne from his Intimate Friend and Contemporary The Rev. John Mulso*: (London 1906). All correspondence between Mulso and White quoted is from Rashleigh Holt-White.
8 Daines Barrington (1727-1800) Lawyer, antiquarian and naturalist.
9 Letter XCII to the Honourable Daines Barrington: *Natural History of Selborne*, p.226: (Macmillan and Co., Ltd: London 1897).

Chapter 4: A Wider World

1 The South Sea Bubble 1720. Many investors were ruined by speculation in The South Sea Company which traded with South America.
2 Alexander Pope (1688-1744) Prolific poet and satirist.
3 Letter I dated September 11, 1749: *The Posthumous Works of Mrs Chapone*, Vol.1 (1807).
4 Catherine Talbot (1721-70) Writer and Bluestocking.
5 Letter dated January 28, 1741. *A Series of Letters Between Mrs Elizabeth Carter and Miss Catherine Talbot: 1741-1770*, Vol.1: (London 1809).
6 Letter dated April 28, 1750 to Catherine Talbot. *Ibid.*
7 Letter dated December 17, 1750 from Catherine to Elizabeth. *Ibid.*
8 Letter dated December 28, 1750 from Deal: Elizabeth's response to Catherine. *Ibid.*
9 Letter IV dated March 25 no year, from Hester to Elizabeth Carter. *The Posthumous Works of Mrs Chapone*, Vol.1 (1807).
10 *Life of Mr Richardson: Correspondence of Samuel Richardson*. 6 Vols.: Anna Laetitia Barbauld (ed.) (1804).
11 *Sonnet to H.M.* 1751: *The Works of Mrs Chapone*: (Edinburgh 1807).
12 28 February, 1752: *Correspondence of Samuel Richardson*; ed. Barbauld. (1804) Vol. 3 pp. 36-37.

Chapter 5: 'Never was woe drest out in gayer colours'

1 Letter V to the Duchess of Portland: *Mrs Delany*. R. Brimley Johnson. (London. 1925).
2 Edward Montagu (1692-1775) Grandson of the 1st Earl of Sandwich, m. Elizabeth Robinson 1742. Wealthy landowner, estates and coalmines in Northumberland.
3 Thomas Tonkin: *The Natural History of Cornwall*; 1736-39.
4 Letter IV: *Mrs Delany*. R. Brimley Johnson. (London. 1925).
5 Letter V: *Ibid.*
6 Letter VI: *Ibid.*
7 William Lloyd Fox: *War Prisoners at Falmouth and District* as reprinted from The Royal Cornwall Polytechnic Society's report (1927)

Chapter 6: 'I never was a writing lady till you made me one'

1 John Burrows: (1733-86). m. to Maria Culling Smith, 1762. Member of the Bluestocking circle. Student at Middle Temple. Took holy orders in 1760. 1764-73 incumbent of Berkeley Chapel; 1773 rector of St Clement Danes. 1767 Rector of Millbrook, nr. Southampton, through Hester Chapone's influence with her uncle, Bishop of Winchester. Rector of Hadley, nr. Barnet 1770-86. Buried at Hadley.

2 North-End, Richardson's house, The Grange, in North End Road, Hammersmith.
3 Anna Laetitia Barbauld, née Aiken (1743-1825) Educationalist, writer of hymns and essays, poet, political and social concerns. Contributed as Anna Aiken to *The Monthly Magazine* (1796-1807)(ed. John Aiken). Edited *The Correspondence of Samuel Richardson* in 6 volumes: (1804). Married M. Rochemont Barbauld in 1774. They managed a very successful boys' school until 1785 when he became mentally ill. He attacked her in 1808. They separated and he committed suicide in the same year.
4 Sarah Fielding (1710-68) The sister of Henry Fielding with whom she collaborated on several novels.
5 Jane Collier (1714-55) Novelist, *An Essay on the Art of Ingeniously Tormenting* (1753).
6 Dorothy, Lady Bradshaigh (1705-85) Her correspondence with Richardson started in 1748 when she wrote two anonymous letters begging him not to subject Clarissa to 'rapes, ruin and destruction'. They met in 1750 and became very close. She was an extremely influential member of his circle and closely involved in his work on *Sir Charles Grandison*.
7 Sarah Chapone née Kirkham (1699-1764) Wife of Rev. John Chapone, mother of John. Hester's mother-in-law.
8 Letter III dated January 10, 1750 no address. *The Posthumous Works of Mrs Chapone*, Vol.1 (1807).
9 *Selected letters of Samuel Richardson*: ed. John Carroll: (Clarendon Press, Oxford 1964).
10 Letters to Richardson: *The Posthumous Works of Mrs Chapone*: Vol. 2. (London 1807).
11 John Locke (1632-1704) English philosopher, influential thinker of the Enlightenment, empiricist, *The Second Treatise of Civil Government* 1690.
12 John Chapone (1725-61) Attorney, Clement's Inn. Son of Sarah Kirkham Chapone and Reverend John Chapone. One brother and two sisters: Catherine and Sarah. Sarah Chapone married Reverend Daniel Sandford in 1752. Lived at Delville near Dublin, the home of Dean and Mrs Delany. In 1766 Catherine married Sir John Boyd. According to Mrs Delany: 'What a providential and great match for her! … having at least £9000 a year.' Brimley Johnson: *Mrs Delany* p210.
The surname Chapone is French in origin: Capon derived from '*caponier*' a gamekeeper. Introduced by Norman invaders, post 1066 and subsequently by Huguenot protestant refugees in C17.
13 Samuel von Pufendorf (1632-94) Political philosopher, historian, economist, defender of the concept of natural law.
14 Colley Cibber (1671-1757) Poet Laureate 1730. Actor-manager and prolific playwright.
15 Letter IV: March 25, 1750 no address. *The Posthumous Works of Mrs Chapone*, Vol.1 (1807).
16 Letter V: May18, 1750 no address. *Ibid*.
17 Benito Jerónimo Feijóo y Montenegro (1676-1764) Benedictine monk, Spanish philosopher and theologian. Wrote *Defensa de las mujeres*: an essay defending women and wives in *Teatro crítico universal* Vol. 1 (1726).
18 This was an early draft to which many changes were made. The poem was published in 1818 after Gilbert White's death.
19 Letter dated June 6, 1751 as from King [sic] Square Court, London, Vol.1 (1807), enclosed in John Mulso's letter. Rashleigh Holt-White (ed.) *The Letters to Gilbert White of Selborne from his Intimate Friend and Contemporary the Rev. John Mulso* (London 1906).

Chapter 7: 'a kind of flower garden of ladies'

1 Letter XI: undated: Canterbury, Monday. *The Posthumous Works of Mrs Chapone*, Vol.1 (1807).
2 Letter XII: undated: Canterbury, Wednesday. *The Posthumous Works of Mrs Chapone*, Vol.1 (1807).
3 Letter VII dated September 9 from Peterborough: *The Posthumous Works of Mrs Chapone*, Vol.1 (1807).
4 Anne Donellan. She never married, the title Mrs is an honorific. A close friend of Mary Pendarves (later Mrs Delany). Corresponded with Jonathan Swift. She criticised Hester Mulso for her lack of 'politeness and manners'.
5 There are two extant versions of Susanna Highmore's sketch: one in pencil and wash in a bundle of Richardson's correspondence in The Morgan Library in New York, recorded as made in 1751, MA 1024B. The other, in The National Portrait Gallery, London, dated 1804, NPG D5810, an aquatint by Sadler after Susanna Highmore, in which the faces, dress and figures are very different from the New York sketch. A portrait of Mrs Chapone, made 1812, NPG 2046 is copied from Sadler's aquatint, not Highmore's original, so may not be a likeness.
6 John Duncombe (1729-86) Son of William Duncombe. Writer. *The Feminiad*: (1754) in praise and celebration of eminent C18 women. He includes Susanna, and Hester whom he refers to as 'Delia' citing her 'genius and goodness'. Married Susanna Highmore 1761.
7 Susanna Highmore (1725-1812) m. John Duncombe. Artist, poet and writer. Daughter of the portraitist Joseph Highmore.
8 *Correspondence of Samuel Richardson*: ed. Barbauld (1804). She dates it 1754 but the date 1751 would fit the subject and reference later in the letter to Hester's then being in Deal with Elizabeth Carter.

9 *Ibid*. Vol.3:171-75.
10 *Ibid*. p. 176.
11 *Ibid*. p. 195.
12 *Ibid*. p. 215-216.

Chapter 8: A Matrimonial Creed

1 First published in *The Posthumous Works of Mrs Chapone*: Vol. II. London (1807).
2 *Reading Daughters' Fictions 1709-1834*: Caroline Gonda: p. 83. Also p.540 *The Monthly Magazine, or British Register*, Vol. XXXIII, Part I for 1812, London.
3 Robert Harley (1661-1724) 1st Earl of Oxford and 1st Earl Mortimer, opposed Hanoverian succession.
4 Sent from Welsbourne, July 8, 1850 *Correspondence of Samuel Richardson*: ed Barbauld (1804) Vol. IV p.6.
5 *Ibid*. p. 20.
6 Letter dated 15 February 1752: *Mrs Delany*. R. Brimley Johnson. (London. 1925). p. 195.
7 Letter XVII: Hampton, July 10 to Elizabeth Carter. *The Posthumous Works of Mrs Chapone*: Vol.1 (1807).
8 James Boswell: *The Life of Samuel Johnson LL.D.* (London 1791) Vol. 1, p. 144.

Part Two: The Bluestocking Connection

Chapter 9: 'Come in your blew stockings'

1 Elizabeth Vesey (1715-91) Anglo-Irish wealthy hostess of informal literary and political discussions of the Bluestockings. Married first in 1731 to William Hancock MP (d.1741); secondly, 1748 to Agmondesham Vesey (d.1785).
2 Benjamin Stillingfleet (1702-71) Botanist and publisher, popular intellectual.
3 Mrs Vesey to Stillingfleet: "Come in your blew stockings" reported by Ethel Rolt Wheeler: *Famous Bluestockings* (Methuen, London 1910) p. 22.
4 Letter dated March 8,1757: Matthew Montagu (ed.): *Letters of Mrs Elizabeth Montagu With Some Of The Letters Of Her Correspondents*: Vol. III. (Boston 1825).
5 David Garrick (1717-79) Actor, playwright and theatre manager.
6 Hester Lynch Thrale (née Salusbury) later Mrs Piozzi (1741-1821) Leading Bluestocking and hostess. Close friend of Samuel Johnson.
7 Hannah More (1745-1833) Teacher at her sisters' school, evangelical philanthropist, playwright and poet: *The Bas Bleu; or Conversation*, Bluestocking. Protégée of Mrs Montagu. Lived with David Garrick and his wife Eva, when in London.
8 Frances "Fanny" Burney, later Madame D'Arblay (1752-1840). Described in 1918 by Virginia Woolf as 'the Mother of English Fiction'. Diarist and novelist: *Evelina: or The History of a Young Lady's Entrance into the World* (1778), *Cecilia …* (1782), *Camilla …* (1796). Protégée of Hester Thrale.
9 William Pitt "the Elder", 1st Earl of Chatham (1708-78) Whig Patriot Party, Prime Minister 1766-8.
10 *HMS Dreadnaught* or *Dreadnought*: Boscawen's and his ship's spelling in the historical records varies.
11 *Admiral's Wife*: Cecil Aspinall-Oglander (Longmans, London 1940).
12 Under the Cruizers [sic] and Convoys Act, 1708, captured enemy ships were valued at court and the value as prize money was divided between the ship's captain, two eighths; fleet admiral, one eighth; the ship's officers shared one eighth; surgeon and warrant officers shared one eighth; junior warrant officers shared one eighth; the crew sharing the last two eighths in descending order of rating. An admiral thus benefited from all of the prizes taken by his fleet. A line of battle ship might have several hundred crew and the most junior boy might be lucky with the price of a drink.
13 *Hatchlands: The Building of Hatchlands*: Christopher Rowell (The Cobbe Collection Trust in association with The National Trust. 2002) p. 36.
14 Matthew Montagu (ed.): *Letters of Mrs Elizabeth Montagu With Some Of The Letters Of Her Correspondents*: Vol. III. (Boston 1825).

Chapter 10: 'the little fidget'

1 *Mrs Delany*: R. Brimley Johnson (London. 1925). p. xxxviii.
2 Lawrence Stone: *The Family, Sex and Marriage in England 1500-1800*: p. 224. 'The need for supportive assistance in this time of psychological and physiological crisis shows how strong was the social attraction for each sex for its own company…'
3 Sir George Lyttelton (1709-73) Whig politician, became Lord Lyttelton in 1756 while Chancellor of the Exchequer.

Chapter 11: Beau Nash

1 Letter dated January 7, 1740 to the Duchess of Portland: *Letters of Elizabeth Montagu*. Vol. I.
2 Melville, Lewis: *Bath under Beau Nash* (London 1907).
3 Letter dated December 27, 1740: *Letters of Elizabeth Montagu*. Vol. I.
4 Letter from Tunbridge Wells dated September 8, 1749 to her close friend Mrs Donellan: *Ibid*. Vol. II.
5 Letter from Tunbridge Wells dated September 26,1749 to Mrs Donellan: *Ibid*.
6 Letter dated September 8,1749 to Mrs Donellan. *Ibid*.

Chapter 12: 'the Sylph'

1 Anne-Marie Fiquet du Boccage (1710-1802) Writer, poet and dramatist. *Letters concerning England, Holland, and Italy* 2 Vols. (1770) i. 7.
2 Letter to Gilbert West dated July 9, 1755: *Letters of Elizabeth Montagu*. Vol. III.
3 *Ibid*. Dated July 13.
4 Letter CCX dated May 10, 1778 from Clarges Street, London to Elizabeth Montagu. Montagu Pennington (ed.): *Letters from Mrs. Elizabeth Carter, to Mrs. Montagu, Between the Years 1755 and 1800. Chiefly Upon Literary and Moral Subject*: 3 Vols. (London 1817) Vol. III, p.68.
5 Agmondesham Vesey (?-1785) Second husband of Elizabeth Vesey. Wealthy Irish MP who in 1767 became Accountant General of Ireland and then Privy Councillor.

Part Three: Marriage and Heartbreak

Chapter 13: 'The frivolous bolt of Cupid'

1 Letter dated November 11, 1743: *A Series of Letters between Mrs Elizabeth Carter and Miss Catherine Talbot*: Vol. I. (London 1809).
2 *Ibid*.
3 Letter dated November 4, 1749. *Ibid*.
4 Letter dated May 3, 1756. Vol. II. *Ibid*.
5 Letter XXV. *The Posthumous Works of Mrs Chapone*: Vol. I (1807).
6 Letter XXXII: undated. *Ibid*.

Chapter 14: 'Give me your congratulations'

1 *Life of Mr Richardson: Correspondence of Samuel Richardson*: 6 Vols. Anna Laetitia Barbauld (ed:) (1804) Vol. 3 p. 230.
2 Letter XXIX dated August 29, 1757 from Canterbury. *The Posthumous Works of Mrs Chapone*: Vol.1 (1807).
3 Letter XXXI dated August 4, 1758 from Canterbury. *Ibid*.
4 Tobias Smollett (1721-1771) Naval surgeon and author of picaresque novels and outspoken opinions.
5 Lewis M Knapp: *Rex versus Smollett: More Data on the Smollett-Knowles Libel case* in *Modern Philology*, (University of Chicago May 1944) Vol. 41, No. 4, pp.221-227.
6 Letter XXXIII dated April 28, 1759, no address. *The Posthumous Works of Mrs Chapone*: Vol.1 (1807).
7 Letter XXXIV dated July 15, 1759 from London. *Ibid*.
8 Ann Yearsley (1753-1806) Poet. Hannah More published by subscription Yearsley's poems in *Poems on Several Occasions*, Thomas Cadell: (London1785). Mrs Montagu initially held Yearsley's profits in trust, to protect the money from Mr Yearsley, causing a rift.
9 Letter XXV dated August 28, 1759 from Salisbury. *The Posthumous Works of Mrs Chapone*: Vol.1 (1807).
10 Letter XXXVI dated December 9, 1760, London. *Ibid*.
11 Letter XXXVII dated February 4 1761 from Carey Street, London. *Ibid*.
12 Letter XXXVIII dated July 31, 1761, London. *Ibid*.

Chapter 15: 'her presence was judged injurious to him'

1 Culling Smith (1731-1812) Knighted baronet in 1802.
2 Letter XXXIX dated September 17, 1761 from Tunbridge Wells: Miss Burrows to Mrs Carter. *The Posthumous Works of Mrs Chapone*: Vol.1 (1807).
3 Letter XL dated September 22, 1761 from London. *Ibid*.
4 *Letters to Mrs Montagu, Between the Years 1755 and 1800. Chiefly Upon Literary and Moral Subjects*, 3 Vols. ed.

Montagu Pennington (London 1817) Vol. 1 pp. 122-23.
5 Letter XLI dated October 5, 1761. *The Posthumous Works of Mrs Chapone*, Vol.1 (1807).
6 Letter XLII dated October 11, 1761. *Ibid.*
7 Letter XLIII dated October 15, 1761. *Ibid.*
8 Letter XLIV dated November 11, 1761, no address. *Ibid.*
9 Letter XLV dated December 6, 1761, from Southampton-street, London. *Ibid.*
10 *The Posthumous Works of Mrs Chapone*, (London 1807) Vol. 1 p. 144.
11 Matthew Montagu (ed.): *Letters of Mrs Elizabeth Montagu With Some Of The Letters Of Her Correspondents*: Vol. III. (Boston 1825).
12 Written from Westhorp, 2 July. *Mrs Montagu Queen of the Blues*: Reginald Blunt (ed.) (London 1923) p. 30 Vol. I.
13 *Ibid.* p.129.
14 *The Monthly Magazine* No. 13 (February 1802) Quoted in Cole: *Memoirs of Mrs Chapone*.
15 *The Posthumous Works of Mrs Chapone*, (London 1807) Vol. 1 pp. 126-9.
16 *Ibid.*

Chapter 16: 'I begin to love her so much'

1 Letter XLVI dated July 6, 1762, no address. *Ibid.*
2 William Pulteney, 1st and last Earl of Bath (1684-1764) Politician and pamphleteer. Prime Minister for "Forty eight hours, three quarters, eleven minutes and seven seconds." Described as "cool and unsteady in his friendships, warm and immovable in his hate." Predeceased by his son Viscount Pulteney. Left £1,200,000.
3 Letter XLVII December 11, 1763 from Frith Street. *Ibid.*
4 Letter XLVIII undated, no address. *Ibid.*
5 Mathew Montagu (ed.) *Letters of Mrs Elizabeth Montagu With Some Of The Letters Of Her Correspondents:* Vol III (Boston 1825).
6 Letter XLVIII undated, no address. *The Posthumous Works of Mrs Chapone*: Vol. 1 (1807).
7 Dr Newton Ogle (1726-1804) Dean of Winchester 1769-1804.

Chapter 17: 'I am grown as bold as a lion'

1 Letter XLIX dated August 19, 1770 from Denton. *Ibid.*
2 Dr John Gregory (1724-73) Scottish academic: *A Father's Legacy to his Daughters* (1775).
3 Mary Wollstonecraft (1759-97) Writer, and advocate of women's rights. Excoriated by Horace Walpole as a 'hyena in petticoats'. Died in childbirth aged 38.
4 David Hume (1711-76) Sceptical Scottish empiricist philosopher and historian. Influenced Adam Smith, Kant, Bentham, Darwin and Huxley.
5 Letter L dated October 12, 1770 from Denton. *The Posthumous Works of Mrs Chapone*, (London 1807).
6 Letter to the Rev. Mr Friend, 1749 from Tunbridge Wells: *Letters of Mrs Elizabeth Montagu With Some Of The Letters Of Her Correspondents*: Matthew Montagu (ed.)Vol. II. (Boston 1825).
7 Term applied to young men who adopted outlandish dress, wigs and manners: from *maccherone*, meaning boorish fool in Italian.
8 Letter dated May 28, 1773 to Mrs Port of Ilam: *Mrs Delany*: R. Brimley Johnson: (London. 1925) p. 236.
9 Eva Maria Garrick, née Viegel (1724-1822) Austrian singer, m. David Garrick 1749.
10 Walter Scott: *Bluestocking Ladies* (London 1947) p. 168 quotes Madam D'Arblay: *Memoirs of Dr. Burney*. (1832).

Part Four: A Model of Conduct for Young Ladies

Chapter 18: Letters on the Improvement of the Mind

1 Chapone, Hester: *Letters on the Improvement of the Mind, Addressed to a Young Lady* (London 1773).
2 Philip Stanhope, 4th Earl of Chesterfield (1694-1773) *Letters to his Son:* Written 1734 onwards, published by the son's widow in 1774.
3 *Admiral's Wife: Being the Life and Letters of The Hon. Mrs. Edward Boscawen from 1719 to 1761* Aspinall-Oglander (ed.) (Longmans, London1940).
4 *Ibid.* pp. 44-45.
5 *Ibid.*p. 105.

6 23 December, 1756: p. 243. *Ibid.*
7 Letter LX dated November 1782 from Wardour Street: *The Posthumous Works of Mrs Chapone* Vol 1: (London 1807).

Chapter 19: Letters VI to VIII

1 In the 1815 edition of *Letters on the Improvement of the Mind* there is a footnote by the editor: 'There has been lately published a work particularly adapted to the use of young ladies entitled "A Dictionary of Polite Literature, or Fabulous History of Heathen gods and Illustrious Heroes." 2 Vols. With Plates.'

Chapter 20: Letters IX and X

1 American Declaration of Independence, July 4, 1776.
2 Letter XLVII dated December 11, 1763 from Frith Street. *The Posthumous Works of Mrs Chapone:* Vol 1: (London 1807).

Chapter 21: 'ye great Harvest of her Fame'

1 Letter LIII, July 20, Farnham Castle. *Ibid.*
2 R. Brimley Johnson: *Mrs Delany* (London. 1925) p. 195.
3 *Ibid*. p. 234.
4 *The Works of Mrs Chapone in Four Volumes*: p.162.Vol.II *Miscellanies*. (Boston 1809).

Part Five: Fame, Family and Friends

Chapter 22: Miscellanies in Prose and Verse and William Weller Pepys

1 William Weller Pepys (1740/1-1825) Baronet 1801. Master in Chancery. Correspondence collected in *A Later Pepys*: Alice Gaussen (ed.) 2 Vols. (London 1904).
2 Gaius Laelius: friend of Scipio and commander of the fleet in the Roman assault on Cartegena in 209 BC.
3 Letter dated September 25, 1770 to William. *A Later Pepys* 2 Vols.: Alice Gaussen (ed.) (London 1904) Vol. 1.
4 Letter dated July 16, 1771 from Millhill. *Ibid.*
5 Letter dated August 3, 1771 from Farnham Castle, Surrey. *Ibid.*
6 James Boswell: *The Life of Samuel Johnson LL.D.* (London 1791) Vol. 1, Ch. 13.

Chapter 23: 'That one talent which is death to hide'

1 Letter VII dated August 22, 1776 from Farnham Castle: no named recipient. *Miscellaneous Letters*: Vol. II. *The Works of Mrs Chapone in Four Volumes*. (Boston 1809).
2 Letter dated 1773 to Mr Burrows. *Ibid.*
3 Letter dated June 15, 1777. *The Posthumous Works of Mrs Chapone*. Vol.1. (London 1807).
4 Jonathan Swift (1667-1745) Anglo Irish satirist, essayist, political pamphleteer, poet: Dean of St Patrick's Cathedral, Dublin.
5 Jonathan Swift: *Letter to a Young Lady, on her Marriage Written in Year 1723* published in *The Works of Jonathan Swift D.D.D.S.P.D. in Eight Volumes* (Dublin 1742) Vol. I, p. 265.
6 Henry Thrale (1724?-81) m. Hester Salusbury 1763. Wealthy brewer, Anchor Brewery, Southwark, MP for Southwark.

Chapter 24: 'belonging to the flying squadron'

1 Letter dated July 23, 1775 from Farnham Castle: *A Later Pepys*: 2 Vols. Alice Gaussen (ed.), (London 1904) Vol.1.
2 Letter dated December, 1775. Miscellaneous Letters: Vol. II. *The Works of Mrs Chapone in Four Volumes*. (Boston 1809).
3 Letter dated October 14, 1777. *A Later Pepys*: 2 Vols. Alice Gaussen (ed.), (London 1904)Vol. 1.
4 Letter LIX undated from Old Alresford, Hants: *The Posthumous Works of Mrs Chapone*. (London 1807) Vol.1.

5 Guillaume Thomas François Reynal (1713-96) FRS 1754. French Jesuit writer: *L'Histoire du stathoudérat* (The Hague, 1748), *L'Histoire du parlement d'Angleterre* (London, 1748), *Histoire Philosophique et Politique des Établissements et du Commerce des Européens dans les deux Indes*: (1770).
6 Letter LVIII dated July 30 from Hadley: *The Posthumous Works of Mrs Chapone*: (London 1807) Vol.1.
7 Walter Scott: *The BlueStocking Ladies*: (London 1947). p. 17.
8 Hannah More's plays, *The Inflexible Captive* opened in Bath in 1775, *Percy* opened at Covent Garden in 1777.
9 Annette M B Meakin: *Hannah More: A Biographical Study* (Smith, Elder & Co. 1911) p. 6.
10 *Diary and Letters of Madame D'Arblay Edited by her Niece* (Henry Colburn, London 1842) Vol. II, Part V 1781 to 1786 p.222.

Chapter 25: Hester Thrale and Fanny Burney

1 James Boswell: *The Life of Samuel Johnson LL.D.* (Dilly, London 1791) Vol. 2, p.465.
2 Sophia Streatfield (1754-1835) Scholar and beauty.
3 Woolsey, Sarah Chauncey (ed.): *Diary and Letters of Frances Burney Madame D'Arblay*: Vols I & II (Boston 1880). Vol.1.
4 Burney, Fanny: *Diary and letters of Madame d'Arblay edited by her niece* (Charlotte Barrett) (Bickers and Son, London 1842-46) Vol. I. p.563. April 24, 1784.
5 *Ibid.* Vol. I. p.550. December 19, 1783.

Chapter 26: 'such a here and thereian'

1 Letter dated August 20, 1778: *Miscellaneous Letters*: Vol. II. *The Works of Mrs Chapone in Four Volumes*: (Boston 1809).
2 The Gordon Riots of 1780 were against The Papist Act 1778 which restored some of the disadvantages to Catholics of The Popery Act 1608.
3 Letter dated June 18 but no year given. The reference to Charleston would place it in 1780 but placed much later in *A Later Pepys*: 2 vols. Alice Gaussen (ed.), (London 1904) Vol. 1.
4 Figures from p.103 Aspinall-Oglander: *Admiral's Widow: Being the Life and Letters of the Hon. Mrs. Edward Boscawen from 1761 to 1805*: (London 1942).
5 Letter LX dated November 1782 from Wardour Street: *The Posthumous Works of Mrs Chapone*: (London 1807) Vol.1.
6 Woolsey, Sarah Chauncey (ed.): *Diary and Letters of Frances Burney Madame D'Arblay*: Vols I & II (Boston 1880). Vol.1.
7 *Mrs Delany*: R. Brimley Johnson. (London. 1925). p. xli.
8 Samuel Crisp (1707-83) Wealthy playwright :*Virginia, a Tragedy*.
9 Letter from Great Russell Street dated Oct 12, 1783. *A Later Pepys*: 2 Vols. Alice Gaussen (ed.) (London 1904) Vol. 1.

Chapter 27: 'such mighty overbearing Passions are not natural in a Matron's bones'

1 Gabriel Marco Piozzi (1740-1809) Italian singer.
2 Streatham, Thursday, May-1781: *Diary and Letters of Frances Burney Madame D'Arblay*: Vols I & II (Boston 1880). Vol.1.
3 Letter dated August 24, 1784 from Dean of Winchester's, Southampton: *A Later Pepys*: 2 vols. Alice Gaussen (ed.) (London 1904) Vol. 1.
4 Thrale, Hester Lynch: entry dated 25 July, 1803: *Thraliana, The Diary of Mrs Hester Lynch Thrale (later Mrs Piozzi) 1776-1809*: 2 Vols Katherine Balderston (ed.) (Oxford University Press 1942).
5 Letter LXI dated June, 1783 from London: *The Posthumous Works of Mrs Chapone*: (London 1807) Vol.1.
6 *Memoirs of Mrs Chapone*: John Cole: (London 1839). p. 59.
7 Letter LXII dated June, 1784. *The Posthumous Works of Mrs Chapone*: (London, 1807) Vol.1.

Chapter 28: 'I shall be good and happy': The Bluestockings in Decline

1 Hayden, Ruth: *Mrs Delany her Life and her Flowers*: (London 1980) p. 162.
2 *A Later Pepys*: 2 Vols. Alice Gaussen (ed.), (London 1904) Vol. 1, p. 412.
3 *Diary and Letters of Frances Burney Madame D'Arblay*: (Boston 1880) Vols I & II.
4 Warren Hastings (1732-1818). The first Governor General of India.

5 Edmund Burke (1729-97) Irish political philosopher, Whig politician and statesman, father of modern conservatism.
6 Richard Brinsley Sheridan (1751-1815) MP, Irish-born playwright, poet, owner of the Theatre Royal, Drury Lane.
7 Charles James Fox (1749-1806) Whig politician and historian.
8 Catherine Macaulay, née Sawbridge (1731-91) Political activist and historian. *The History of England from the Accession of James 1 to that of the Brunswick Line*: 8 volumes, (1763-83).
9 Erasmus Darwin (1731-1802). (Grandfather of Charles Darwin). *The Botanic Garden, Part 2; The Loves of Plants*: (London 1791).
10 Letter dated December 27, 1791. *Diary and Letters of Frances Burney Madame D'Arblay*: Vols I & II (Boston 1880). Vol.II.
11 Letter from Pall Mall, dated June 15th (no year). *Miscellaneous Letters*: Vol. II. *The Works of Mrs Chapone in Four Volumes*: (Boston 1809).
12 The French Revolution of 1792: Storming of the Tuileries in dispute between the Commune de Paris and monarchy: ineffective.
13 Edmund Burke: *Reflections on the Revolution in France* (1790).

Chapter 29: 'Your irreparable loss'

1 Letter dated July 3, 1794 to Elizabeth Carter. *Miscellaneous Letters*: Vol. II. *The Works of Mrs Chapone in Four Volumes*: (Boston 1809).
2 Letter to Elizabeth Carter dated October 12, 1794 from Southampton. *Ibid.*
3 Letter to Elizabeth Carter, June 29, 1795 from Francis Street. *Ibid.*
4 Thomas James Mathias: *The Pursuits of Literature; a satirical poem in four dialogues*: (1794).
5 Letter LXIII dated November 1797 from London: final letter to Elizabeth Carter. *The Posthumous Works of Mrs Chapone*: (London 1807) Vol.1.
6 *Diary and Letters of the author Madam D'Arblay*: Austin Dobson (ed.) (1904-05) Vol. 5. pp. 434-35.

Chapter 30: 'enlighten my understanding'

1 *The Posthumous Works of Mrs Chapone:* (London 1807) Vol.II p.159.
2 *Gentleman's Magazine*: (Supplement 1801) pp. 1216-17.
3 Madame D'Arblay: *Memoirs of Doctor Burney*: (London 1832).

Part Six: Epilogue

1 William Hazlitt (1778-1830) Literary critic, humanist philosopher, grammarian, painter and satirist. '*On Great and Little Things*' (in *Table Talk, Essays on Men and Manners*: 1821).

Chapter 31: The Backlash of Satire: The Anti-Chapone, or Grandmothers in the Wrong

1 I am indebted to Melissa Hardie of The Hypatia Trust for lending me an early handwritten version of the text of *The Anti-Chapone*. Published as *The Anti-Chapone, or Grandmothers in the Wrong, Proved by Incontestible Facts in a Letter from Aunt Lorincia, in Town, to her Young Niece in the Country*: (Brodie, Dowding, and Luxford, Salisbury 1810).
2 Rev. Richard Polwhele (1760-1838) Cornish clergyman and poet: *The Unsex'd Females, a Poem*: (1798).
3 Mary Wollstonecraft: *A Vindication of the Rights of Men, in a letter to the Right Honourable Edmund Burke; occasioned by his reflections on the Revolution in France* (London 1790), *A Vindication of the Rights of Woman: With Strictures on Political and Moral Subjects* (Johnson, London 1792), *The Wrongs of Woman* published posthumously with other Wollstonecraft works in 1798. Hannah More called *The Wrongs of Woman* a "vindication of adultery".
4 Joanna Martin: *Wives and Daughters*: (London 2004) p. 227.
5 While wit was highly valued at this time, 'witling' was used disparagingly of the self-styled wit or one of little wit.
6 *A Traitor's Kiss*: O'Toole, Fintan, (Granta Books 1998) p. 311
7 Louisa Henrietta Sheridan, (?-1841) daughter of Capt. William B Sheridan, married Lt. Col. Sir Henry Wyatt, British Embassy Chapel, Paris, 1840.

Bibliography

Addison, Joseph, with Steele, Richard (eds.): *The Spectator* (1711-12)

Aiken, Anna, maiden name of Mrs Barbauld, contributed to *The Monthly Magazine*

Aiken, John: (ed.) *The Monthly Magazine* (1796-1807)

Armstrong, Nancy and Tennenhouse, Leonard (eds.): *The Ideology of Conduct* (Methuen & Co., New York 1987)

Aspinall-Oglander, Cecil: *Admiral's Wife: Being the Life and Letters of The Hon. Mrs Edward Boscawen from 1719-1761* (Longmans, London 1940)

—*Admiral's Widow: Being the Life and Letters of The Hon. Mrs Edward Boscawen from 1761 to 1805* (The Hogarth Press, London 1942)

'Aunt Lorincia': *The Anti-Chapone, or Grandmothers in the Wrong* (Brodie, Dowding, and Luxford, Salisbury 1810)

Austen, Jane: *Mansfield Park* (J. M. Dent & Sons Ltd., London 1980)

Barbauld, Anna Laetitia: *The Correspondence of Samuel Richardson*, 6 Vols. (Richard Phillips, London 1804)

Blunt, Reginald (ed.): *Mrs Montagu "Queen of The Blues"* 2 Vols (Constable and Company Ltd, London 1923)

du Boccage, Anne-Marie Fiquet: *Letters concerning England, Holland, and Italy*, 2 Vols. (1770)

Boswell, James: *The Life of Samuel Johnson LL.D.*, 2 Vols. (Dilly, London 1791)

Brimley Johnson, R: *Mrs Delany* (Stanley Paul & Co. Ltd., London 1925)

Brimley Johnson, R.(ed.): *Bluestocking Letters* (Bodley Head, London 1926)

Burney, Fanny: *Evelina: or The History of a Young Lady's Entrance into the World* (1778)

—*The Witlings: A Comedy By A Sister of the Order* (1779)

—*Cecilia: Or, Memoirs of an Heiress* (London 1782)

—*Camilla: Or, A Picture of Youth* (London 1796)

—*The Woman Hater* (1801)

— *The Wanderer: Or, Female Difficulties* (Longmans, London 1814)

— *Memoirs of Doctor Burney* (Moxon, London 1832)

— *Diary and letters of Madame d'Arblay as edited by her niece* (Charlotte Barrett) (H. Colburn, London 1842-46) There are several later editions with commentaries by others.

— see also D'Arblay, Madame

Byron, George Gordon, Lord: *The Blues: A Literary Eclogue*, (written in 1821) *The Liberal*, (1823)

Carter, Elizabeth: *All the Works of Epictetus, Which are Now Extant* (1758)

— *Poems on Several Occasions* (London 1762)

Cave, Edward (ed.): *The Gentleman's Magazine* (founded in 1731)

Chapone, Hester: *Letters on the Improvement of the Mind, Addressed to a Young Lady* (London 1773)

— *The Posthumous Works of Mrs Chapone*, 2 Vols. (John Murray, London 1807)

— *The Works of Mrs Chapone* (John Thomson and Co., Edinburgh 1807)

Chapone, Sarah: *The Hardships of the English Laws in Relation to Wives, with an Explanation of the Original Curse of Subjection Passed Upon the Woman, in an Humble Address to the Legislature* (London and Dublin 1735)

Chesterfield, Philip Dormer Stanhope, Earl of Chesterfield: *Letters to his Son as Letters written by the late Right Honourable Philip Dormer Stanhope, Earl of Chesterfield, to his son, Philip Stanhope Esq; …* (London 1774)

Clarke, Norma: *The Rise and Fall of the Woman of Letters* (Pimlico, London 2004)

— *Dr Johnson's Women* (Pimlico, London 2005)

Cole, John: *Memoirs of Mrs Chapone* (London 1839)

Collier, Jane: *An Essay on the Art of Ingeniously Tormenting; with Proper Rules for the Exercise of that Pleasant Art* (London 1753)

Connelly, Willard: *Beau Nash: Monarch of Bath and Tunbridge Wells* (Werner Laurie, London 1955)

D'Arblay, Madame: *Memoirs of Doctor Burney* (London 1832)

— *Diary and Letters of Madame D'Arblay Edited by her Niece*, 7 Vols. (Henry Colburn, London 1842-46)

Dadswell, Ted: *The Selborne Pioneer* (Ashgate, Aldershot 2006)

Duncombe, John: *The Feminiad* (Augustan Reprint Society, William Andrews Memorial Library, University of California 1981)

Eger, Elizabeth and Peltz, Lucy: *Brilliant Women* (National Portrait Gallery Publications, London 2008)

Eglin, John: *The Imaginary Autocrat: Beau Nash and the Invention of Bath* (Profile Books Ltd., London 2005)

Fielding, Henry: *Tom Jones* (Oxford World's Classics, Oxford 1996)

Foreman, Amanda: *Georgiana Duchess of Devonshire* (HarperCollinsPublishers, London 1998)

Fox, Wilson Lloyd: *War Prisoners at Falmouth and District* Reprinted from *The Royal Cornwall Polytechnic Society's Report 1927*

Gaussen, Alice C. C: *A Later Pepys* Vols. I & II (Bodley Head, London 1904)

Gonda, Caroline: *Reading Daughters' Fictions 1709-1834* (Cambridge University Press, Cambridge 2005)

Gregory, Dr. John: *A Father's Legacy to his Daughters* (Printed for W. Strahan; T. Cadell, in the Strand; and J. Balfour, and W. Creech, Edinburgh 1774)

Halifax, Lord: *The Lady's New-Year's Gift: Or, Advice to a Daughter* (Matt. Gillyflower and James Partridge, London 1688)

Harman, Claire: *Fanny Burney* (HarperCollinsPublishers, London 2000)

Hayden, Ruth: *Mrs Delany her Life and her Flowers* (British Museum Publications Ltd., London 1980)

Hibbert, Christopher: *The Personal History of Samuel Johnson* (Longman, London 1971)

Holt-White, Rashleigh (ed.): *The Letters to Gilbert White of Selborne from His Intimate Friend and Contemporary The Rev. John Mulso* (R.H. Porter, London 1906)

Johnson, Samuel: (ed.): *The Rambler* (1750-52

— (ed.): *The Adventurer* (1752-59)

—*A Dictionary of the English Language* (London 1755)

— *The Lives of the Most Eminent English Poets or Prefaces, Biographical and Critical to the Works of the English Poets*, Vols. I-IV (1779) Vols. V-VI (1781) then as *The Lives of the English Poets* 6 Vols. (1781) and as *The Lives of Poets*

Jones, Vivien (ed.): *Women and Literature in Britain 1700-1800* (Cambridge University Press, Cambridge 2000)

Knapp, Lewis M: *Rex versus Smollett: More Data on the Smollett-Knowles Libel case in Modern Philology*, Vol. 41, No. 4 (University of Chicago, May 1944)

Langford, Paul: *A Polite and Commercial People: England 1727-83* (Clarendon Press, Oxford 1989)

Laurence, Anne: *Women in England 1500-1760: A Social History* (Phoenix Press, London 1996)

Mabey, Richard: *Gilbert White – A Biography of the author of the Natural History of Selborne* (Profile Books, London 2006)

Martin, Joanna: *Wives and Daughters: Women and Children in the Georgian Country House* (Hambledon and London, London 2004)

Meakin, Annette M. B: *Hannah More: A Biographical* Study (Smith, Elder & Co. 1911)

Melville, Lewis: *Bath under Beau Nash* (London 1907)

Montagu, Elizabeth: *An Essay on the Writings and Genius of Shakespear* (London 1769)

Montagu, Matthew (ed.): *Letters of Mrs Elizabeth Montagu With Some Of The Letters Of Her Correspondents*, 3 Vols. (Wells and Lilly, Boston 1825)

Musgrave, Toby; Gardner, Chris and Musgrave, Will: *The Plant Hunters* (Ward Lock, London 1998)

Myers, Sylvia Harcstark: *The Bluestocking Circle: Women, Friendship and the Life of the Mind in Eighteenth Century England* (Clarendon Press, Oxford 1990)

Nicolson, Harold: *The Age of Reason (1700-1789)* (Readers Union Constable & Co. Ltd., London 1962)

O'Toole, Fintan: *A Traitor's Kiss* (Granta Books 1998)

Pennington, Lady: *An Unfortunate Mother's Advice to her Absent Daughters* (Peter Wilson, Dublin 1761)

Pennington, Montagu (ed.): *Memoirs of the Life of Mrs Elizabeth Carter, with a New Edition of her Poems, to Which are Added some Miscellaneous Essays in Prose, Together with her Notes on the Bible, and Answers to Objections Concerning the Christian Religion*, 2 Vols. (F. C. & J. Rivington, London 1808)

— (ed.): *A Series of Letters between Mrs Elizabeth Carter and Miss Catherine Talbot from the year 1741-1770 and Letters from Mrs Carter to Mrs Vesey between the years 1763 and 1787* 4 Vols. (London 1809)

'A Person of Quality': *The Young Lady's Companion; Or, Beauty's Looking Glass* (London 1740)

Piozzi, Hester Lynch (Thrale): *Anecdotes of the Late Samuel Johnson LL.D. During the Last Twenty Years of his Life*, Arthur Sherbo (ed.) (London and Oxford, 1974)

Porter, Roy: *English Society in the 18th Century* (Penguin Books, England 1991)

Reynal, Guillaume Thomas François: *Histoire Philosophique et Politique, Des Éstablissements & du Commerce des Européens dans les deux Indes*, 4 Vols. (Amsterdam 1770)

Richardson, Samuel: *Pamela: or, Virtue Rewarded, in a Series of Letters from a Beautiful Damsel to her Parents*, first published 1740-41 (Penguin Classics, London 1985)

— *Clarissa, or, The History of a Young Lady*, first published 1747-48 (Penguin Classics, London 1985)

— *The History of Sir Charles Grandison*, 7 Vols., first published 1753-54 (Oxford Paperbacks, Reprint edition 1986)

Rowell, Christopher: *The Building of Hatchlands*, in Cobbe: *Hatchlands Park* (The Cobbe Collection Trust in association with The National Trust, 2002)

Scott, Walter: *Bluestocking Ladies* (Green & Co., London 1947)

Scudéry, Madeleine: *Le Grand Cyrus*, 10 Vols. 1649-53

— *Clélie, histoire romaine*, 10 Vols. 1654-60

Sheridan, Louisa Henrietta: *The Comic Offering; or Ladies' Melange of Literary Mirth*, (Smith, Elder and Co. London, annual 1831-35)

Sheridan, Richard Brinsley: *The Rivals* (1775)

Steele, Richard, with Addison, Joseph (eds.): *The Tatler* (1709-11)

— *The Spectator* (1711-12)

Steele, Richard (ed.): *The Guardian* (1713)

Stone, Lawrence: *The Family, Sex and Marriage in England 1500-1800* (Pelican Books, England 1978)

Swift, Jonathan: *A Letter to a Very Young Lady, on her Marriage; Written in the Year 1723* (London 1727) also referred to as *Letter to a Young Lady*

Tague, Ingrid H: *Women of Quality: accepting and contesting ideals of femininity, 1690-1760* (The Boydell Press, 2002)

Thackeray, W.M: *Vanity Fair*, first published 1847-48 (Penguin Books, London 2001)

Thrale, Hester Lynch: *Anecdotes of the Late Samuel Johnson LL.D. During the Last Twenty Years of His Life* (1786).

— *Thraliana, The Diary of Mrs Hester Lynch Thrale (later Mrs Piozzi) 1776-1809*, 2 Vols.: Katherine Balderston (ed.): (Oxford University Press 1942)

Todd, Janet: *Mary Wollstonecraft – a Revolutionary Life* (Phoenix Paperback, London 2001)

Tonkin, Thomas: *The natural history of Cornwall 1736-39* (Manuscript)

Trevelyan, G. M: *History of England* (Longman Group, London 1973)

Turner, Cheryl: *Living By the Pen: Women Writers in the Eighteenth Century* (Routledge, London 1994)

Vickery, Amanda: *The Gentleman's Daughter: Women's Lives in Georgian England* (Yale University Press, Newhaven and London 1998)

— *Behind Closed Doors: At Home in Georgian England* (Yale University Press, Newhaven and London 2009)

Wheeler, Ethel Rolt: *Famous Bluestockings* (Methuen, London 1910)

White, Gilbert: *The Natural History and Antiquities of Selborne* (B. White & Son, London 1789)

Wollstonecraft, Mary: *A Vindication of the Rights of Men, in a letter to the Right Honourable Edmund Burke; occasioned by his reflections on the Revolution in France* (London 1790)

—*A Vindication of the Rights of Woman: With Strictures on Political and Moral Subjects* (Johnson, London 1792)

Woolsey, Sarah Chauncey (ed.): *Diary and Letters of Frances Burney Madame D'Arblay*, Vols. I & II (Roberts Brothers, Boston 1880)

Zuk, Rhoda (ed.): *Catherine Talbot and Hester Chapone, Bluestocking Feminism: Writings of the Bluestocking Circle, 1738-1785*, Vol. 3, general editor Gary Kelly (London, 1999)

Index